YOUTH MINISTRY
NUTS & BOLTS

Zondervan/Youth Specialties Books

Adventure Games
Amazing Tension Getters
Attention Grabbers for 4th-6th Graders (Get 'Em Growing)
Called to Care
The Complete Student Missions Handbook
Creative Socials and Special Events
Divorce Recovery for Teenagers
Feeding Your Forgotten Soul
Get 'Em Talking
Good Clean Fun
Good Clean Fun, Volume 2
Great Games for 4th-6th Graders (Get 'Em Growing)
Great Ideas for Small Youth Groups
Greatest Skits on Earth
Greatest Skits on Earth, Volume 2
Growing Up in America
High School Ministry
High School TalkSheets
Holiday Ideas for Youth Groups (Revised Edition)
Hot Talks
Ideas for Social Action
Intensive Care: Helping Teenagers in Crisis
Junior High Ministry
Junior High TalkSheets
The Ministry of Nurture
On-Site: 40 On-Location Programs for Youth Groups
Option Plays
Organizing Your Youth Ministry
Play It! Great Games for Groups
Teaching the Bible Creatively
Teaching the Truth about Sex
Tension Getters
Tension Getters II
Unsung Heroes: How to Recruit and Train Volunteer Youth Workers
Up Close and Personal: How to Build Community in Your Youth Group
Youth Ministry Nuts & Bolts
Youth Specialties Clip Art Book
Youth Specialties Clip Art Book, Volume 2

YOUTH MINISTRY
NUTS & BOLTS

MASTERING THE MINISTRY BEHIND THE SCENES

Duffy Robbins

ZondervanPublishingHouse
Grand Rapids, Michigan
A Division of HarperCollins*Publishers*

Youth Ministry Nuts & Bolts

Copyright © 1990 by Youth Specialties, Inc.

Youth Specialties Books, 1224 Greenfield Drive, El Cajon, California 92021,
are published by Zondervan Publishing House, Grand Rapids, Michigan 49530

Library of Congress Cataloging-in-Publication Data

Robbins, Duffy.
  Youth ministry nuts & bolts : mastering the ministry behind the scenes / Duffy
Robbins.
    p.   cm.
  "Youth Specialties."
  ISBN 0-310-52571-3
  1. Church work with teenagers. 2. Church work with youth. I. Title. II. Title: Youth
ministry nuts and bolts.
BR4447.R637 1990
259'.23—dc20   90-41526
                                                                              CIP

Edited by J. Cheri McLaughlin and Kathi George
Cover illustrations by Jay Wegter
Designed by Mark Rayburn
Typography by Leah Perry

Printed in the United States of America

    92 93 94 95 96 97 98 99 / CH / 10 9 8 7 6 5 4 3

ABOUT THE YOUTHSOURCE™ PUBLISHING GROUP

YOUTHSOURCE™ books, tapes, videos, and other resources pool the expertise of three of the finest youth-ministry resource providers in the world:

Campus Life Books — publishers of the award-winning *Campus Life* magazine, who for nearly fifty years have helped high schoolers live Christian lives.

Youth Specialties — serving ministers to middle-school, junior-high, and high-school youth for over twenty years through books, magazines, and training events such as the National Youth Workers Convention.

Zondervan Publishing House — one of the oldest, largest, and most respected evangelical Christian publishers in the world.

Campus Life
465 Gundersen Dr.
Carol Stream, IL 60188
708/260-6200

Youth Specialties
1224 Greenfield Dr.
El Cajon, CA 92021
619/440-2333

Zondervan
5300 Patterson Ave., S.E.
Grand Rapids, MI 49530
616/698-6900

To Pastors David Madeira and David Seamands. I've worked alongside these two men of God as a youth minister and it was with their grace and patience that I learned many of the principles discussed in this book.

TABLE OF CONTENTS

INTRODUCTION:

GETTING THEM THROUGH THE ROOF

The gospel writer Mark tells the fascinating story about the time Jesus was giving his homecoming address at a friend's house in Capernaum (Mark 2:1-12). Hoards of people jammed the main room of the house, with hundreds more waiting outside, hoping for a glimpse of this man Jesus about whom they had heard such incredible stories and rumors.

The room is hot, the air close, and the crowd is absolutely silent as they strain to catch every word of the Master. Suddenly, those nearest to Jesus feel pieces of roofing fall on them, showering them with clods of dirt, twigs, and finally larger slabs of tile. Heads tilt back as the amazed crowd watches a ragged hole opening up in the ceiling and a mat lowering into the house. The glare of the sunlight shining through the hole at first obscures the four men lowering this first-century elevator down so that its paralytic passenger stops just in front of Jesus.

All over the room there is whispering and excited conversation. But Jesus' voice silences the crowd with a strong and clear verdict. Looking directly into the eyes of the paralytic he proclaims, "Son, your sins are forgiven."

At this point there's probably as much confusion up on the roof top as down below.

"Did you hear what he said?"

"Yeah, Jesus said his sins are forgiven."

"Well, that's just great. A lot of good that's going to do him. If we went to all this trouble just so Cyrus [names have been changed to protect the innocent] can have a clear conscience, I'm gonna to be ticked off!"

Then the Son of Man speaks again. With all the authority of heaven, he calls to the paralytic, "Get up, take your mat, and go home." And to everyone's amazement, he gets up, takes his mat, and walks out in full view of them all. Meanwhile, up on the roof, four guys are laughing and yelling and giving each other "high fives."

✻   ✻   ✻

I would like to say that the crowded room and hushed mob of Mark's account reminds me of my Sunday night youth fellowship. (To be honest, when I read about the ceiling damage and the hapless man being lowered from the rooftop, I'm reminded of my first junior high lock-in!) But this story is more than an account of divine power—it's a drama of determined friendship. Four men went to incredible pains to see that their friend got to the feet of Jesus. Jesus was impressed by their faith. I am too.

But I'm equally impressed by their ingenuity and determination. Absolutely convinced that Jesus can heal their friend, they overcome all of the logistical, interpersonal, and physical obstacles to get their friend to the feet of Jesus. It wasn't enough that they had faith and that Jesus had power. For the healing to take place, they were going to have to plan, organize, and pull off a complex strategy.

MEANWHILE, BACK AT THE YOUTH GROUP

The task faced by those four men is the same task that volunteer and professional youth workers face every week—behind-the-scenes work that ushers our kids into the excitement of healing confrontations with Jesus. I wish every book that I write could be about seeing students who have been maimed and paralyzed by sin throw off their crutches and hurts and walk away into new lives of wholeness. It's that kind of excitement that motivates otherwise normal adults to tolerate loud music, loud burps, lost sleep, and lousy food for the privilege of getting a weekend "vacation" with thirty teenagers and thirty "jam boxes" on a church retreat.

But this book addresses instead the unglamorous, behind-the-scenes ministry of youth workers. Paralyzed people don't get around too well on their own. There have to be people willing to go to the trouble of "carrying." Someone has to lay out a strategy for breaking through interpersonal, logistical, and physical barriers so that our students can actually get to the feet of Jesus. We know the kids have a need. We believe Jesus has the power. But how do we get through the roof to bring kids to Jesus? That's the nuts and bolts of youth ministry.

NUTS AND BOLTS

Although the actual healing of kids may take place at a Sunday night youth meeting or during the fall retreat, much of youth ministry happens unnoticed, behind the scenes. Read between the lines of Mark's account (2:1-12), and make a list of the logistics of the dramatic healing of the paralytic, using the four categories below:

Team Ministry   Equipment

Planning   Leadership

Before any healing could take place that day, someone had to have a vision that this paralyzed man could get healed, and he had to believe it strongly enough to recruit and motivate others to take part in his bizarre plan. And of course, that raises the issue of who should be recruited. I would hate to be on a pallet being lowered through the roof by four men whose strength only lasted for half the journey down.

The recruits would also have to understand the plan and receive instruction about how to do their part. This may not have taken more than a sentence or two, but it surely must have happened. Once they know what to do, these recruits would have to work together. One can envision two men lowering quickly while the other two lower slowly. The bed slants down, the body slides off in midair, and someone shouts from above, "Jesus, heeeeeeaaaaal hiiiiiimmm. Heeeeere he cooomes!"

Someone had to give thought to what equipment was needed. What if there had been only enough rope to lower the man part way to Jesus? There above the crowd would be a pallet, suspended in midair with a very frightened paralytic cursing his ex-friends on the rooftop. They also needed a tool to break through the earth and tile roof. Maybe they had to come up with some money to pay for this stuff. Where did the money come from? Who kept it when it was collected? How did they make sure it was handled properly?

Someone had to be in charge. Someone had to give the order to lower and give the order to stop. Was there disagreement over the plan? Did this wild plan meet with some initial resistance? It's hard to imagine the men saying, "Hey, what a great idea! We climb the roof with a paralyzed man, tie his bed to ropes, break through the roof, and drop him down in front of a carpenter!"

Surely they must have considered some other plans for getting this paralytic in the presence of Jesus. In my "nuts and bolts" course on youth ministry at Eastern College, I ask my students to get in groups of three and brainstorm about two other possible ways these men could have gotten their friend at the feet of Jesus. Judging from the passage in Mark (2:4), they must have at least attempted a more conventional approach first. Why was this plan chosen? Why were other plans rejected?

The four men carefully evaluated their strategy. It would have been embarrassing, for example, had they broken through the roof of the wrong house! ("Sorry about the roof folks. We're looking for Jesus.") Or what if they had broken through the roof two feet in the wrong direction? Jesus would be right in the middle of his sermon, and a man on a pallet would land on his head. Not a pretty picture.

Of course, we don't know how any of these issues were handled because they were all handled behind the scenes. What we hear about and celebrate is that four men lowered a sick friend through the roof, and Jesus forgave his sins and healed his paralysis. But we can be sure of this: either formally or informally these questions were dealt with. It may have been done in haste, or it may have been planned for a few days, but none of this wonderful story would have happened if some compassionate people had not taken time to work through the nuts and bolts of their task.

WORDS OF WARNING

It's not true that if we plan and organize enough, good ministry will happen. While these four men had to work through organizational and interpersonal details to get their friend to the feet of Jesus, nothing would have happened if Jesus had not been in that house down below. It is Jesus alone who takes human effort and turns it into life-changing ministry.

The notion that organization is the mark of spirituality or that disorganization marks the lack of spirituality is also untrue. The Holy Spirit works when and how he chooses to work. This book simply describes ways to utilize our resources to set the stage for what God wants to do.

TO THE PROFESSIONAL
ROOF WALKER

Beware the temptation to overprofessionalize youth ministry. There is nothing profane about the word "professional." At its root, it means "promise," a promise to be prepared, to responsibly perform our work with excellence. But, there is a kind of professionalism that is profaned by God. That kind of professionalism—ministry by habit or human effort—yields youth ministry born less of compassion than of know-how and based less on the fruit of the Spirit than on works of the flesh. Frankly, a book like this can lead us in that direction. We need to understand right at the beginning that tightening a few nuts and bolts can make us more efficient, but only the Spirit of God can ignite our ministries with that divine efficiency that yields changed lives.

TO THE VOLUNTEER
ROOF WALKER

After a glance through the table of contents of this book, it would be possible to get totally depressed. Chapters on budgeting, dealing with conflict, decision making, when to leave a ministry—not exactly the stuff of spiritual goose bumps. Overwhelmed and exhausted volunteer youth workers may say, "I've got church three nights a week, a full-time job, no adult friends, and about two nights a week with my family."

This book is not written so that you can discover all of the things you are *not* doing. The history of God's work through his people is that he can do much with little. Rather than being intimidated and paralyzed by discovering in this book all that you could be doing, focus on one or two strategies that might better help you to do what you are already doing.

If your ministry is small in number, some of these issues will not be a problem for you. As a volunteer, there are some issues in this book that may not be pertinent to your situation. Use this book as a resource for troubleshooting in those areas that are presenting some sticky problems. Use it as a manual that will help you avoid time-consuming mistakes, so that you can maximize the time you are able to devote to ministry with kids.

When we shuck it down to the heart, youth ministry isn't a matter of budgeting, publicizing, and organizing. It's a matter of loving teenagers, spending time with them, and helping them hear and understand the gospel of Christ. Volunteer or professional, youth workers involved in that kind of ministry—even when all the nuts and bolts aren't tightened up—will see God work.

SECTION
ONE

OPENING
YOUR TOOLBOX

CHAPTER ONE

STARTING WITH THE HEART

We begin the task of organizing a youth ministry not by tightening a few nuts and bolts, but by talking about the hand and the heart that turn the wrench. If we don't begin working from the inside out, we are in danger of functioning like an artificial fireplace flame—it's quiet; it's clean; there are never ashes or scorch marks; but neither is there any warmth. The warm heart makes a ministry work. Flow charts, buildings that stay neat and clean, advance scheduling, and files in alphabetical order are important only as they enable us to exercise our spiritual gifts to impact teenagers. We need people exercising their spiritual gifts because their hearts are stoked by the grace of Christ.

I used to work with a godly preacher, Roy Putnam, who groomed his staff and congregation with Ephesians 2:8-10.

> For it is by grace you have been saved, through faith—and this not from yourselves, it is the gift of God—not by works, so that no one can boast. For we are God's workmanship, created in Christ Jesus to do good works, which God prepared in advance for us to do.

"Effective ministry comes not just through greater efficiency," he would often say, "but through greater 'Ephesiancy.' "

GIFTED FOR MINISTRY
WITH TEENAGERS

J. R. R. Tolkien's *The Fellowship of the Ring* tells of the hobbit, Frodo, who receives the mysterious ring of power and who must journey to almost certain death in Mount Doom to destroy the Ring. The wizard

Gandalf, who guides him in his quest, listens as Frodo responds to the weight of his mission.

> "I am not made for perilous quests," cried Frodo. "I wish I had never seen the Ring! Why did it come to me? Why was I chosen?"
>
> "Such questions cannot be answered," said Gandalf. "You may be sure that it was not for any merit that others do not possess; not for power or wisdom, at any rate. But you have been chosen and you must therefore use such strength and heart and wits as you have."

The greenest of rookie volunteers and the most sage veterans of youth work have all wondered if they are, in fact, suited to this "perilous quest." They wonder because youth ministry is not merely a nuts and bolts operation. It begins with people who need to be reminded that any ministry happens through God's grace—that God has gifted us with such "strength and heart and wits" as we need to be faithful to Christ. Our ministries differ stylistically, but each of us has an important ministry with students. God gifts us in different ways to do different kinds of ministries.

STRENGTH AND HEART AND WITS

The New Testament gives no evidence that the lists of spiritual gifts appearing in 1 Corinthians 12 and in Romans 12 are exhaustive. In fact, I'm sure that many youth workers are discovering that they exhibit spiritual gifts that are every bit as vital as they are nontraditional—gifts like sketching, playing games, song-leading, and hanging out. God has not chosen us for any merit that we possess. But we have been chosen, and like Frodo, we must use such strength and heart and wits as we have.

Mike Yaconelli of Youth Specialties suggests that a number of spiritual gifts have been overlooked and underappreciated when it comes to youth ministry.

THE GIFT OF HELPLESSNESS
EPHESIANS 2:8–10

Some of you are thinking, This is it! I've found my gift!! And you might be right. Believe it or not, helplessness is a tremendous asset in youth ministry. Helplessness opens us to new ideas and strategies, keeps us teachable, and moves us to innovation. Veteran youth workers can become stale or burn out when they are not motivated by helplessness to reach out for new strategies.

I am reminded of my helplessness when I walk into a room full of teenagers. Not only do I know I'm not one of them, but they know I'm not one of them! I do not listen to Q-106, Power-105, or Z-99. I like public radio. I am not into wrestling with the guys. I don't even enjoy pizza! They don't see me seated at a cafeteria table and nudge a neighbor to say, "Hey, who's the new kid? And what happened to his hair?" Attached to my balding head is a body whose lines are written more in cursive than in a sharp, block print. In the normal currency of the adolescent world, I'm no Tom Cruise.

But that's good — sort of. Since I'm not among those Tom Selleck/ Barbie Doll youth workers who can be just like one of the kids, I'm forced to bank not on my appearance but on the hard work of building caring relationships with teenagers. And that's healthy. That keeps me ministering with teenagers by the power and the grace of God. I admit that for me praying is more important than pranks, caring is more important than coolness.

THE GIFT OF TRUTHFULNESS
EPHESIANS 4:15; 6:13,14

Having observed Roman soldiers firsthand, the apostle Paul likens the Christian's armor to Roman battle gear. The first piece of armor that he mentions is the belt of truth. It was the part of the Roman armor to which all other pieces of the armor were attached. Into this girdle-like belt, the soldier tucked up the loose ends of his tunic. He attached his breastplate to that belt to hold it firmly in place, and his sword was also attached to that belt. If his belt were not buckled tightly in place, even the most experienced centurion might trip over his tunic or fall because his breastplate had slipped into shin-guard position.

In a day when we are as apt to read about a preacher in the *National Enquirer* as in *Christianity Today*, youth workers must root their strengths, wits, ideas, and resources in truthfulness. It is essential that we in youth ministry be people of integrity—people committed to not only speaking the truth, but living it.

Tim, a volunteer in our youth ministry, possessed few of the traditional skills of gifted youth ministers. He wasn't funny. He couldn't play guitar. He had little public speaking experience. And he didn't have any kind of facial hair. But the way he lived backed up his claim of commitment to Christ, and that gave him a potent ministry with the kids in our group. They respected his integrity. What he talked, he walked. That's truthfulness.

Jason exhibits truthfulness in another way. Even under pressure, even when it may make some of his students angry, Jason consistently speaks the truth. But even more remarkable is Jason's willingness to admit when he does not know the answer to a question. In a setting where not knowing leaves a person vulnerable, that kind of truthfulness takes courage. As volunteer youth workers, we are especially intimidated when kids ask questions for which we have no answer. But we are not working with teenagers because we are theological experts. We are working with students because we love Christ and we love teenagers.

THE GIFT OF LISTENING
EPHESIANS 4:2

Amy sat in my office intense and confused. Over two years I had developed genuine respect for her as a Christian. Now she was seriously dating a non-Christian who was putting pressure on her to have sex. She had resisted so far. She didn't want to go against God's word. But she honestly confessed that part of her wanted to have sex with her boyfriend.

I listened to her, nodding occasionally, asking questions about where God fit in with all of this. After a half hour we prayed, and she left my office. I felt the encounter had been positive. She had talked freely and I had responded to her struggle with restraint and support. Then it hit me—this eighteen-year-old girl was somebody's daughter. I grimaced at how different my attitude might have been if she had been *my* daughter.

Daughter: "Dad, me and my boyfriend are trying to decide whether we should have sex or not. What do you think?"

My response: "I can fix that for you, honey. I'll kill him."

For whatever reasons, teenagers are often afraid to be completely open with their parents. They feel, justifiably in many situations, that if their parents knew about their lives, that knowledge would create worry, fear, distrust, or outright panic in their household. "I can't tell my mom that," they say. "She'll freak." Through the gift of listening, we can offer our students the advantage of experienced counsel guided by a heart of concern, without the sometimes sharp edge of parental overconcern and panic.

THE GIFT OF LIKING TEENAGERS
EPHESIANS 1:15–17

On a recent cross-country flight, I noticed in the departure lounge a large crowd of teenagers preparing to take the same flight that I was taking. As other adults made the same observation, I felt a wave of sheer dread flooding over them. Businessmen asked if there were later flights. One lady wondered aloud if there was a no-kids section on the plane. Others downed a few extra drinks so that they wouldn't even notice that they were on the flight at all. One irate businessman remarked to me with some relief as he took his seat on the plane, "I was afraid they were going to put me up there in that section with all the teenyboppers." I felt like smiling and saying, "I usually throw up every few minutes when I'm flying, but other than that, I bet it will be pretty quiet back here."

The average adult has a certain disdain for teenagers. But God has gifted some of us with an appreciation for teenagers—an ability to look beyond some of the typical marks of adolescence and see real people. Liking teenagers, however, is not the same as acting like a teenager. Teenagers do not need us to be adults who act like teenagers. They simply need us to be adults who don't hyperventilate when teenagers act like teenagers.

THE GIFT OF NURTURE
EPHESIANS 4:11–13

Steve works in a military school with students who have virtually no relationship with any religious organization. He is often the first Christian these students have ever met. Some are curious. Some are suspicious. Some are openly hostile. Patiently, Steve returns to the campus to build and nurture these relationships—braiding thin lines of friendship into thick cords of caring. Having earned the right to talk with these students personally about their walks with Christ, he leads some into relationships with Jesus. It is a painstaking process that he will start all over again this week as he goes back on campus, even as he encourages and meets with those who have already made a commitment. It is not a ministry that just anyone can do.

Sometimes Steve confronts his students one on one. Other times he offers encouragement after a racquetball game or a rebuke and correction during halftime of the televised ball game. Sometimes he communicates through a note or a phone call. Through the entire process, Steve is clear about his goals. He is called to be a pastor to these students, not a peer.

THE GIFT OF AFFIRMING
EPHESIANS 4:15, 29

In a culture that scrawls crude graffiti on the self-image of most teenagers, youth workers offer kids a vision of who they are in Christ. Asked to speak on the topic of self-image in Soweto, South Africa, youth minister and missions expert Paul Borthwick faced a formidable challenge. His teenage audience had grown up under the oppression of apartheid, being told from birth that they are nonpersons. Bringing the students back to the heart of the gospel, he reminded them that self-worth is not calculated by government ruling or media images, but by the God who made them in his image.

We occasionally get so busy managing ongoing youth programs that we forget the power and impact of a simple word of affirmation—especially for average teenagers, who are constantly being reminded that they are not smart enough, not athletic enough, and not beautiful enough. Writing a quick note to a student, offering public praise for a job done well, posting on the bulletin board a newspaper clipping or announcement about the achievement of a student—all these actions express affirmation to a teen.

Affirm students by identifying the talents that they possess, and then discover ways for them to display their gifts in ministry. We occasionally do that with students talented in music or public speaking. But what about the student who is good in photography? or computers? or poetry? Can we encourage that student to use her talents in photography to prepare a special slide show to correspond with the hymns on an upcoming Sunday? Could we utilize that student's ability with computers to help in a tutoring program? Why not invite that young poet to read his poetry as part of the worship service or youth meeting?

THE GIFT OF A SENSE OF HUMOR
PROVERBS 17:22

After twenty years of youth ministry, I'm convinced that this gift is vital. Having a sense of humor doesn't necessarily mean we must be funny; it means that we must be able to recognize what is funny. It doesn't mean always making people laugh; it means knowing when to laugh. We need to have the ability to see the humor in various situations.

A sense of humor is crucial because anyone involved in youth work will be laughed at occasionally—usually when we are not trying to be funny! The fact is that kids sometimes laugh *at* us and not just *with* us. Nearly all adult youth workers reading these words have some physical feature, for example, about which they feel self-conscious when they are around teenagers. Of course, most of us believe that we disguise these features by the way we dress and compose ourselves. The safest bet, however, is that all of the kids in our youth groups have not only noticed the asymmetrical placement of our ears or the relative largeness of our noses, but they have discussed it, and they even have a name for it!

The gift of a sense of humor shows students that we don't take ourselves so seriously. From the teenager's point of view, taking oneself seriously is the most telling trait of terminal adulthood. Losing the ability to laugh at ourselves makes us boring people. But the real dividend of being willing to laugh at ourselves is that we can help teenagers develop that same perspective for themselves. My jokes about my bald head help the students I'm speaking to develop a more positive and healthy perspective about their own imperfections. Joining in a good laugh communicates acceptance. We don't laugh with our enemies.

THE GIFT OF FLEXIBILITY
EPHESIANS 5:15–20

Anyone who has ever driven a church vehicle has learned the importance of flexibility. Youth ministry is fraught with pitfalls and potential disasters. Sometimes it is the mechanical surprise—a projector bulb that blows just before the special slide show; sometimes it is the more human element—you've planned to break the kids into six teams of four, and ten students show up for the meeting. But there are always enough bumps to make the journey interesting. A youth worker who has the gift of flexibility will be able to absorb the shocks with enough finesse to go the distance.

Flexibility is critical not only for prolonging the youth worker's sanity and survival, but also for teaching students a mind-set that guards their sanity and survival in an unpredictable world. Students glimpse our faith in the sovereignty of God most clearly through the situations that turn out wrong. Grace is easy to exhibit when there are no problems. When we are flexible enough to bounce back under negative circumstances, however, we authenticate our testimony. As Paul wrote to Timothy, "You know all about my teaching, my way of life, my purpose, my faith, patience, love, endurance" (1 Tim. 3:10). And where did Timothy learn these lessons? Through Paul's "persecutions, sufferings—what kinds of things happened to [him] in Antioch, Iconium and Lystra, the persecutions [he] endured" (1 Tim. 3:11).

Blessed is the youth worker who stays cool when the bus breaks down, for his is the ministry that keeps on rolling.

THE GIFT OF PERSEVERANCE
EPHESIANS 1:15–17

Perseverance is that gift of God's grace that allows us to hang in with a student when we really might prefer to just hang that student!

The kids in the youth group called him B.J. The leaders called him Trouble. Sitting in on several meetings of the youth group as a consultant, I identified him almost immediately as one of those teenagers that makes career youth workers decide to become senior pastors. Talking when he was supposed to be quiet, hushed when he was supposed to be singing, laughing when he was supposed to be sober—in terms of spiritual potential, anyone would have guessed that B.J. stood for "Biiiig Job."

But Pete Berner showed the gift of perseverance. He hung in there with B.J.—kept loving him, having him into his home, allowing him to hang out at his office. He wouldn't give up on B.J. All through B.J.'s high school years, Pete and his wife Dorothy were there, through the occasional times of promise and through the frequent occasions of doubt.

I spoke at a retreat recently at which Pete was leading the music. When he stood up with his guitar, I couldn't believe who his partner was. Right there, next to him, leading the worship was—you guessed it—B.J., now a college graduate serving as an intern and training to become a youth minister.

The Associated Press some time ago carried a laser photo depicting a male emperor penguin standing alone among the rocks with an egg balanced on his feet. The caption explained that when the female emperor penguin lays the egg, she rolls it over to the male and then gingerly places it on top of his feet. The article went on to say that the male then stands there without moving for the next two months until that egg hatches. That is a picture of perseverance.

On promotion Sunday, we youth ministers often find ourselves looking into the eyes of a parent dropping off a seventh-grade son or daughter with the words, "Trust me. There's life in there." Meanwhile, we have to stand there and pray and wait and be patient and pray some more and persevere as a young person matures. When it is all said and done, tightening the nuts and bolts of a youth ministry is sometimes more a function of heart than muscle. When we might be tempted by a lack of results to stop fooling with the nuts altogether, it is the gift of perseverance that heartens us as we press on.

MEASURING YOUR MOTIVATION

Besides being equipped with diverse gifts, youth ministers use their gifts under the influence of differing motivations.

• Paul, a youth-ministry veteran in the Northeast, is charged by a motivation to achieve new goals. He is constantly exploring new areas, writing new articles, trekking new realms in his ministry. His has been a large ministry marked by keen organization and thorough planning.

• Scott is motivated by building relationships. His ministry with Urban Young Life in Washington, DC, may not be the model of smooth efficiency and organization, but Scott's ability to get close to students and leaders has given him a broad and effective ministry.

• Kristen is a youth-ministry student mobilizing student volunteers from her campus to work with a ministry in inner-city Philadelphia. An intense desire to impact the lives of others through leading people into various service opportunities motivates her. She coordinates people for tutoring, youth ministry, home visitation, and other ministries.

The unique gifts and motivations of each of these youth workers affect the way they minister: how they set their priorities, how they spend their time, how they plan their budgets, how they recruit other leaders. Virtually no area of their ministries is left unaffected.

What are the inner motivations that direct us in our ministries with teenagers? Why does one youth worker concentrate on smooth operation, while another is content to allow planning time to be nudged off the schedule to spend extra time with students? Why is another intent on calling out students to become more involved in affecting their community for Christ?

NEEDS AS MOTIVES

Dr. Em Griffin, Professor of Communications at Wheaton College and a member of the Board of Young Life, has written about how our particular motivations tend to affect our ministries.

As a Christian, I believe God has built in this innate need for meaning, and this gnawing desire is satisfied only in relationship to him. But even if we weren't willing to credit God as the source of this longing, the will to meaning is the best umbrella to explain the why's of daily existence. This meaning comes in three ways. We can accomplish worthwhile tasks, develop satisfying relationships, or exercise an impact on another's life. The corresponding motives are need for achievement, affiliation, and power.[1]

NEED FOR ACHIEVEMENT ("nAch")

People who are nAch motivated seem to be moved by self-imposed standards of excellence. Those standards affect the way they plan, the time they put into setting up retreats, and even the time they spend preparing the publicity pieces for retreats. Their programs are apt to be well-planned and organized. Pastors, boards, and treasurers love nAch youth workers because they always get their reports in on time, and don't yield too many surprises.

Of the gospel writers, Griffin identifies Matthew as the nAch author. Perhaps Matthew's background in tax collecting led him to marvel at how Jesus could get things done, how he fulfilled the expectations of the Old Testament prophets. Matthew seems to view Jesus as the ultimate achiever.

Those who are nAch, quite frankly, aren't often attracted to youth ministry. Perhaps it's because the stereotype of the youth minister as the "wild and crazy, seat-of-the-pants, good ol' boy" doesn't match up to the way we see ourselves if we are nAch. On the other hand, some of the most effective youth workers I've known have been men and women who were predominantly nAch. They organized their ministries not only for efficiency, but also "Ephesiancy."

NEED FOR AFFILIATION ("nAff")

More commonly, youth workers are those who are motivated through satisfying relationships. In fact, part of the reality that breeds the stereotype mentioned earlier is that youth workers tend to be more concerned about being with students than about filling out the bus usage report, balancing the youth group checkbook, or notifying parents that there is a week-long work project planned for the up-coming month. We don't sweat the details. We're into relationships. Those who are motivated by the need for affiliation typically have ministries that are strongest in fellowship, small group ministries, and contact work. John's gospel reflects the heartbeat of the nAff person—a strong emphasis on love, friendship, and fellowship.

One advantage volunteer youth workers have is that they can focus on relationships without being obligated to sweat the details. Many paid youth workers who might by nature be more nAff are forced by the obligations of their position to focus on numbers, meetings, forms, and reports when they would rather be knocking around with a group of kids. A respected youth worker in our area just left his church staff position recently, not because he wanted to leave the church, but because he felt he could spend more time with students if he served as a volunteer youth worker. When volunteers are feeling ignored or unnoticed by the official governing bodies of the con-gregation, it's good to remember that this neglect allows them to concentrate on what ultimately matters—spending time with students.

NEED FOR POWER ("nPow")

Youth workers who are nPow desire to have a direct impact on others. They are apt to be strongly motivated for evangelism and social outreach. They want to see the youth group wield a kingdom influ-ence in the high school and in the community. Like the gospel writer Mark, they are moved by a Jesus of power and action. Jesus speaks and things happen—waves stop rolling, the storm stops raging. His words ring with authority.

Bart Campolo is working with inner-city teenagers in Norristown, Pennsylvania. His strong motivation for power led him to begin a ministry equipping students for serving Christ in the nation's cities. Sponsoring workshops for inner-city youth workers and training college volunteers, he seeks to have an impact for the kingdom. It's not an ego trip. He just wants to see something happen for kids in the city.

ALL MOTIVATIONS ARE
CREATED EQUAL

No one gift or motivation is more important than any other in youth ministries that value "Ephesiancy" more than simple efficiency. Folks who exhibit any one of these gifts or motivations each possess their own inherent assets and liabilities.

The need for achievement, for example, can become a pride ride that degenerates into a ministry so intent on accomplishing something for God that people get stepped on, rolled over, and mowed down. Youth workers motivated by the need for affiliation can become sloppy in their jobs, using "time with the kids" and "contact work" as excuses for avoiding tedious but necessary tasks. Those motivated by the need for power can easily overlook the ongoing, long-term responsibilities of follow-up and nurture once the big goal is met or the big event is over.

Foolish is the youth worker who ranks doing above being. God has always reminded us that what we do is rooted in who we are. Examining our gifts and our motivations is a wise place to start if we hope to build solid ministries. We start with hearts and build from there.

CHOSEN FOR A
PERILOUS QUEST

A book about how to budget, how to do publicity, and how to work out staff conflicts can become intolerably stale if it isn't kept fresh by the vision of our calling. Each of us is called to ministry and gifted for ministry; for "in him we were also chosen, having been predestined according to the plan of him who works out everything in conformity with the purpose of his will, in order that we, who were the first to hope in Christ, might be for the praise of his glory" (Eph. 1:11-12).

In Dan Taylor's book, *Letters to My Children*, he recounts for his son an episode that took place in school when he was a sixth grader. Miss Owens, the substitute teacher, wanted to teach young Danny a lesson about life. She decided to do it in the context of the weekly square-dancing classes. On square-dancing days the boys lined up at the door of the classroom, and one by one they chose which of the girls to grace with the pleasure of their company.

Needless to say, these could be very cruel moments for the girls as the sixth-grade boys surveyed their options with all of the romance of nomads buying camels. "Believe me," Taylor writes, "the boys did not like doing this—at least I didn't. But think about being one of those girls. Think about waiting to get picked. Think about seeing who was going to get picked before you. Think about worrying that you'd get picked by someone you couldn't stand. Think about worrying whether you were going to get picked at all!"

Mary didn't worry about getting picked last—she expected it. Mary was neither pretty nor smart, neither witty nor athletic. Taylor recalled that she was nice, but of course "nice" didn't account for much in sixth grade. While some of the other girls in class had beauty marks and dimples, Mary's distinguishing characteristics were a large stomach and an arm and leg disfigured by polio.

Midyear Miss Owens suggested that on the next square-dance day young Dan should choose Mary as his partner. Taylor remembers greeting her suggestion with complete shock—as if she had suggested that he fly to Mars. And to make matters worse, she said that it was what a Christian would do. To this young man it was a low blow because he thought Miss Owens was probably right. "It was exactly the kind of thing Jesus would have done," he writes. "I was surprised, in fact, that I hadn't seen it on a Sunday school flannel board yet: 'Jesus choosing the lame girl for the Yeshiva dance.' It was bound to be somewhere in the Bible."

Taylor's only hope was that on square-dancing day he would be the last guy to make a choice. That way Mary would be the only girl left. He could choose her without losing face. Unfortunately, when SD-day came again, Dan was first in line to choose his partner. With all of the enthusiasm of someone anticipating oral surgery, he mumbled the words, "I choose Mary."

> Never has reluctant virtue been so rewarded. I still see her face undimmed in my memory. She lifted her head, and on her face, reddened with pleasure and surprise and embarrassment all at the same time, was the most genuine look of delight and

even pride that I have ever seen before or since. It was so pure that I had to look away because I knew I didn't deserve it.

Mary came and took my arm, as we had been instructed, and she walked beside me, bad leg and all, just like a princess.

Mary is my age now. I never saw her after that year. I don't know what her life's been like or what she's doing. But I'd like to think she has a fond memory of at least one day in sixth grade. I know I do.[2]

Taylor's account is reminiscent of the gospel of Christ. We, like Mary, misshapen and homely, have little to make us attractive to a righteous God. And yet, the Lord of the Dance has called us by name. In the words of Jesus, "You did not choose me, but I chose you and appointed you to go and bear fruit—fruit that will last" (John 15:16).

It's our privilege to invite those who have been maimed by sin and crippled by fear and guilt to come and dance at the banquet of the King. It is, indeed, a perilous quest. But we have been gifted and charged to go and bear fruit. We must use such wits and heart and strength as we have to do so.

CHAPTER TWO

PASSPORT TO EXCELLENCE

Being Christians who mean well does not guarantee that we are Christians who manage well. Whether coordinating the leaders of a three-hundred-member youth group or leading three to five students in informal, regular Bible study, we need to remember that a church organization does not function automatically. To be all that we can be for the glory of Christ, we need to learn how to knit together our flow charts, paid staff, volunteer staff, job descriptions, and the inspiration of the Spirit, to fit the tasks to which God has called us. Our opportunities with students are too few, and the time we can devote to our ministry is too precious to waste with muddled plans, lack of communication, and unproductive activity.

Len Kageler, youth pastor at the North Seattle Alliance Church, recounts an occasion after six years of full-time ministry on which one of his volunteers approached him with a pointed and painful evaluation.

> He explained, in exquisite detail, my deficiencies in handling the youth staff. My main problem, as he saw it, was communication. I repeatedly failed to give adequate direction. I also failed to help him see his role as important. Did I really need him in the youth ministry, or was this a one-man show?
>
> As I reflected later, other incidents came to mind that corroborated what he had said. Just a month earlier, a young couple had resigned from the team saying they didn't feel they knew enough about what was going on to be of any help.[1]

Len's honest report reminds all of us that even veteran youth ministers can waste valuable time, resources, and leaders if they fail to give adequate attention to their management skills.

NOW JUST ONE MINUTE . . .

To many of us, "management skills" sounds like something that sidetracks us from our drive to minister to kids. Does this management stuff really matter to youth workers? In 1982, the hot book in corporate board rooms and management meetings was a book by Thomas Peters and Robert Waterman, *In Search of Excellence*. These two men based their findings on some assumptions basic to all people. I believe a look at their assumptions will answer the question of relevance for us.

All of us want to think of ourselves as winners. But most of us are amazingly normal. We win some and we lose some. And there's no question that we respond better when those in leadership emphasize the ones we win more than the ones we lose. We are, in the words of Waterman and Peters, "suckers for a bit of praise."

Our imaginative, symbolic right side of the brain is at least as important as our rational, deductive left. That means it's often more important to ask "Does it feel right?" than "Does it add up?" My wife taught me this truth early in our marriage. We would discuss some matter of finance or calendar and I would state my case succinctly, logically, and reasonably. She would profoundly respond: "I know. But I still think you're wrong." We may be doing our youth ministry the way they said to do it in seminary or the way that appears to be most logical, but if it doesn't feel right to the ministry team and the students, it probably won't work well.

God has given us a wonderful capacity to learn and store information. However, most of us find that we are better at remembering stories than facts, better at remembering movie plots than sermon outlines. Therefore, it's to everyone's advantage to make plans, strategies, and goals that are as simple as possible. Elaborate ones may work out great on paper, but if we want them to play out in the everyday arena of a youth ministry, we should keep the vision and procedures basic.

We respond to external rewards and punishments. I can talk to leaders and students about God calling us to a mission project in order that many will experience the love of God. The response: polite enthusiasm. What actually kicks the fund-raising campaign into high gear is my offer to reward the ten best fund-raisers with free youth group T-shirts.

This is not to say that people are not motivated from within. They are. Nor that my students and leaders lack genuine zeal for Christ. They have it. But we should never underestimate the motivation of the small carrot (or T-shirt) dangling out front.

People judge our beliefs more by our actions than by our words. If we give lip service to the notion that "every person on this student-leadership team is important" but never relinquish responsibility to any more than two or three trusted students, students draw their own conclusions about our truthfulness and their gifts.

We will sacrifice a lot to institutions that will provide meaning for us. Anyone who has seen a normal adult put on a pig face and yell "Go Hawgs" in the stands of RFK Stadium at a Redskins game knows this is true. As a young college student on student staff with Young Life, I spent forty-plus hours a week doing contact work with students through Young Life clubs—even when it meant cutting college classes one or two days a week—all for the exorbitant salary of sixty dollars a month. Why? To be sure because of my commitment to Christ. But there were a lot of different ministries through which I could have served Christ. In the fellowship and work of Young Life, however, I found deep friendships and a sense of purpose. I felt it was my niche. I belonged there. If we want to develop students and volunteers who are committed to our youth ministry, they need to sense that our youth ministry is committed to them.

DOES THIS STUFF REALLY MATTER IN YOUTH MINISTRY?

We can see ourselves in the assumptions Waterman and Peters used to approach their management skills research. But how does *In Search of Excellence* parallel our search for excellent youth ministries? Their research in the business world shows that the organizations that function with excellence cultivate these seven variables: **structure, strategy, people, management style, systems and procedures, shared values, and present/hoped for organizational skills.** Let's categorize some typical issues of youth ministry within these variables.

- *Structure.* How will we divide the youth group? Should we have junior highers and senior highers together? When, if ever, is a group too big to be effective?
- *Strategy.* Do we use the Sonlife approach, the Son City approach, the Reach Out strategy, the Catch the Rainbow strategy, or does it matter? Do we need to do a work project, a Bible study, a prayer warrior weekend, or a banana night?
- *People.* How do we find effective leadership for a growing youth ministry? How can we motivate students to be involved in leadership? How can we nurture and effectively train the kind of adult leaders that we need?
- *Management style.* What should be our posture in working with the church board? the pastor? other staff members? other volunteer staff? How do we decide how to do what? and when? Does my leadership style encourage others to use their gifts or discourage them from doing so?
- *Systems and procedures.* Is there any ongoing process we can use to evaluate our youth ministry? What sort of procedure should we use for budgeting effectively?
- *Guiding concepts and shared values.* Why do we have a youth ministry? Do we have a clearly stated vision that helps our leaders, our students, and the parents of our students to understand why we do some of the things we do? And why don't we do some of the things we don't do? What do we want students to look like when they have come through our ministry? If we have to cut back our youth budget, which areas should be cut least? What are our priorities?
- *Present/hoped for strengths and skills.* What can we as a small youth group offer to students who can choose from two other mega youth groups in our area? What are some areas in which our students still lack a biblical understanding of the Christian life?

YOUTH MINISTRY—
AN EXCELLENT ADVENTURE

The critical question that confronts us if we take seriously the analysis of Waterman and Peters is how can we implement some of these marks of excellence in our ministries with teenagers? Chances are that Waterman and Peters have never put eggs in their armpits, but some of their writing is relevant to organizing a youth ministry. The following exhortations concerning effective youth ministry are based on four characteristics they observed when researching excellent organizations.

A GOOD YOUTH MINISTRY
PUTS PEOPLE AT THE CENTER

"The good news from the excellent companies," the researchers write, "is the extent to which, and the intensity with which, the customers intrude into every nook and cranny of the business."[2] Regardless of how busy we become, how zealous our vision is, or how demanding our other responsibilities are , we need to remember that we cannot have a youth ministry without youth. (Some of us would have to confess that the thought has occurred to us on occasion.) For a youth-ministry organization to be excellent it must cater to the students' needs and be sensitive to individual student's well-being. It must put people ahead of programs by accomplishing the following tasks:

Focus on the number of volunteer leaders as much as on the number of students involved. We tend to ignore students "after the sale." A good leader-to-student ratio that allows for full and frequent interaction among kids and leaders is approximately one adult for every ten high school students, and about one adult for every six junior high students. Increasing student rosters without boosting the leadership roster assures that we will involve more students than we can care for.

Urge volunteer leaders to spend time with the students outside of organized meetings. Not every adult volunteer can juggle family and job responsibilities to budget in the fifteen hours weekly of informal contact that Young Life asks of its volunteers. The critical emphasis for the volunteer youth worker who wants to stay "close to the customer" is to spend time on a regular basis with some student apart from the regular meeting, even if it is only thirty minutes a week. Sad to say, that will probably be thirty minutes more than that student will spend with any other adult they know. But that thirty minutes will make a difference.

Follow-up first-time visitors within a week of their initial visit to youth group or Sunday school. Typically this is done through a mailing, a phone call, personal contact, or a combination of the above. Some youth ministries enlist student hosts to look after first-timers, to greet them as they enter the meeting, and to fill out visitor cards with them. One Georgia youth worker told me of his "A&P Squad," a team of students and leaders who practice the kinds of hospitality and caring that were seen in the lives of Aquila and Priscilla, a couple mentioned often in Paul's letters (Acts 18:2, 18, 26; Rom. 16:3, 4; 1 Cor. 16:19). Those on the A&P Squad contact visitors within seven days of their first visit. Follow-up doesn't have to be a youth group "Welcome Wagon," but it should go beyond the usual letter addressed to "Dear Occupant in Christ."

Survey (informally or systematically) students as well as adult leadership about what types of activities might be planned, what types of topics might be studied, and any kinds of changes that might be made. The survey can be as simple as posing to the group this assignment: "On a blank sheet of paper, write down four topics you would like to see the group study, three activities you would like to see our group do, two ways we could make the youth group better, and one way you feel you could be better used or involved in this ministry." As a youth program becomes larger, it is at the same time increasingly important and increasingly difficult to get feedback and suggestions from those involved in the program. Waterman and Peters note that one of the strengths of corporate giant IBM is the company's policy that every customer complaint be answered within twenty-four hours. (See Chapters Seven and Eight for other evaluative strategies.)

Send birthday cards to students on their birthdays. It's not a big deal, but I discovered early in my own ministry that this is a gesture that kids notice. More than that, I began to realize that this birthday note was one of the most significant notes I could write to that student all year. I could offer words of encouragement and challenge to them in that letter that might not be accepted from me at any other time of year. It was as if they perceived their birthdays as appropriate occasions for looking back and looking ahead, for evaluation and challenge.

A GOOD YOUTH MINISTRY
FREES PEOPLE OF VISION

Waterman and Peters judge the most discouraging fact of big corporate life to be "the loss of what got them big in the first place: Innovation."[3] As the company grows, it typically becomes more careful, less willing to take risks. They note that in a National Science Foundation study reported in *Inc.*, researchers found that "small firms produced about four times as many innovations per research-and-development dollar as medium-sized firms, and about twenty-four times as many as large firms."[4]

Excellent companies have mastered the ability to be big and act small through leaders who foster autonomy and stimulate entrepreneurship. They favor employees who discover better ways to do what they do by giving them the freedom to try new strategies to reach their goals. Employees are allowed to act on their ideas without submitting them in quadruplicate so that all the higher-ups can send them a memo saying why it won't work.

When a youth program is small, the leadership is hungry and desperate, willing to try anything. Sparks fly. Some mistakes are made, but creativity happens, and kids start to get excited. As the group grows, however, the leadership often becomes more conservative, less willing to try new ideas, more conscious of trying to maintain the standard than of trying to reach for new goals. The price for maintaining is usually loss of innovation.

A ministry full of encouragement and risk taking reflects a humble leader. Most of us have seen the poster entitled "The Seven Last Words of the Christ" on which is written this statement: "We've always done it this way before." One of the dangers of having successful youth ministry is the tendency to think that the way we are doing things is the best way, that we have nothing to learn from other ministries. That kind of myopia blinds us to innovations that might strengthen our ministries. An excellent youth ministry has an organizational climate that allows for autonomy and entrepreneurship. We can free people of vision in the following ways:

Sow seeds of encouragement. There is no better way to warm up an organizational climate than through encouragement. Bob and Joani Miller were giving musical performances at youth retreats and conferences throughout the Northeast. When they were in town, they helped lead worship on Sunday mornings in their home congregation. With the encouragement of Associate Pastor Wayne Buchanan, they began to plan special outreach services for one Sunday night a month—services through which Christians could witness using drama, music, photography, video, and comedy. It was rough at first. Technical glitches had to be worked out. Sketches and skills had to be refined. But Wayne continued to support and encourage them every step of the way.

Within a year this unique, once-a-month "Church Shock," as it was called, became one of the most innovative worship services in the area. Non-Christians, attracted by the music, the fun, and the unpredictability, began to crowd the community center on Church Shock night. Bob and Joani encouraged the innovative and creative skills of other Christians who utilized their artistic gifts in this dynamic outreach. Now over fifteen people, high school age and up, consistently work alongside the Millers in the Church Shock performing troupe. The secret to the creative atmosphere at Church Shock is an attitude that says, "Try it; I bet it will work," rather than, "Do you think we should try it; what if it doesn't work?"

Give away ownership. Volunteers or students to whom we delegate a project, a Bible study, or game leadership, often sense that we expect them to do the jobs our way. We communicate that expectation by taking the project back if they try something different, by ignoring their suggestions, or by "riding in" like the cavalry to rescue them when they encounter difficulty. After all, we are seminary trained and thereby more experienced and semimessianic. They may comply with our wishes regarding the projects, but in so doing they short-circuit the innovations that might be sparked if they were convinced that the assignments were theirs, start to finish.

One of the best ways to encourage either students or leaders to be innovative in a ministry is to allow them ownership. That is what Waterman and Peters mean by autonomy. If we really want to see something new happen with youth group outreach, we need to challenge a group of students and adult leaders to genuinely own that program. To be creative, people need to feel that no one is breathing down their necks. Just as it's nearly impossible to work on a car if the owner is still driving it, it's difficult to be innovative with a program when leadership has not really been given over to us. Ownership encourages innovation.

Don't be afraid to fail. For the youth-ministry volunteer lost in the maze of *Ideas* books, discussion guides, game resources, and Bible studies, the possibility of failure stifles innovation. Sure, the game sounds good, but will it work with our kids? What will we do if it doesn't work? We must be willing to accept some bombs as the cost of a direct hit. Failing at something new doesn't mean that we or our students are incapable. It's merely a matter of timing, of group personality, or any of fifty other variables.

Every effective youth minister has occasions on which a game plan has to be changed after the opening whistle. Many of us don't believe that, however—mistakes don't happen to the really experienced, really good, really talented youth workers who lead seminars and share ideas, right? Of course, the reason behind the misconception is that these really experienced, good, talented youth workers couldn't get anyone to come to a workshop called "Ten Worship Ideas that Totally Died." People want to know what does work, leaving unspoken all of the mediocre ideas that fell between strokes of genius.

Those who attempt anything new will occasionally fail. Those who never fail never attempt anything.

Allow time for incubation. One of the reasons that youth ministers seldom innovate is that they simply don't have time. The average youth worker programs to survive, but innovation takes time. People need adequate time to formulate and incubate new ideas; they need to be allowed the luxury of long-term planning.

We planned the basic sketch of our Sunday night Breakaways at least nine months in advance. Well before laying out specific programming for an evening, we knew what our theme for a particular night would be. Generally speaking, the specific planning for a Sunday night took place one month prior to the date.

At the meeting to plan the October 31 Breakaway, we planned how to develop the "fear" theme we had chosen to capitalize on the Halloween coincidence. In the course of the conversation, someone suggested doing a slide show about what teenagers fear. Beyond that there was little specific guidance. One of the volunteers talented in photography, Thom Scott, was assigned to prepare the show. He had one month to complete the job. What he eventually produced was a remarkably entertaining and creative piece of work, including background music, narration, and humor, all the while involving several of our students in the filming. It was a masterpiece.

Aside from Thom's talent, the two keys to his completing such a blockbuster slide show were ownership and time. By giving him a month to work on the project, we showed that we took him seriously. We were saying, "We don't already have in mind some idea that we want you to carry out. We trust your ability. We sincerely want you to be innovative, and we know that this takes some time."

Our normal approach to delegation is to say to someone, "We really need you to come up with some wild, creative stuff for an upcoming event. The sky's the limit. It's your baby. Go for your dreams. Anything goes. And . . . it needs to be ready for tonight's meeting." Not only is this an insult, but it's an excellent way to stifle innovation.

A GOOD YOUTH MINISTRY
DEVELOPS AND DEPLOYS WORKERS' GIFTS

Waterman and Peters consistently found that excellent secular companies develop and utilize the strengths of their employees, treat their people with respect, and take them seriously. The Navy, however, is apparently another story. The authors quote Elmo "Bud" Zumwalt, the ex-chief of Naval Operations: "The Navy assumes that everybody below the rank of commander is immature."[5]

Unfortunately, the church echoes the Navy's sentiment when it treats people as if those below the rank of pastor or under eighteen are immature and unfit for real ministry. Before any Wall Street wunderkind articulated the principle of productivity through people, Jesus himself said,

> I tell you the truth, anyone who has faith in me will do what I have been doing. He will do even greater things than these, because I am going to the Father. And I will do whatever you ask in my name, so that the Son may bring glory to the Father. You may ask me for anything in my name, and I will do it (John 14:12-14).

Likewise, Paul writes,

> It was he who gave some to be apostles, some to be prophets, some to be evangelists, and some to be pastors and teachers, to prepare God's people for works of service, so that the body of Christ may be built up until we all reach unity in the faith and in the knowledge of the Son of God and become mature, attaining to the whole measure of the fullness of Christ (Eph. 4:11-13).

We in the church talk about the concept of productivity through people. Our Scriptures explicitly state it. But when it comes right down to the way we function, the way we do youth ministry, we act on our true beliefs: productivity through profit ("We need a bigger budget"); productivity through preaching ("We need to give these kids more doctrinal teaching; I better take care of it"); or productivity through program ("Only a few students came to our peer-ministry class and we get huge crowds out for our Friday night outreach; we may have to cut the peer-ministry program").

Following are some practical questions that we can ask of ourselves and our ministries to evaluate our adherence to the principle of productivity through people, to discover if we are taking seriously the gifts and abilities of those involved with our ministries.

Do we attempt to provide our teachers with the kind of classroom environment and instructional equipment that allows them to do their best?

OR

Do we communicate that their jobs are unimportant by allowing them to walk into classrooms lacking all basic supplies — except blackboards which haven't been cleaned since the apostolic age and Marconi-era movie projectors with burned-out bulbs?

Do we meet with our student-leadership core on a regular basis to get feedback on the program and meet regularly with our volunteer team for the same purpose?

OR

Do we meet with them only occasionally, when we need their blessing on something we already have planned?

Do we treat the volunteers with respect?

OR

Do we frustrate capable ministers by entrusting them with responsibility for the teenagers, but not the key to the church kitchen, or by requiring leaders to pay out of their pocket to participate in youth group activities instead of recognizing their contribution as being worthy of free pizza or a roller-coaster ride?

Are we facilitating the ministries of others by helping students and volunteers discern their gifts and giving them opportunities to test and sharpen those gifts?

OR

Do we hold to the motto "If you want it done right, you've got to do it yourself"?

Are we enhancing the morale of our leadership by communicating with words and actions that we take seriously their potential and contributions?

OR

Do we undermine these people (who hold responsible jobs, create personal momentum, organize their homes, make decisions, and gain the respect of their coworkers on a daily basis) by entrusting them only with the responsibilities of inflating balloons and performing skits?

At the heart of biblical Christianity is our belief in the priesthood of all believers—the notion that all believers, whether adult or adolescent, whether ordained or nonordained, whether paid or volunteer, are capable of and called to ministry. This means that we need to structure our youth ministries to discern, develop, and deploy gifted people.

Beyond carefully training leaders and plugging them into slots suited to their gifts, deploying gifted people requires trusting their abilities and ideas—believing that they can make significant contributions. More than trusting people, we in Christian ministry must also have a bedrock trust in a God who does extraordinary feats through ordinary people. We've got to have a basic belief in the ability of kids and adults to live lives of kingdom significance.

A sixteen-year-old girl was handing out sandwiches to homeless people on the streets of Los Angeles, recounts Ridge Burns, Director of the Center for Student Missions in southern California. In the course of a conversation with a grizzled-faced homeless man, she found out that the man had at one time been a medical doctor who, because of his alcoholism, had lost his license to practice medicine. She surprised even herself as she boldly shared her faith with him and invited him to ask Jesus into his life.

That man is still walking the streets with the homeless but now does so because he feels God has called him to be a doctor for the street people—all because some youth worker dared to believe that a sixteen-year-old girl could make a difference.

Stories like this one remind us that we underestimate God when we are reluctant to let youths lead singing, simply because we lead better. They make us realize that we may be overlooking crucial gifts when we refuse to let adult leaders teach because they don't have adequate formal training.

There are so many ways to say that we trust and value the contributions of others. We need to make every effort to enhance among volunteers a sense of family, of team membership. Some youth programs do this with baseball caps that say "Youth Staff." Others provide youth-staff T-shirts. I remember speaking at Camp Oswegatchie in upstate New York a few summers ago; there, every adult leader at the camp was awarded a special counselor's T-shirt that read,

> OS·WE·GAT·CHIE STAFF/os-we-GA-chee staf/ v. [Am Indian: black waters and a bent stick; or long, skinny bacteria] 1: adults running around in the woods acting as if they were teenagers 2: the cause of the disease Oswegatchicus exhausticum, characterized by hysteria, exhaustion, hoarse voice, and a fear of bears (see Ursusophobia) 3: the group of people allegedly supervising KP, classes, and night activities 4: the Christian servant-leaders of the greatest senior teen camp in the world syn: see fools for Christ's sake

It was more than a T-shirt; it was a badge of camaraderie and affirmation. It may have been corny, but it said, "We appreciate you."

A GOOD YOUTH MINISTRY
MAKES ITS CLEAR PURPOSE KNOWN
THROUGHOUT THE ORGANIZATION

The writer of Proverbs 29:18 puts it this way: "Where there is no vision, the people perish" (KJV). People tire of moving forward when there is no goal ahead of them. The shape of any excellent organization, whether in business or in youth ministry, is determined not by changing circumstances or the ups and downs of passing opinions, but by long-term vision. Waterman and Peters are adamant on this point. "Every excellent company we studied is clear on what it stands for, and takes the process of shaping values seriously. In fact, we wonder whether it is possible to be an excellent company without clarity on values and without having the right sorts of values."[6]

This mark of excellence is the most critical. Without a vision, staying close to the customer degenerates into a namby-pamby political game of trying to please everybody and accomplishing nothing of substance. Autonomy and entrepreneurship become little more than tinkering—an empty drive to perfect technique without any purpose. Productivity through people becomes a confusing chaos in which everyone does their own thing without any common head to direct the parts of the body. Thomas J. Watson wrote a book some time ago based on his experiences as a chief executive at IBM. Waterman and Peters draw from that book a lengthy quote that defends the importance of an organization deciding what it stands for.

> One may speculate at length as to the cause of the decline and fall of a corporation. Technology, changing tastes, changing fashions all play a part . . . No one can dispute their importance. But I question whether they in themselves are decisive. I believe the real difference between success and failure in a corporation can very often be traced to the question of how well the organization brings out the great energies and talents of its people. What does it do to help these people find common cause with each other? And how can it sustain the common cause and sense of this direction through the many changes that take place from one generation to another? Consider any great organization—one that has lasted over the years—I think you will find that it owes its resiliency not to its organization or administrative skills, but to the power of what we call "beliefs" and the appeal these beliefs have for its people. This then is my thesis: I firmly believe that any business, in order to survive and achieve success, must have a sound set of beliefs on which it premises all its actions and policies. Next, I believe that the most important single factor in corporate success will be the faithful adherence to those beliefs. And, finally, I believe if an organization is to meet the challenge of a changing world, it must be prepared to change everything about itself except those beliefs as it moves through corporate life. In other words, the basic philosophy, spirit and drive of an organization have far more to do with its relative achievements than do technological or economic resources, organizational structure, innovation and timing. All these things weigh heavily in success. But they are, I think, transcended by how strongly the people in the organization believe in its basic precepts and how faithfully they carry them out.[7]

Watson's statement is remarkable. Except for a few business-type terms, and the lack of even one mention of pipe cleaners and pizza, it could have been a mission statement for a youth ministry. (Try reading it again while humming "Pass It On.")

One of the gravest mistakes in modern youth ministry is ministering without vision—being stimulated into action through the latest resource, nudged into submission by some ruling elder, or halted by some bored teenager who doesn't consider the ministry adequately entertaining. There is no shortage of youth-ministry books on the market that define and clarify some sort of youth-ministry philosophy. Some use funnels. Some use pyramids. Others use circles. Virtually every geometric shape has been called into service. And yet, defining a philosophy is only the first step. Not only must we have a vision in youth ministry, but we must openly and frequently communicate that vision to everyone involved in the youth program—to the adults involved in leadership, to the students who attend every week, and to the parents of teenagers involved.

CORRECTING BLURRED VISION

One day in my fourth-grade classroom as I was clowning around with a buddy and putting on his glasses, I made an incredible discovery: I needed glasses. All of a sudden the world came into focus. Trees had leaves instead of green blobs. Cafeteria signs became clear enough to read. The blackboard suddenly made sense. All along I assumed that everyone saw things the way I saw them. It took glasses to expose the inaccuracy of my assumption.

Below are some tests that will help us evaluate the clarity of the vision in our youth programs.

What are we here for? Pose this question to the volunteer leaders, the pastor, the parents of students in the program, and the students themselves. Ask them to write out specific examples that demonstrate what they think you are trying to accomplish in the youth program. On one occasion, after I explained our youth-ministry vision to our Council on Ministries, the whole room erupted into applause. I could sense dawning understanding around the room—

"Eureka. So that's why we're here!" These faithful congregational workers, church leaders, and sincere Christians had been working without a real sense of purpose until they heard my ten-minute statement on our vision for ministry.

What do others see? If someone were to observe your youth program for a one-month period, what sort of values might they deduce that you hold? What sort of values would you want them to witness? What might someone observe about the values that drive your youth group if they were part of a leadership planning session? How about if they witnessed a game night? a retreat? a parents' meeting? a fund-raiser? We communicate our values most accurately when we are not intentionally doing so.

How do we make decisions? Observing the kinds of criteria we use to evaluate our ministries uncovers our values. Did we cut out the discipleship program because "there weren't enough kids involved"? Did we conclude the Bible study was a success because "the kids were really quiet"?

How precious are our methods? Listen to the discussions in planning sessions or staff and committee meetings. Ministries in which techniques and methodologies are precious are seldom guided by vision.

Are we taking our pulse every year? Frequent checks alert us early to inaccurate and unclear vision. We need to schedule periodic meetings with our youth-ministry constituency—students, parents, leaders, and congregational leaders—to inform them about our vision.

We need to consistently preach our vision, model our vision, remind ourselves of it as we plan, and make it known unashamedly to our leaders, our students, and their parents. Does our youth ministry have a clear, written vision statement? The first question we need to ask is not "Will it work?" or "Can we do it?" but "How does it help us reach our goal?" and "Does it fit our vision?" This is a mark of an excellent ministry.

A DESIRE FOR EXCELLENCE

To be sure, our vision and mandate as ministers of the gospel take us into realms that cannot be touched by the secular business consultant. Ours is a realm in which the report of the prophet carries more weight than the annual profit report. However, even if it takes listening occasionally to the counsel of two high-powered business types, the development of excellence is worth our time. We are working with precious human lives, helping teenagers grow into the image of Jesus. We are serving Christ, his Excellency himself. He desires and deserves our best.

Be very careful, then, how you live [and work] — not as unwise but as wise, making the most of every opportunity, because the days are evil (Eph. 5:15, 16).

CHAPTER THREE

GETTING IT DONE — MISSION IMPOSSIBLE?

I watched with a combination of awe and pity as Terry and I shared a week together at his home. A typical youth worker, it was the third night in a row Terry had been out late with some of his kids. It must have been two in the morning before he finally staggered into the bedroom of his small apartment. I awoke just long enough to thank the Lord that Terry wasn't married. I knew I would have been a witness to murder.

I could hardly believe it when he woke me up at six the next morning to tell me where to find everything in the kitchen. He whispered that he was on his way to the church to get everything set up for the car rally that was to be held later that day. I whispered a prayer of thanks that I didn't have to get up yet.

Terry was an absolutely sold-out brother, giving his life to teenagers, loving them creatively, intensely, and personally, sprinting through his day at a breakneck pace that took him over a nineteen-hour obstacle course every day. It seemed sad that someone that in love with Jesus and with kids would probably be sick, burned-out, divorced, or all of the above within five years.

* * *

When I think of people like Terry, I am reminded of a newspaper story reported by Robert Banks in his book, *The Tyranny of Time*.

> Horace Whittell, a dock worker in Gillingham, England hated his alarm clock. Everyday for forty-seven years, its bell had jarred him awake. For forty-seven years, he had longed to ignore it. For forty-seven years, he had felt the pressure of time. Then he got his revenge.
>
> On the day he retired, Mr. Whittell flattened the clock under an

eighty-ton hydraulic press.

"It was a lovely feeling," he said.[1]

The art of time management has many practitioners and they produce no small amount of material on the subject. Unfortunately, much of it really isn't so helpful. For example, author G. M. Lebhar offers this hot tip: If we reduce our sleep time by two hours a night, devote at least one hour a day less to mealtime chatter, friendly conversation, and leisure activities, and recover an additional hour of work by moving closer to the workplace, thereby reducing the time spent commuting, we could add five and a half years of usable time to our lives![2]

Particularly for Christians, the bulk of time management material misses the point entirely. Banks argues persuasively that most of what we read about time management, even from Christian writers, emphasizes a view of time that underlines urgency—that time is fleeting, and we must grab from it what we can before it's gone. Banks reminds us that Scripture never encourages a "busy use of time at all," but challenges us to discern appropriate timing. The apostle Paul never counseled in Colossians 4:5 that we see as many outsiders as possible, or for that matter, that we limit the number of outsiders we see. Paul's counsel is that we "act wisely" toward outsiders. The key here is discernment.

In a second set of passages (Rom. 13:11-12; Rev. 22:20) from which we are often taught that we must work furiously and quickly in light of Christ's imminent return, Banks redirects our focus to what he describes as a more biblical theme of alertness.

> The implication drawn from this is not that we should speed up our activities, but that we should refuse to allow ourselves to become "anxious" about anything (Phil. 4:6). This is the very opposite of the state of mind of the busy person. We are also enjoined to conduct ourselves "becomingly" in the light of our knowledge of Christ's coming, not to rush around trying to do everything before it is too late (Rom. 13:13).[3]

PRACTICING DISCERNMENT AND ALERTNESS

As the Christian management consultant Fred Smith reminds us, there are basically two approaches to time use.

One is the technological: minutes as units. The other is the philosophical: minutes as meaning. It's possible to grasp the technological view so tightly that you end up with no meaning. Technology should always be the servant of philosophy.

Too often people don't know the difference between a fast track and a frantic track.[4]

Especially youth workers, facing the constant and unending demands of our work with teenagers, need to reshape our thinking about personal management. When we are overly concerned about how much time we're spending, we will be overly concerned about time running out, leading to depression and pointless, feverish activity. As Smith points out, this mind-set breeds a mid-life crisis— "thinking about all the time already gone, the things you haven't done, won't get to do"—makes you frantic.

The inexperienced youth worker is often a blur of busyness, always going somewhere and late for the next place, playing catch up and praying that someone will cancel an appointment. Effective youth workers pace their ministries and live balanced lives that allow them to have identities apart from youth work. They have learned to practice disciplines of discernment and alertness. As one youth minister said when asked how his ministry had most changed over the course of his twelve years in youth work: "I've learned to work smarter, so I don't have to work harder." Smith sums up the principle: "Opportunity is not a mandate to do."

TIME TO MAKE CHANGES AND CHANGES TO MAKE TIME

Paul Borthwick, currently serving as Minister of Missions at Grace Chapel in Lexington, Massachusetts, is one of the most thoroughly organized youth ministers I know. He wrote the book on organization.[5] Judging from his youth ministry, he seems like the kind of person who has his T-shirts arranged by color. During my first full-time youth-ministry position, Paul and I attended the same monthly support group. Through that group I learned the significance of wisely managing my life and ministry.

That's where effective time management begins—with a decision to make some changes. We must

Realize poor time management is our *problem.* It's not the youth group's fault or the church's fault or our family's fault that we run out of time. If we own the problem, then we can influence the outcome of the problem.

Utilize all of the resources available to us in Christ. We have capacities for wisdom and discernment beyond our own human limitations. Make better personal and ministry management a matter of prayer. Instead of focusing on why the situation can't change, approach the matter with a sense of trust and challenge.

Specifically identify the benefits of better personal and ministry management. Anticipating more personal time, more study time in the Word, more family time, more time with students, a smoother ministry operation, survival beyond the age of thirty-five—the benefits you list are your incentive for change!

FACING THE PARADOXES

The first step in the process of effectively managing your time is taking an honest look at some common myths that govern the way we plan our time. Marlene Wilson, author of *Effective Management of Church Volunteers*, refers to these as paradoxes in time management.[6]

The open-door paradox. We youth workers practice an open-door policy that says to the students in the youth group, "I am available at any time if you need to talk." That means we always have students hanging around in our office. Our intent is good, but paradoxically, students who really need to talk about their problems are embarrassed to bring them forward in a place crawling with other kids. Consequently, they may never get to discuss them with us at all. The result is that we have discouraged the very thing we hoped to accomplish.

Tyranny-of-the-urgent paradox. Youth ministers tend to scamper around putting out fires instead of doing the kind of long-range planning that effective ministry requires. The result is that long-range planning is neglected, thereby ensuring future crises and more fires to fight.

Cluttered-desk paradox. We leave items on our desk so that we won't forget them. But as the pile of important materials mount up, the items on the desk get lost or misplaced, and we forget them altogether. Or occasionally a critical note resurfaces as the pile changes shape, reminding us that we need to act on an important matter, and that matter of urgency distracts us from what we were originally doing.

Telephone paradox. We call a fellow youth minister to give her information about an upcoming event and her secretary answers. Since we consider the information too important to give to the secretary (and risk a breakdown in communication), we offer to call back. Following an afternoon of telephone tag, we finally decide to stop trying for a day or two. Eventually we forget to make the call altogether, and the important event passes without the colleague ever getting the message.

Moral: A left message is better than no message.

Delegation paradox. We don't bring on new team members or student leaders because we don't have time to train them. But if we spent the time in recruitment, training, and delegation, we would have far more time in the long run.

TIME TO PLAN

Essentially, good personal management is a process of indentifying goals, organizing the goals into key areas, establishing clear objectives, developing a plan of action, setting priorities, and making a "To Do" list.[7] To find out what this looks like in a youth ministry, let's consider the following case study:

Jim and Sally are the loving parents of twenty-two kids—two of them by birth, ages three and five, the other twenty by "adoption," ages twelve to eighteen. Jim and Sally are the volunteer youth leaders at Christ Community Church. Jim is an electrician by trade and runs his own business. Having two young children keeps Sally pretty well occupied, even though she is not employed outside of the home.

This is their third year with the youth group, and it has been their most satisfying and productive year yet. The group is growing in breadth and in depth. In fact, that's part of the problem. Some students are asking if Jim and Sally would be willing to have an extra weekly discipleship group in their home. This would be in addition to teaching the weekly Sunday night youth group and Sunday school lesson. Jim's career is demanding, and he doesn't know if he can afford another night with the youth group every week. As the children get older, Sally is more concerned that the family have adequate time together.

They're not on the point of panic—not by a long shot. But they have discussed the busyness that seems to keep them ever on the run, and they are concerned that they are just holding on now and feel it isn't going to get better. They are excited about what God is doing with the youth group. They have no desire to end their involvement there.

STEP ONE:
IDENTIFY GOALS

Jim and Sally began to take control of their time by separately writing down some of their goals. They divided them into three categories: goals for the family, goals for the ministry, and goals for Jim's business. After discussing their individual goals, they agreed on some mutual goals. For the sake of example, we will chart their goals in the areas of family and ministry only.

Goals:
Family
    Maintain our strong marriage and family life
    Increase our time for family activities involving both children
    Make sure that we *both* have adequate time to stay healthy physically, emotionally, and spiritually

Youth Ministry
Continue our current level of youth group involvement
Continue to see the youth group grow numerically and mobilize the students to do outreach at the high school
Nurture the spiritual growth of those students who are seeking discipleship

STEP TWO:
ORGANIZE GOALS INTO KEY AREAS

Their next step is to organize their various goals into key areas so that they can establish objectives—specific actions that are steps toward the goals.

Key Areas:
Family
Time as a family
Exercise
Hobbies
Church/spiritual growth
Fellowship
Youth Ministry
Better youth-ministry training
More adult leadership in the youth program
Added time for discipleship of interested students

STEP THREE:
ESTABLISH CLEAR OBJECTIVES

Having developed from their goals some clear statements of need, Jim and Sally are ready to talk about specific objectives. It is critical at this stage that the objectives be measurable, achievable within the allotted time period, and compatible with the other goals.

Objectives:
Family
1. Hold at least four evenings a week for time at home as a family.
2. Save two Saturdays a month for family activities.
3. Walk, jog, or swim at least three times a week.
4. Sally will continue to pursue her crafts, Jim his fishing.

5. Attend church consistently, read one good Christian book a month, and attend one retreat just for our growth as Christians.
6. Go to dinner with adult friends once every two weeks.

Youth Ministry

1. Attend at least two youth-ministry training workshops/seminars.
2. Draw up a job description to use for recruiting some more leaders.
3. Investigate what kinds of curricula are available for discipling students.
4. Set aside one breakfast per week for discipleship group— 6:30 to 8:00 on Wednesday mornings.
5. Cancel Sunday night youth group every eighth Sunday night.
6. Recruit another couple to take primary responsibility for youth Sunday school class.
7. Twice a year, hold leadership training for more mature youth group kids (four-week series) culminating with an overnight retreat.

STEP FOUR:
DEVELOP AN ACTION PLAN

By defining specific objectives, Jim and Sally are saying, "We won't do everything; we won't allow our goals to be crowded out by the urgencies that press in on us everyday. We'll do instead only the objectives we listed, because we believe reining ourselves in will help us to meet the family and youth-ministry goals on which we've agreed."

Taking each of the objectives one at a time, Jim and Sally now plot out a strategy that allows them to fulfill their objectives. This action plan involves bite-sized chunks. The bigger the plan, the less likely it is to be carried out. It is discouraging to anticipate eating a whole elephant, but we can picture taking one bite at a time. A good action plan describes the action to be taken, assigns someone to be responsible for the action, gives a deadline for having completed the action, and assigns to someone the task of working out the logistics so the plan can be carried out.

Action Plan:
> *Objective:*
>> To attend at least two youth-ministry training workshops/ seminars
>
> *Who:*
>> Jim and Sally will both go
>
> *When:*
>> Within next six months
>
> *How:*
>> Sally will investigate by getting info from Christian bookstore; Sally will handle registration, etc.
>
> *Cost:*
>> About two-hundred dollars

STEP FIVE:
SET PRIORITIES

After Jim and Sally have worked through their action plan, they go back over the list of objectives and decide which is most important. Since they can't do everything right now, they discuss what is the *best* investment of their time right now. Going back through the list, Jim and Sally agree that their first priority with the youth group is setting up the Wednesday morning discipleship group. They decide to take action on the plans that will open up some time for that. As a family they decide to spend fewer nights out with the youth group. Feeling that their next critical need is for additional leadership, they decide to begin pursuing that goal as well.

STEP SIX:
MAKE A "TO DO" LIST

Based on their chosen priorities, Jim and Sally are now ready to put together a "To Do" list that will help them take action on their plan. Since they have decided to move forward with the Wednesday morning discipleship group, Sally prepares the week's "To Do" list with that objective in mind.

Things to Do:
> Go to Christian bookstore and find material we can use for discipleship

Prepare flyer to hand out at youth group announcing the new Wednesday morning meeting

FIRST THINGS FIRST

Our willingness to set firm priorities and to stick with an action plan that gives those priorities expression is one of the toughest tests of leadership. As Alec MacKenzie says:

> One of the measures of a manager is his/her ability to distinguish the important from the urgent, to refuse to be tyrannized by the urgent, to refuse to be managed by crisis. They must forget the unnecessary and ignore the irrelevant.[8]

The difficulty of sticking with priorities confronted me in my first youth-ministry position. At the interview I articulated that I felt called to disciple students and that this would determine the way that I programmed for the youth ministry. Everyone agreed with this policy—until I cut the traditional summer camp that the students went to every year, in favor of some activities that would better achieve our primary purpose of discipleship. The retreat, a family-camp affair up in New Hampshire, was a nice idea, but it didn't fit our immediate goals and objectives concerning discipleship. While I wanted to take advantage of some summer camp ministry, I was not prepared to spend budgeted money on that particular site, with the traditional group of students who took part in that particular retreat.

It was uncomfortable during the three-day blizzard of phone calls and complaints. People were happy for me to have objectives and goals as long as they didn't interfere with the way they'd always done things. But I came out of the experience with few wounds and a valuable lesson: Any time we take a stand for something, we can almost guarantee we will be standing on somebody's foot. If we take priorities and goals seriously, we should be prepared for a few screams and gasps. Our willingness to set priorities grows out of a confidence in who we are called to be and what we believe God has called us to do.

CHAPTER FOUR
TIME BUSTERS

Some business executives were once asked to respond to two questions: How do *others* waste your time? How do *you* waste your time? Before reading any further in this chapter, jot down your own responses to these questions.

Time management experts suggest recording in fifteen-minute segments exactly how we spend a week—at least—of work days. The discipline of writing our activities out helps us discern what could be done, what should be done, what must be done, and what should be left undone. Alec MacKenzie helps us to understand the importance of this kind of personal research and accountability.

> The time inventory, or log, is necessary because the painful task of changing our habits requires far more conviction than we can build from learning about the experience of others. We need the amazing revelation of the great portions of time we are wasting to provide the determination to manage ourselves more effectively in this respect . . . we think our time wasters are primarily external forces until we see a picture of ourselves . . . One surprise will be that time is generally wasted in the same way every day and another surprise is the small fraction of the day that is free and uncommitted.[1]

Businessmen and youth workers alike cite some of the following issues as Time Busters.

TIME BUSTERS

TELEPHONE
Priority Management, a consulting firm in Pittsburgh, reports that we spend about two years of our lifetime just trying to make phone

contact with people who are either on the phone or unavailable. And I have noted that it's difficult for Christians to make phone calls short—to inform or question and then hang up. Right or wrong, we feel compelled to ask how the callers are doing, query for prayer requests, invite them to share a memory verse, and review their life goals.

Telephones are dictatorial. Every time they ring, they insist on an answer, regardless of what we are doing or who we are with. And then it's usually someone calling to ask about an activity that was discussed in the bulletin every Sunday for the last month. Our family fights back by refusing to answer the phone during dinner. This nightly appointment with each other is so important to us that we don't let anyone barge in to interrupt. At work we can fight back by requesting a secretary or office receptionist to screen our calls so that other work is not disrupted to pass on common-knowledge information.

One youth minister in Chicago (who shall remain nameless) has discovered he can turn on his answering machine when he's at home and screen out calls he doesn't want to answer at the moment. Then when he is going to be out for a while, he turns the machine off so that he won't have any calls to return when he gets home! Pray for this guy.

Author Les Christie has given us some practical tips on using the phone more profitably.[2]

Keep a functioning pen and a pad of paper by the phone. Nine out of ten of us forget messages or make phone calls to people for reasons we forget. Get something to write with and write on!

Keep a personal phone book of frequently called numbers. Most of us look up the same numbers over and over again. Be sure to have a special section for youth-ministry resource people: crisis-pregnancy center, suicide-prevention hot line, Christian counselors, substance-abuse resources.

Let your phone do the driving. Locate needed materials, make reservations, order take-out food, all by phone. At best, you will average maybe fifty miles per hour by car. Using the phone, you can easily travel up to 186,000 miles per second.

Jot down what you wish to talk about before you make the call. It saves time for both the caller and the one called. And you'll never embarrass yourself by getting someone on the phone and saying, "I needed to talk with you about something, but now I can't think of what it was."

An answering machine is meant to serve you, not distract you. I know some youth ministers who spend so much time recording their phone greetings that they could have written every caller a personal letter in the same amount of time.

MAIL

How do you feel about spending approximately eight months of a normal lifetime just opening junk mail? That's what one consulting firm estimates. The worst are the youth-ministry resource packets— fifty index cards at a shot. One youth minister told me she feels guilty tossing those packets in the garbage. She could be ditching *the* idea or resource that will help her students find Christ. Most of us know the feeling of waking up in the middle of the night in a cold sweat, having dreamed we were before the throne of God, and having him ask, "Why did you throw away all those inspiring ideas I sent your way?"

Our tendency is to read mail as soon as possible, even if we are in the middle of other projects. The mistake is that doing so forces us to read through the mail twice—once out of curiosity and once to actually respond. We should try to handle mail items just once. Except for items of correspondence that one can't answer immediately, a good rule of thumb is to open the mail when you are able to answer it, and answer it as soon as you open it.

MEETINGS

Christians apparently like to have meetings. A quick skim through the New Testament, however, shows only two real business meetings— one described in Acts 1:12-26 and a second in Acts 15:1-29. Reading these two passages, it seems reasonable to suggest that Scripture gives us only two situations in which a meeting is called for: one for replacing an apostle and one for discussing circumcision.

Why do we meet so much? Partly from a fear of making our own decisions. Although Scripture instructs us that there is wisdom in the counsel of many, more often than not we meet, not to make a better decision, but so that there will be more to share the blame if we make a poor or unpopular decision. The proverb of reference for this principle is, "The more necks in the noose, the longer it takes to choke."

But we could probably preserve our necks by utilizing work groups and subcommittees to hammer out policies in advance of group meetings and then circulating the written proposals or policy statements. Generally speaking, the smaller unit is more effective in planning anyway. Also, we need to courageously make our own decisions, without trying to gather other targets in case of a shootout. Make meetings a last resort, scheduled only if someone has a concern about decisions being made.

PUBLICITY

Youth ministers spend an inordinate amount of time just trying to get kids' attention. They make one of two mistakes in the area of publicity: they either do none at all, or they spend tremendous amounts of time doing the kind of promotion that might, at best, bring ten additional people to the program. The key to effective publicity is knowing whom we are trying to reach and identifying a few good ways to reach them. (We will discuss publicity more thoroughly in Chapter Eleven.)

PAPERWORK

Hell will be a place where ministry reports, expense statements, and requisition forms are due on an hourly basis. On earth, however, paperwork is merely a necessary evil. My strategy is to prepare some of these forms progressively through the report period. Rather than wait until the end of the month to fill out an expense statement, for instance, I keep up-to-date tallies throughout the month. At the end of the report period, all I have to do is summarize. I use the same approach with monthly departmental reports, adding a paragraph or so to the report each week. By the end of the month, when the report is due, it's virtually ready to be typed up and sent out.

MEALTIME APPOINTMENTS

We often use an hour at lunch discussing matters that could have been dealt with in twenty minutes, not because we want to be thorough, but because we want to try and enjoy our lunch. Fred Smith puts it this way:

> In my judgment, eating together is generally only a preface to conversation. You eat for forty-five minutes before you ever get down to business. It might establish rapport, but it's hard to do serious business. I would rather have thirty minutes eyeballing somebody in an office than two hours over a dinner table. Eating is a social occasion, not the most productive business occasion.[3]

CIVIC "DUTIES"

Beware the civic dinner circuit—we're invited to offer the opening prayer and then keep our mouth shut. Early in my ministry, I was flattered by invitations to be a guest pray-er at the Rotary Luncheon or the Christian Women's Club. While the gesture was well meant, these activities were so time consuming that I almost had to change my job title to Minister of Mealtimes. Eugene Peterson says it best:

> One of the indignities to which pastors (and occasionally youth ministers) are regularly subjected is to be approached as a group of people are gathering for a meeting or a meal with the request, "Reverend, get things started for us with a little prayer, will ya?" I am not prescribing rudeness: the bellow does not have to be audible. I am insisting that the pastor who in indolence or ignorance is politely compliant with requests from congregation and community for cut-flower prayers forfeits his or her calling. Most of the people we meet inside and outside the church think that prayers are necessary, but harmless, starting pistols that shoot blanks and get things going. It is an outrage and a blasphemy when pastors adjust their practice of prayer to accommodate these inanities.[4]

FOUL-UPS

Coworkers, secretaries, team members, or even leadership kids make mistakes that cost us time. It happens. Welcome to youth ministry.

LACK OF PLANNING

Good long-range planning can actually save us time in the long run. Henry Ford once said, "People who have no time do not think; the more you think, the more time you have." When it comes down to it, we don't take time for planning because we don't feel it's worth the time. Most volunteer youth workers will tell you quite candidly that their long-range goal for the present is survival!

Veteran youth workers can fall into the trap of not planning because we've learned to think on our feet. We can pull off a respectable program even without much planning. We may manage to finesse our way through the program without embarrassing ourselves, but does it do justice to the kids and the God we serve? We forget that God blesses our ministries sometimes in spite of us, and not because of us. But perhaps the greatest loss from seat-of-the-pants youth work is the volunteer leadership. We have to run the whole show by ourselves because we're making up the show as we go along!

Another reason for lack of planning in youth ministry is that typically youth workers are oriented to action. Something about youth ministry attracts folks whose basic response to problems is: "Ready. Fire. Aim." True, if we throw ten activities on the calendar, one of them is bound to work. In the meantime, though, we have run ourselves ragged through nine other activities that have used our money, time, and energy. It's not a good trade-off. The apostle Paul counsels us to "be wise in the way we act" (Col. 4:5).

COMMUTING/DRIVING

Youth workers seem to spend a lot of time driving around. One youth volunteer told me that he never goes on any errand alone. He always takes one of his students. "I get more youth ministry done that way," he claims, "and it allows me to spend time with students." Or keep some good teaching tapes in the car to make your time on the road work for you and not against you.

OVERCOMMITMENT

Steve, a wonderful Christian with a contagious faith and a heart that is open to serve, is on a ministry treadmill that is leaving him exhausted and, on occasion, even resentful. He's working with the youth group, heading up the youth committee, serving on the church board, and, inconveniently enough, also holding down a full-time job. His good humor ("If it's Wednesday, this must be prayer meeting; if I'm home, you must be my wife.") won't last forever.

A person may be overcommitted because they have broad interests. The irony is that conscientious church workers will be of more help over the long haul by pacing themselves, by devoting their energies and attentions to one or two areas only. We have only so many fingers to plug the holes in the dike.

Sometimes we are overcommitted because we think that is the way spiritual people operate. I've heard youth ministers say, "I'd rather burn out than rust out." And I suppose if I had to choose between the two, I would agree. But those are not the only options. Donald Bloesch is right when he says that in modern Christianity "busyness is the new holiness." Lack of time has become a badge of spirituality. John Wesley wrote, "Though I am always in haste, I am never in a hurry, because I never undertake more work than I can go through with calmness of spirit."

According to the gospel writers, Jesus was determined and single-minded, but he never seemed to be in a hurry. Even in those situations when haste might have seemed appropriate (the death of his friend Lazarus, for instance), Jesus took his time. He had three years to establish the kingdom, three years to recruit and train his disciples, three years to prepare for the redemption of all mankind, and yet he never seemed to feel the pressure of time.

A third contributor to overcommitment is our inability to convincingly use the word *no*. Any *yes*es we are serious about have to be protected by sincere *no*s. Why are we so uncomfortable using the "n" word? Maybe because we want to please everybody, or we like to be in on the action or thought of as "can do" people. Maybe because we have a genuine burden for the task or maybe because we know the committee is desperate. Or maybe it's because our egos are tickled by the person who says, "You're the only person who can pull this off. We need you." It's easy to think, "Y'know, they're probably right. It's going to be a severe blow to the kingdom if I don't ride in and save these people." We can't allow our judgment to become clouded by pride, though. Wilson is right: "The true measure of a leader is not what he or she does, but what he or she decides to leave undone."[5] *No* may be one of the most important words in youth ministry.

GENERAL UNDISCIPLINE

The greatest single mismanagement of our time is rooted in inadequate self-discipline.

Double-mindedness. We waste time thinking about the next project while we're working on this project, and thereby take twice the time to complete this project.

Being sidetracked. I find the demon of browsing lurking in hardware stores, bookstores, and libraries. I make a "quick trip" to find one item, and an hour later I am still perusing the shelves.

Compulsive behaviors. Sometimes we waste time adding unnecessary touches. For example, it's worthwhile to make the new promotional mailing attractive. It's *not* vital that it merit an art award in the category of "Composition, Art Work, Creativity, Profundity, Social Consciousness, and Hilarity." You're just trying to get students to come to the event, for heaven's sake.

Fellowshipping. Youth workers are sociable people. We like to talk and visit, even when we have other work that deserves our attention. I used to work in a ministry in which the normal routine of the morning was an extended coffee break. None of us intended to be shirking our duty; the breaks just got longer and longer. (We finally had to limit the coffee break to forty-five minutes because it was interfering with our lunch hour.) And there was an unwritten assumption that someone who passed on the coffee break in favor of doing necessary work was angry or upset about something.

Poor organization. One study shows that we spend an average of one year of our lives looking for lost objects. For youth workers, perhaps this can be explained as a personality type that is more interested in spending time with a student than rummaging through a file cabinet. (Or perhaps it's because churches don't provide file cabinets for people who do youth ministry.) Whatever—youth ministers waste a lot of time trying to find "that study we did two years ago," "the letter we wrote to the deacons last quarter," "the balloons." A little better organization could allow us to invest that time more profitably.

Procrastination. This should probably have been mentioned much earlier in the chapter, but we just never got around to it. Procrastination is not always as clear-cut as blatant postponement of a task. We're creative. We procrastinate by over-researching, over-praying, over-waiting-on-God. Procrastination is an especially attractive option when we don't want to complete the task anyway. We sometimes procrastinate because we feel the assignment is a waste of time. Ironically, the greater waste of time occurs because we don't just plunge into the task and get it done.

Indecision. Sometimes, the more sensitive we desire to be to God's leading, the slower we are to follow it. Bill was a younger youth-minister friend who was so zealous to wait on God that he never did anything. I used to jokingly say, "I think God is the one waiting on you." He loved Christ and he loved the ministry; but he was so fearful of making a wrong decision that he never made any decisions. It cost him several significant ministry opportunities before he learned to start moving. Faithfulness is not waiting until everything is clear and absolutely certain. Faith is acting on what we know and trusting God to help us with what we don't know and might face. It's easier to steer a *moving* vehicle.

WAITING

We can turn everyday frustration into a pleasant surprise of added time by planning to make waiting work for us. We can bring a student along when we go to the store or to the dentist and use that time in the line or the lobby for talking. Or if we find ourselves stuck in traffic, waiting in line, or delayed at an appointment, we can whip out Tom Clancy or C.S. Lewis and take in a chapter of that book we've been wanting to read. We can even use waiting time to respond to some of the letters we've been meaning to answer.

SLEEP

Most of us would like to waste a little more time on this activity. And while an ample amount of sleep is critical for good health, our wants often argue louder than our needs. One of the consistent factors among most of the great saints in church history is that they were people who went to bed early and rose early. Granted, very few of them were doing youth ministry. But more often than not, our late hours are dictated by time spent in front of the tube and not by time spent with family members or kids.

PEOPLE

The student who drops in "just to hang out" is both the glory and the bane of the youth worker's existence. Sometimes we sense that these drop-ins are ordained of God, and that whether we or the kid or our schedule is aware of it, this student has a divine appointment. Those opportunities are precious.

At the same time, there are other students for whom we are responsible, other precious opportunities for which we must plan, and that means we need to help people to understand that our investment of time is serious business. The average parishioners don't hesitate to drop in on the youth minister, because they feel the youth minister doesn't do anything anyway. But they would never make that same assumption about a doctor or lawyer or any other professional.

We shouldn't find it surprising that a teenager or two drops by the house on our free nights. The assumption is that we were sitting at home, bored, waiting for something to happen anyway. From the adolescent perspective, that's basically what it's like to be at home with just your family on a weekend night. If they were home alone, it's likely that they would be thrilled if some friends dropped by. They assume the same is true for us. But there is no rule that says, "Thou shalt always allow teenagers from the youth group to come into thine house and eat thine food even if thou hadst planned a family night."

Even if others don't take our time seriously, we must. That doesn't mean that we can't be spontaneous, and it doesn't give us an excuse to ignore genuine need. But the best and most responsible spontaneity grows out of good planning. No one else is responsible for our schedule but us. If we do not honor our time, no one else will.

TIMELY TRUTH

Though the chapters that follow in this book offer guidance in youth ministry behind the scenes, helping us to better manage our youth ministries, there is no management more important than personal management. More important than the nuts and bolts is the control and discipline of the hand that turns the wrench.

The following extreme paraphrase of Proverbs 24:30 reminds us that effective personal and ministry management is a sacred responsibility:

I passed by the church of a sluggard, by the youth group of a man without sense; and lo, the kids were facing some thorny issues; their hearts were tied and tangled with all kinds of worldly concerns, and the sense of community in the group had broken down altogether. Then, I saw and considered it; I looked and received instruction. "A little wastefulness, a little disorganization, a little mismanagement, a little pride, and a youth ministry will be greatly impoverished, robbed of potential as an armed man robs his victims" (BVD: Bible Version according to Duffy).

SECTION
TWO

DRAFTING
YOUR
BLUEPRINT

CHAPTER FIVE

MAKING DECISIONS WITHOUT MAKING ENEMIES

Devon and Erin had been working with the youth ministry at Third Church for almost five years. Because of their seniority, they were widely recognized within the congregation and among the core of seven volunteer leaders as the couple in charge of the youth ministry. When plans went well, the credit eventually trickled back to them. When there were problems, the blame usually found them as well. Despite their status as volunteers, they were clearly in charge.

In a December meeting, the youth-ministry team discussed plans for the upcoming summer. The youth group traditionally had a full summer program, and Devon and Erin liked to stake down some of the important dates in December. Their progress, however, screeched to a halt when they came to assigning a date to the summer youth-choir tour.

The youth choir was an integral part of this church's ministry to teenagers and the summer choir tour was the cornerstone of the youth-choir program. There was no question that it was the dangling carrot that kept those kids singing the rest of the year.

The questions to be settled surrounded the timing of the tour. Katie Barton, the choir director, had been on the staff for three years and had nurtured the kids into a flourishing choir. Her popularity with the students had made her a valuable member of the youth-ministry leadership team.

Occasionally, the schedule of the youth choir conflicted with the schedule of the youth program, but Devon, Erin, and Katie always worked something out. But this year there appeared to be the seeds of a major standoff. Katie insisted that the youth choir needed to tour during the month of June. Too many churches shut down or drastically cut back their programs in July and August, making it almost impossible for Katie to line up enough performances to fill out the itinerary.

As Devon explained to the youth-ministry team, that was precisely the reason he had always appreciated the choir touring during the month of July. It never interfered with the traditional dates of youth camp during the third week of June. "It's hard to catch many students in town during July," he told them, "and during the month of August, the students who are in town are tied up with band camp, cheerleader camp, or football camp." Since the choir was a special constituency that didn't involve the whole youth group, Devon couldn't see altering the youth program schedule to fit the choir schedule.

"You'll be impressed by our board. They're tops when it comes to decision making."

Ron and Terry sided with Devon. They had already made some family vacation plans based on the normal June camp week, and it would be very difficult to change them now. Dave and Maggie were fairly open either way, although their fifteen-year-old Ashley was a member of the youth choir, and should there be a conflict of dates, it would land them in a dilemma. Carolyn, a young single woman who had been working with the group for about a year, was open to both positions, but had already talked to the team about perhaps doing a student work project this year rather than the traditional camp week.

Here were eight sincere people, all committed to ministry with teenagers, and all willing to give up some of their summer vacation time to the youth program. There were no hard feelings—yet. These people were good friends and cared about one another. But a decision had to be made, and relatively soon. How could these folks on the ministry team make these decisions without making enemies?

AN OCCUPATIONAL HAZARD OF LEADERSHIP

Making decisions is, all at the same time, the loneliest, the most exciting, and the most critical part of leadership. As we begin talking about decision making, we can start with these premises:

• Any effective leader will eventually make some hard choices.
• The one who makes decisions will sometimes disappoint and anger those who wanted the decision to go another way. While we are always looking for "win-win" solutions, it's impossible to give both parties their way if the preference of one party negates the preference of the other party.
• No one is always right. Therefore, we must be humble in our decision making, and as often as possible utilize the counsel of others, not for protection against blame, but for guidance.
• If you make enough decisions, you will eventually make a bad decision. That is the price we pay for being human. When we make bad decisions, the proper response is to ask forgiveness of God, our constituency, and ourselves, and then move on, rejoicing that our God can make crooked ways straight.

DIFFERENT SOLUTIONS
FOR DIFFERENT PROBLEMS

Working in youth ministry with others who have a common vision and love for Christ is no guarantee of agreement on every issue. In fact, that is the splendor of the church of Christ—we can have remarkable diversity and still share a basic unity in Jesus. Our call as a church is not uniformity, but unity. Organizing everybody to walk in lockstep may be more efficient, but it's not at all "Ephesiant." As the apostle Paul put it:

> Be completely humble and gentle; be patient, bearing with one another in love. Make every effort to keep the unity of the Spirit through the bond of peace. There is one body and one Spirit— just as you were called to one hope when you were called—one Lord, one faith, one baptism; one God and Father of all, who is over all and through all and in all (Eph. 4:2-6).

In youth ministry we face dilemmas that require decisive action. Some are as simple as what theme to use for the next game night or which movie to show at the lock-in. Others are more complex: How will we lay out the summer youth-program schedule? How will we deal with the discipline problems of the two tenth-grade girls? How will we allot the youth budget? Will we allow Steve to stay on the youth-ministry team if he and Sherry get a divorce?

Whether simple or complex, every decision has two stages: creativity, getting input about what might be done; and judgment, deciding what should be done. Both elements are critical. Creativity is like a miner directing the streams of runoff from several sources into one spillway. Judgment is when he uses his pan to sift through the ore to find the real gold. The more streams he draws from, the more likely he is to find his treasure. On the other hand, if he keeps everything that runs down the spillway, he'll end up with tons of mush. Any decision-making process needs both creativity and judgment.

GO FOR THE GUSTO
OR PLAY IT SAFE?

The degrees of creativity and judgment required depend on the decisions that need to be made. For instance, it doesn't matter much how you carry a log from Point A to Point B. We may even allow two small children to try to carry it. They might try several different ways of moving the log, but since the risk of failure is not so severe, we let them try virtually whatever they will. We're not sure if they can pull it off, but there seems to be little harm in letting them give it a shot.

Likewise in youth ministry, if the decision we are making is not so serious, we may decide to put more weight on the creativity side of the equation. The stakes for failure are no big deal, so we allow ourselves the freedom of extra creativity. If we are planning a lock-in, for example, we don't have a heavy agenda for the evening. As long as we maintain a wholesome Christian environment where we can be with students, we're not that uptight about the programming for the evening. This is a lock-in, after all. "It ain't brain surgery," as they say.

So we may allow a group of students to plan the entire event. We give them a few guidelines, and then say, "It's your call. All decisions are up to you." We are willing to allow for more creativity in a situation like this, even if a little mush gets mixed in with the runoff. As long as the students stay within the prescribed guidelines, the consequences of poor decisions will not be that costly.

CREATIVITY AND JUDGMENT

But what if our decision is how to carry a tray full of iced-tea glasses across the room to the guests in the den? We may be more cautious this time. There is less room for experimentation here, and the consequences of a wrong approach will be more messy. The stain on the carpet won't be the end of the world, but it will be small consolation to encourage the lady of the house that if she looks at the stain long enough she will see the face of Jesus.

Using judgment, we decide to allow one of the children to carry the tray if he will accept help from one of the adult guests. The child still gets practice carrying the tray, but in judgment we've added the steadiness of an older hand.

Some decisions in youth ministry demand this same blend of creativity and judgment—most short-term programming decisions, for instance. What topics will we study in Bible study? What activities will we plan for the next six months? We need to allow the students opportunities to bear the weight of responsibility. That's the way they learn. Students add creativity and freshness to our more mature steadiness. And while they may make choices on the basis of personal likes and dislikes, we exercise judgment that comes through experience to come up with a plan that is best for the whole youth group. Besides, at the very worst, their decisions will affect only the next six months.

HANDLE WITH CARE

Taking our tea-tray example further, what happens if Aunt Gertie passes out in the parlor as she reaches for the iced-tea tray? The child, fresh from his victory with the tea service, offers to carry Gertie upstairs with the help of his adult teammate, but this is deemed too risky. This is no time for creativity and learning. The child's offer is refused. One of the guests, a doctor, steps in and takes control of the situation, suggesting that Aunt Gertie not be moved at all for the time being.

At times in our youth ministries, lives are at stake, and wrong decisions will have serious consequences. Will the group proceed with the planned ski trip even though the highway patrol says the weather is unsafe for driving? Will we allow John to continue working with the youth group even though he admits to being arrested for molestation? In these cases, the equation will be weighted far more on the side of judgment. One element of decision making is discerning the appropriate blend of creativity and judgment for a particular decision.

HEADS I WIN, TAILS YOU LOSE

In the case of the summer youth program schedule, it would probably be the kind of scenario in which judgment will weigh a bit more heavily than creativity. We are talking about two major events that have traditionally played a large part in the summer youth program.

They will want to be open to new ideas, but they will want to proceed with some measure of caution. It will obviously affect the whole thrust of the summer program, and, perhaps even more important, it has the potential for disrupting the unity of the leadership team. That would be the most serious consequence of all. Is it fair to allow Devon and Erin to call the shots throughout the year and then yank that authority from them when it comes to summer planning? Can they pull off a July retreat without Ron and Terry? Do they want to? What about a summer retreat without Katie and her musical contribution? No one would look forward to that. Maybe Carolyn's suggestion of a completely different kind of summer event is worth looking at.

According to Robert Moskowitz, there are basically four types of solutions to any kind of problem.[1]

TYPE-A SOLUTION

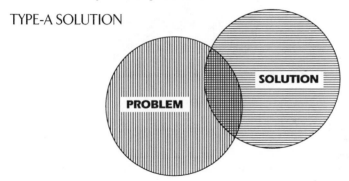

While solving some of the aspects of the problem, this type solution leaves others untouched. Type-A solutions may also have the side effect of additional problems.

If the group goes with Carolyn's suggestion, for instance, taking the entirely new approach of a week-long work project, it would offer some appeasement to both Devon and Katie. Because of the limited number of students who would be interested in a trip like this, Katie would not feel as if her choir tour is threatened by massive camp participation. At the same time, this would still allow Devon to offer the group a major June event. Carolyn's suggestion would also take care of Ron and Terry's scheduling problems. So it would resolve some of the problems.

On the other hand, it would resolve *only* some of the problems. It would still preclude all of the choir kids from being involved in the work project. And it would disappoint all of the students who are not in choir and are not interested in doing a work project. After all, this is a church and the summer camp in June is a tradition! That might arouse the ire of a whole new core of people who believe they are facing the prospect of a summer with neither a choir tour nor a camp week.

TYPE-B SOLUTION

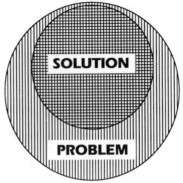

Like Type-A, a Type-B solution resolves only some elements of the problem, leaving others untouched. Type-B solutions, however, open no new cans of worms.

A Type-B solution to our case study is to run both the choir tour and the summer camp week simultaneously. Katie would have her way with the tour schedule, and Devon could schedule the retreat for the usual June dates. This would help Ron and Terry who have been holding these dates in anticipation of the normal summer schedule.

What this solution would *not* do is resolve Dave and Maggie's dilemma. Ashley will still have to decide which event she is going to participate in, and that will put them on the spot. What if she doesn't go to the summer camp? Should they go as leaders anyway? And what about all of the other students who have traditionally been involved in both youth choir and summer camp? This solution is no solution at all for them.

TYPE-C SOLUTION

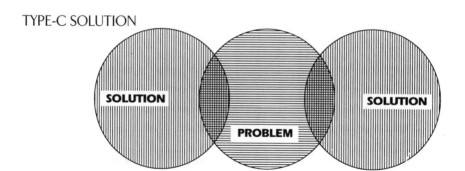

A Type-C solution is really two or more Type-A solutions brought together and applied simultaneously. The good part of a Type-C solution is that it may solve all or most aspects of the problem. The bad part is that it usually brings unwanted side effects.

In the course of the discussion, Dave and Maggie suggested that perhaps all three events could be offered. The choir could tour in June, during which time the youth group would also sponsor a week-long work camp. Then in July, the group would proceed with the traditional summer camp. That would please everybody, at least partially.

Devon's response was almost immediate. "Yeah, but what about the extra money for three trips? We just don't have it in the budget. And what are we going to do about leadership for three events? I can't take anymore time away from work. I'm already giving up one week of vacation for camp. Does that mean I have to take off a week for the work camp as well? And if Erin and I aren't there, and Katie's with the choir, are you guys going to be willing to put it all together?"

The room was quiet. All of a sudden, they all shouted at the same time, "What we need is a Type-D solution!"

TYPE-D SOLUTION

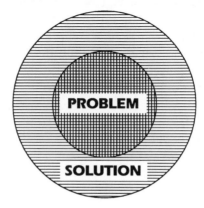

A Type-D solution is a total solution, dealing with all aspects of the entire problem, even in some cases providing some added benefits and side effects that no one thought about. In Never-Never Land, every problem has a Type-D solution.

Just when it appeared that Katie and Devon were going to raise their voices, Maggie came up with an alternative idea. "Katie, what would happen if we did the choir tour during spring break this April? That way everybody would be around still, and it would allow us to keep our usual date for summer camp."

Ron smiled and said, "Yeah, and that would allow us to chaperon on the choir trip without taking any vacation because we teachers get the same Easter break as the students get. That would give us extra time with the students."

Devon, looking around at the others said, "I like it. That would allow Erin and me to take some time off from the youth group during Easter week. We've always wanted to do that but felt that we had to be here to do something with the youths."

And a mighty wind filled the room and tongues of fire appeared above their heads as they began to speak in other tongues. . . .

MEANWHILE, BACK IN REALITY

Unfortunately, defining different kinds of solutions is much easier than finding them. Typically, ministry teams get bogged down in the decision-making process because those involved have preconceived notions of what a solution looks like. We spend our time and energy always looking for an elusive Type-D solution when we might be able to break the decision gridlock by understanding that solutions don't always look the same way. When a planning meeting seems hopelessly snagged on some issue, we may be able to craft a compromise proposal by playing out how the issues might look if we sought a solution other than the "perfect" one.

CHAPTER SIX

DECIDING HOW TO DECIDE

In the case history of Third Church in the previous chapter, Devon and his team of volunteers escaped into decision-making nirvana through a process of consensus. While this is an effective and satisfying way to reach a group decision, it is not always the best way. Nor will it always work. Difficult decisions may require us to choose among several good ideas or settle for the best of four unattractive options. We are looking for a solution that gives us the maximum amount of benefit with the minimum amount of negative side-effects. But Type-D solutions are not always available to us in youth ministry. If they were, we would all be well-liked by everyone, never face criticism, never have to make tough choices, and have a full head of hair.

In his article, "Four Ways to Make Group Decisions,"[1] Em Griffin outlines five criteria for evaluating the methods we use to make group decisions:

- *Quality.* Have we made the best possible decision?
- *Time.* Will the process allow us to reach a decision in a reasonable amount of time?
- *Commitment.* Will the decision-making process encourage our ministry team or student leadership to own the decision? Will they support it?
- *Attractiveness.* Did the process build the morale of our group?
- *Learning.* Have we learned through the process of making this decision?

Ideally we want to make the best possible decision in the shortest amount of time with the least amount of animosity and the most possible esprit de corps.

"Now this little model is special-made for committees . . . it comes equipped with one gas pedal, four steering wheels, and ten sets of brakes."

CHOOSING BETWEEN GOOD IDEAS

Consider the following case study adapted from a situation that actually occurred with a youth ministry in the Northeast.

First Church received an anonymous thousand dollar gift with the donor's stipulation that the money be used in direct ministry with teenagers, and that it be used within six months, not sit in some account for several years. No problem, right?

Wrong. When the chairperson of the youth committee made her announcement, all nine strong-minded leaders offered different ideas about how the money could be used to the glory of God. Sarah, the chairperson, spoke first, recommending the purchase of youth-ministry resources: a set of *Ideas* books, several videos, some tapes, and a few hundred dollars of various other resource materials. "There's a lot of stuff out there that will help this ministry program for years to come, but we just haven't had the money to put into resources until now."

That prompted Jim to speak. "Do we want to invest money into books or into people? Why don't we use it to send one of our students to the mission field this summer with Teen Missions? We can pay for almost all of the expenses with a gift that size."

Guy and Mary smiled at each other, both thinking the same thing. "We saw God use that weekend backpacking trip last summer to change kids," Mary said. "With a thousand dollars we could upgrade the youth group's gear supply."

Stan wanted to hold the money as a scholarship for some students who would not be able to afford the summer camp. Bill felt strongly that the church bus needed overhauling. (He was usually the one driving it.) Cindy thought a new keyboard/synthesizer would give a face-lift to the youth choir. Bob and Pat, a couple whose teenage son was in the youth group, listened to all the ideas before Pat suggested, "I think we ought to let the kids decide what to do with the money. After all, it was given to the youth group, not the leadership committee."

Murmurs and mumbles circulated around the room. This was not going to be an easy decision. How should they proceed?

DECISION-MAKING STRATEGIES

If we want to make decisions without making enemies, we need to consider that there are four different strategies for coming to a group decision.[2] We could vote; we could appoint an expert; we could use the Delphi method; or we could try to reach consensus.

VOTING

Ah yes, the American way. Sarah, in our example, could lead the entire group to discuss the various options as presented by their advocates and take a vote on the matter. Voting works best if the chairperson sets a time limit for discussion. Since Sarah's deadline is six months away, she may encourage an educated decision by allowing people a week to research their choices before reporting back to the group.

There are two approaches to taking a vote. One is to take more than one ballot. Assuming that the proposals to purchase backpacking gear and to purchase resource materials get the two highest vote totals on the first ballot, the chair would then eliminate the other choices and take a second vote on just those two options.

The second approach is for Sarah to propose a vote on the one idea that seems to be drawing a lot of interest from most of the committee members. If her "call for the question" is supported by the majority of the group, they can vote on that one idea. If it's a "yes" vote, the whole process has been cut down considerably.

It almost seems un-American to challenge voting as the best way for a committee to make its decisions, but the question is worth considering. "One person, one vote" sounds good in principle, but there is a downside.

"Our bylaws specifically state that the will of God cannot be overturned without a 2/3 majority vote."

Quality. Using our criteria of evaluation, the first issue is one of quality. Will the voting process help the youth committee make the best possible decision? Maybe yes. Maybe no. To begin with, we're all aware of the fact that the majority is not always right. The lessons of the Holocaust teach us that, and we have reason enough to question the principle by simply asking, "Just because the Supreme Copurt of the land, using democratic principles, legalizes abortion as a means of birth control, does that make it right?" According to the vote, it does. According to Scripture, I think not.

On the other hand, if we suppose that these are nine Spirit-led Christians sincerely seeking the will of God, we might reasonably assume that their collective decision will give us our best chance of discerning the mind of God. One of them alone might be fooled into a wrong decision, but as Scripture reminds us, there is greater wisdom in the counsel of many (Prov. 24:6).

Plus, our chances of a high-quality decision are increased by the sheer amount of discussion that will be involved in this method. Each person will be attempting to hype his or her idea. That will assure that each suggestion gets ample exposure before the group. Just as the group underlines the strengths of good ideas, ideas that are not as strong will have the weaknesses exposed. This should improve the quality of the decision as well.

Time. One of the attractive parts of putting the question to a vote is that the whole process doesn't have to take that long. Voting can be a relatively quick way for the youth committee to reach a decision. Unfortunately, the quicker the process, the lower the chances of a high-quality decision. For that reason, Sarah prefers to let everyone have his or her say on all the issues before any final vote. By the time she has allowed all parties to have their say, the issue has been so thoroughly talked through that the vote is little more than a rubber stamp of an obvious consensus.

Sometimes committee members will grow impatient with the committee process at just this point. Bill sometimes complained that Sarah allowed the group to "talk things to death." He would rather just see the issue come up for a vote so that they could move on to other issues. That is, in fact, one of the advantages of a vote: people have to make a choice. It can abruptly end a long drawn-out discussion and force people to take a stand. We're all occasionally frustrated by the committee member who, when asked for an either-or decision, responds, "Well, I feel very strongly both ways."

Commitment. On the other hand, although a swift decision may be more attractive than a drawn-out discussion, if people feel they're been steamrolled into a decision with which they're uncomfortable, they aren't going to support it. Sarah can't afford to have Cindy hurt and angry that her feelings about the needs of the youth choir went unappreciated. Scholarships won't mean anything if Bill refuses to drive the group on a bus that he feels is in disrepair. The group's commitment to the final decision is going to depend on how clearly and fairly everyone feels her or his imput was recieved.

Attractiveness. As we all know from politics, voting can often cause some fairly intense division within a group. By definition, voting always produces a "winner" and a "loser." We can alleviate some of the divisiveness of a vote by allowing more than one round of balloting. That way, as the choices are narrowed down, it's possible that my opponent in the first ballot can become my ally by the final ballot.

Learning. The very fact of debate means that ideas are examined and evaluations exchanged. That's educational, even if it isn't always pleasant. Also, defending one's position before the others on the committee develops leadership and thinking skills.

APPOINTING AN EXPERT

As the discussion of what to do with the gift money intensified, Sarah suggested that the inexperienced, volunteer group seek advice from a professional youth-ministry veteran. Mike Rice, the youth minister at Second Baptist, had given them good counsel on a few other occasions. They considered calling him. Again, this particular approach to decision-making brings with it plusses and minuses.

Quality. A high-quality result depends, of course, on getting the right expert. Many self-styled experts have more willingness than expertise. For the group to support the expert's decision, they have to believe in the expert.

Time. The one immediate benefit of bringing in an expert is that it will save a lot of time. It doesn't take any genius to compute that eight people meeting twice for three hours each adds up to forty-eight man-hours. An expert like Mike Rice could do some pretty thorough investigating of the situation and still give the committee a recommendation in less than a fourth of that time.

Commitment. Will the group be committed to Mike's suggestion? Maybe and maybe not. Even if the entire committee trusts Mike's expertise, individual committee members may feel he cannot fully appreciate their viewpoint. Bill, for example, doesn't expect that anyone but himself can fully appreciate the risk of driving the bus in its current condition. For Bill the decision is not a question of expertise, but of necessity.

Attractiveness. Appointing an expert may be a good move since it eliminates the divisive debate that comes along with the voting process. Once the group has decided to go to the expert, the burden of judgment is on someone else's shoulders. This takes some of the emotional charge out of the decision.

Learning. On the other hand, the group isn't likely to benefit from the learning that comes through debate. The expert comes, he sees, he decides. He hands down the oracle, the group stamps it, and then the one who best understands the decision leaves.

THE DELPHI TECHNIQUE

At first glance, this approach sounds like you call in a group of fraternity members to make the decision. Rather, it is essentially what happens when the judges average their scores for an Olympic figure skater. It works this way.

The chairperson instructs committee members to vote on each of the seven ideas suggested, ranking their preferences for each idea beginning with one for highest preference and seven for lowest preference.

Ideas	Sarah	Jim	Stan	Guy & Mary	Bill	Cindy	Pat & Bob
Purchase resources (Sarah)	1	7	3	4	4	4	4
Missions scholarship (Jim)	3	1	2	3	6	7	6
Backpacking gear (Guy/Mary)	4	3	4	1	7	3	2
Retreat scholarship (Stan)	5	2	1	2	3	5	3
Overhaul church bus (Bill)	2	4	5	5	1	2	5
Youth choir keyboard (Cindy)	6	6	6	6	5	1	7
Let the kids vote (Pat/Bob)	7	5	7	7	2	6	1

Then, Sarah takes this information and gives the voting totals to the youth committee without identifying who voted for what.

Ideas	TOTAL	Ranking
Purchase resources (Sarah)	27	4
Missions scholarship (Jim)	28	5
Backpacking gear (Guy/Mary)	24	2/3
Retreat scholarship (Stan)	21	1
Overhaul church bus (Bill)	24	2/3
Youth choir keyboard (Cindy)	37	7
Let the kids vote (Pat/Bob)	35	6

It was obvious after the first ballot that the committee was not too eager to turn the decision over to the youth group students. Equally obvious is that Cindy and the choir are going to have to delay "funkiness" for a while longer—the committee doesn't like the keyboard idea.

Having cut the list down to five choices, the group then moves through the ranking process again. On the second ballot, a clear preference might emerge. If not, the committee can eliminate one or two more preferences and then vote again by ranking the remaining three. After moving through the cycle three times, it should be possible for the group to come up with a final decision based on the preference with the lowest total.

Quality. The Delphi method brings with it the same quality assurances that voting does, but it has the added advantage of giving everyone an equal voice. Statistics are no respecter of persons. Sarah's opinion as chair is worth no more than Bill's as bus driver. The anonymity and genuine equality in the voting process makes it less likely that someone will be misled by personal biases. In that sense, the quality of the decision is likely to be fairly high.

Time. The Delphi method quickly narrows down a long list of options without wasting a lot of time on unpopular ideas.

Commitment. It is quite possible, however, that the decision made by the group is one on which no one is really sold. For example, according to this method, the number-one option in our case study is using the money to underwrite retreat scholarships. But that was the first choice of only one person (Stan). It was the fifth choice of two people, and the third choice of two people. In other words, of this group of nine, at least half of the people ranked this choice no higher than their third preference. That is not the kind of outcome that evokes group ownership of the final decision.

Attractiveness. Typically the decision reached through this method is one that nobody really hates. That's good. Unfortunately, it's the kind of decision nobody really loves either (except Stan!). It will be hard for the group to really build esprit de corps on the foundation of this kind of decision.

Learning. Obviously, no one learns much about ideas that go undiscussed.

CONSENSUS

The last method the youth committee could use to reach a decision about allocating the thousand dollar gift is working for consensus—a long and tedious process of discussing the matter until the parties can come to some agreement on what should be done. Consensus is probably the decision-making process that most closely approximates the way we are to function as Christ's body. But it is also the toughest way of all to decide an issue. As the parody of the old hymn reminds us, "To dwell above with saints we love, O that will be glory. But to dwell below with the saints we know; that's another story!"

The ultimate question that the youth committee is addressing, however, is not "Which way is easiest?" or "What will make Bill happy?" but "What does God want?" In a meeting of Christians, presumably when we work through these issues, we are seeking to know the mind of God.

To reach consensus, we must keep in mind at least these five guidelines:

- *Announce the intention right from the start.* Let everyone know that we do not plan to move ahead on a matter until we are in relative agreement on how to proceed. Tell our committee, "This is too important to move ahead with only a simple majority."
- *Be prepared to take time to process.* Consensus does not cater to someone looking for a quick decision or impatient with process (and quite often youth-ministry types are).
- *Encourage open expression.* People have to feel free to disagree, or the consensus will yield a false representation of what the committee agrees upon.
- *The chair must not mistake silence for agreement.* The chair must make sure that all voices are heard and stay on the lookout for the person who sits in quiet discontent until five minutes after the meeting is over and then complains that no one cared what she thought.
- *Consensus is not the same as one-hundred-percent total agreement.* It is an agreement among group members that they have arrived at the best solution possible, given the many opinions involved.

While consensus is difficult to reach, it generally produces a *high-quality decision* that encourages *strong esprit de corps*. After hammering out this consensus, the group will be *committed to follow through*, and the give and take of open discussion *will encourage learning*. The only drawback to consensus is the *large expenditure of time*. Consensus doesn't allow microwave decisions. It is a marinate, roast, and simmer approach.

WHY FOUR METHODS?

Various youth-ministry situations call for different decision-making methods. Choosing Sunday school curriculum requires a method that is strong in encouraging commitment to the decision and building group morale. Even if we don't feel the curriculum is the absolute best material, it may be more important that our teachers feel good about what they are teaching. In that case, we may work for consensus.

On the other hand, if we have several ideas on the table for the fall calendar, none of the ideas is really awful, and no one is strongly attached to any one idea, we can quickly narrow our list of options and make choices using the Delphi method. Speed is more important than a precise group decision that everyone feels good about.

BEWARE GROUPTHINK

The greatest threat to sound decisions is the phenomenon Irving Janis describes as "groupthink," a word he uses to describe what happens when well-meaning people hide their true feelings from the group in order to maintain the appearance of group unity and cohesiveness.[3]

As Janis points out, the classic example of groupthink was the Bay of Pigs invasion of Cuba ordered by then-President John Kennedy. The plan was that a small band of Cuban exiles would secretly land on a beachhead in the Bay of Pigs. From there they would launch an offensive with the aim of overthrowing the government of Fidel Castro. The quick result of this ill-conceived scheme was nothing less than a total rout. Within three days, the ragtag band of would-be conquerors had been overcome, and their secret mission directly traced to an embarrassed U.S. government. Later Kennedy said, "It was the perfect failure. How could I have been so stupid as to let them go ahead?"

In the postmortem discussions of the incident, virtually everyone, including Kennedy himself, agreed that the decision to launch the initiative came out of a White House leadership team marked by several factors that made groupthink probable:

- The group had a highly directive and charismatic leader (Kennedy).
- There was a high morale among group members that encouraged them to make decisions as a group they would not have made as individuals.
- There was social pressure on all group members to conform to the wishes of the leader.
- The group had a strong inherent belief in its own morality and had an equally strong belief that their opposition (Fidel Castro) was inept, wrong, and weak.

If we look at the Bay of Pigs debacle, we can see quite easily how this same pattern of groupthink can so easily happen in the church setting, particularly in the setting of a youth-leadership team. While our bad decisions in youth ministry seldom lead to international incidents, we make some costly mistakes because of groupthink.

I made one of my most memorable mistakes in youth ministry at my first full-time position. Young and eager for direction, I highly valued the few strong supporters I had on the youth committee. The unity of that group was so important to me that it clouded my judgment on a key decision involving one high school girl named Mary.

Having only been in this position for a few months, I was approached by some of my strongest and most trusted adult leaders. They recommended to me that Mary not be allowed to go on an upcoming out-of-the-country trip. They explained that because of my newness I had no way of knowing about Mary's moral reputation and her penchant for extracurricular activities on retreats. They had seen the group grow much since my arrival, and they felt that Mary's participation in the mission project might hurt our newfound momentum.

It all made perfect sense—at the time. We talked about it, agreed on it, and I called Mary. What seemed like a good group decision turned out to be a fiasco. Mary cried on the phone for about thirty minutes until her dad took over. His portion of the phone call alternated between extreme anger and occasional crying. Finally, by the time Mary's mom was on the phone, crying and screaming, I was beginning to wish I were floating somewhere in the Bay of Pigs.

Mary's parents phoned around to share their story with some of their friends at the church, and that really opened wide the can of worms. By the next day, everything broke loose, and I was thinking that maybe there had been a change in God's will for my life!

As I look back on that decision, I can excuse it, in part, because of my youth and inexperience. But in retrospect, I can also see that it was a decision that we came to as a group that none of us probably would have made on our own. It was a bad decision born of textbook groupthink.

We are especially susceptible to groupthink in the Christian community because we tend to think of conflict as negative. Sometimes, however, conflict can be greatly used by God. "As iron sharpens iron, so one man sharpens another" (Prov. 27:17). We must not allow our strong desire for group unity to override our willingness to wrestle through a tough decision.

We in the church also tend to think of error as uncharacteristic of a person really in touch with God. This makes it difficult for us to disagree with a Christian brother or sister, particularly one in a leadership role. By our definition, disagreement is saying that we believe them to be in error, and therefore not as in touch with God as we would like to think.

Groupthink is also born partially out of our notion that love is always "nice." We've been taught that if we can't say something nice we shouldn't say anything. And while the Scripture never teaches that kind of "sloppy agape," many have been misled to believe that voicing an opposing view in a meeting or planning session is a sign of a divisive spirit.

All of this is muddled even further by the mistaken but popular notion that a genuine trust in God relieves us from having to exercise our own critical judgment. If we are being led by the Spirit, the thinking goes, we can trust that all of our decisions initiate from his guidance. But the heart is deceitful. John, the Elder, consistently encouraged the leadership in his churches to "test the spirits" to see if they are of God (1 John 4:1-6).

PREVENTING GROUPTHINK

Recognizing some of the causes of groupthink is probably one of the best ways to prevent it. But other steps can ensure that team decisions are sound and not just the result of groupthink.

Assign to one person in the group the role of critical evaluator. One pastor told me that, in an attempt to keep himself and his staff honest in meetings, each meeting he appoints a different staff member to play the role of devil's advocate. This person tries to shoot down new ideas as they arise and questions assumptions.

Periodically divide the decision-making group into subgroups that meet separately under different chairpersons and then come back together to hammer out differences. This exercise reduces the chances that the large group will overly influence the decision-making process. In the smaller group setting, and under the leadership of a different chair, group members feel a bit more at ease about speaking what they believe.

On a regular basis invite outsiders to your meetings. Some youth workers invite parents to sit in on planning meetings so that they can give the ministry team a reality check. Others invite the pastor, a member of the church, or even some of the kids. Outsiders don't have the same bias to group unity. This gives them the freedom to voice opposition when it needs to be spoken.

Require group leaders to withhold opinions and preferences until the group has a chance to hear from others. This diminishes the chances that the group will be overly influenced by these opinions.

CHOOSE YOU THIS DAY

Making decisions is at the heart of our heritage as Christians. In youth-ministry leadership, we face numerous choices—some pleasant, some not so pleasant; some easy, some not so easy. The mark of effective leadership is not always making right decisions. An effective leader uses all possible resources to come to the best possible decision and arrives at that decision in a way that utilizes and affirms the roles of others in the body of Christ. Effective decision making takes creativity, judgment, and courage. But most of all, it takes confidence in the God who promises: "I will instruct you and teach you in the way you should go; I will counsel you and watch over you ... Many are the woes of the wicked, but the Lord's unfailing love surrounds the man who trusts in him" (Ps. 32:8, 10).

CHAPTER SEVEN

EVALUATING YOUR PROGRAM

Greg is a youth minister in the Midwest with about ten years of experience. His track record had been good enough to land him a very exciting position with a large and active congregation. The potential seemed unlimited. Although he had only been in his new position about a year, he felt there were signs of progress. That's why he was so shocked one morning after staff meeting when he was called into the office of the executive minister and informed that the elders of the church had voted to ask him to leave.

Brian experienced the opposite situation. As youth pastor of a downtown church in a large northern city, he had held his position for about two years. The congregation and the senior pastor seemed genuinely pleased with his work. He seldom received any major criticisms from the congregation. Everyone seemed to be happy. Everyone, that is, except Brian. Although he couldn't put his finger on it, he didn't feel his ministry progressing the way he had envisioned. He felt strongly disappointed. Within a few months Brain accepted a call to a new youth-ministry position.

Doris, a volunteer youth worker, angrily approached me after a youth workers' seminar that was being held simultaneously with a high school retreat. "I brought seven girls to the retreat and they have shown absolutely no interest whatsoever," she fumed. "Look at these conference notebooks filled with empty outlines and untouched morning devotionals. I'm so mad at these kids right now, I'm ready to quit. Maybe I'm not seeing something, but it looks like to me like all we've done is just waste of a lot of time and energy."

In one form or another, each of these people is struggling with the issue of evaluation. What are we doing wrong? Why aren't we seeing the results we want? Are we doing anything that really makes a difference?

How *do* we evaluate a youth-ministry program? By the size of the group? the size of the budget? the size of the youth worker's paycheck? What are some practical ways of sizing up the strengths and weaknesses of a youth ministry?

As we begin to sift through the nuts and bolts issues, we need to consider ways to evaluate which nuts and bolts need to be loosened and which need to be tightened. We need to develop strategies for evaluating what we should be doing, what we aren't doing, and what we need to do.

AN UNCOMFORTABLE QUESTION

The way I eat is no different from most children. I like hot dogs, hamburgers, fast food, and special delicacies like Spam, cream of mushroom soup, and rice casserole. What I don't like is pizza, dressing on my salad, and any new dish that I've never tasted. When the subject of my diet is discussed, as it often is, I'm inevitably asked this question: "Duffy, you sure have a different kind of diet. Do you ever have any trouble with your cholesterol count?"

My answer: "No."

"What about your triglyceride level? Are you having any trouble with a high count there?"

Again, I answer: "No."

Astonished, these people glance down at my plate of Hamburger Helper and look back with disbelief. "Man, that's incredible. How do you do it?"

That's when I tell them my secret: "I never get it checked. It's wonderful. I've never had a high reading in my life."

To be completely truthful, I recently had my cholesterol checked (and yes, it was fine, thank you). But I think I avoided it for the same reason heavy people don't weigh themselves and people who haven't brushed aren't eager to go to the dentist. None of us is thrilled to find out where we are missing the mark. One man's performance review is another man's firing squad. Evaluations can be intimidating.

Whether we're talking about a cholesterol level or a youth ministry, ignorance may be bliss but it is also very risky. Serious youth ministers cannot afford to gloss over evaluations. "The wisdom of the prudent is to give thought to their ways" (Prov. 14:8). Evaluation will not always be a pleasant exercise, but it is an important one.

Whether volunteer or professional, there are basically three reasons that we tend to avoid the evaluation-and-review process: myths, fears, and lack of know-how.

YOUTH-MINISTRY MYTHS

God's blessing means God's sanction. There's an unwritten rule in the Christian community that "God's blessing means God's sanction." If our ministry is growing and flourishing, then we must be doing everything right. Flourishing youth ministries, however, are no indication that God sanctions either our methods or our attitudes. In fact, we may even seriously struggle in our ministries precisely because we are doing God's will. (Consider Moses, Elijah, Jeremiah, Jesus, Paul.) God's blessing in our ministries says more about his abounding grace than about whether we have chosen right or wrong courses in ministry. We can't excuse ourselves from evaluation just because God is blessing our work.

We're already doing things the best way they can be done. With that arrogant assumption, we put off evaluation, smugly assured that no one knows how to do the job better than we do. We've peaked. There is no way we can improve on what we're doing. The corporate claim of Hewlett-Packard is, "We never stop asking, 'What if?'" Unfortunately, many of us in youth ministry never stop asking, "Why should we?"

The experts know best. We love the safety of doing what the experts say. That gets us off the hook. That places upon the experts the responsibility for our ministries. We don't have to risk experiments and tough thinking because we only do what the experts say to do. "Expert" has been defined as a word that combines the prefix *ex-*, meaning "former," with *spurt*, meaning "drip under pressure." Just because a method has been published in a youth-ministry book somewhere doesn't mean it's the best one; it just means it's the best one known to that author. Experts are only experts because they've made almost every mistake once.

FEAR

I once made the mistake of looking for a pen under the cushions on our sofa. What I discovered was a nightmare of leftover cookies, popcorn, used Kleenex, and a smashed doughnut. And I was faced with the unhappy prospect of having to clean up the mess. I've since made it my policy to never lift up the cushions on our sofa.

Particularly in the church, we neglect evaluation because we are afraid of what we'll find. And we're afraid of the mess involved in trying to clean it up. It's easier on us not to ask too many questions. I remember feeling that way doing a cost analysis of our youth-ministry basketball program. I was afraid that I was going to discover it was not the wisest use of youth program funds and that we would have to make some very unpopular changes. It wasn't, we did, and they were very unpopular. I thought twice before I did any more cost analyses.

LACK OF KNOW-HOW

How do we effectively evaluate our youth ministry? Students readily evaluate it: either "it's awesome" or "it's boring." The parents may say, "You're doing too much." The deacons may say, "You're doing too little." Some nice old lady might say, "The young people's group is a blessing." But are we equipped to accurately evaluate our program?

GETTING THE KNOW-HOW

The writer of Proverbs counsels us to "give thought to [our] steps" (Prov. 14:15). That means that as thoughtful youth ministers, we should be doing the kind of evaluation that affirms specifically what we're doing right and demonstrates specifically what we're doing wrong.

REAFFIRM THE VISION

It is impossible to evaluate our ministry markmanship if we don't have a clear sense of our target. We must begin the process of evaluation by determining goals. Whether we develop a vision statement or hammer out a philosophy of ministry, it is absolutely critical that we begin the evaluation process with this stage. It's impossible to tell how close we are to the mark if no one is willing to define it. Proverbs 14:15 reminds us that a simple person will believe anything, but the prudent one *looks where he is going*.

LOOK OVER THE PROGRAM

Jim Burns tells of an occasion when two of his students strolled up to him at the conclusion of a Bible study. "Jim, we need to talk to you," they began. "Your Bible studies are really good and everything. It's just that . . . well . . . like . . . we want more meat, y'know?" Jim couldn't believe it. He thought he had been giving the students "meat" in the Bible study. How should he respond to their feedback? What steps should he take?

As we begin the evaluation process, we must keep asking ourselves these basic questions: What are we doing right (our strengths)? What are we doing wrong (our weaknesses)? What can we do better (improvements)? In measuring our ministries against these questions, there are three criteria to use as yardsticks: finances, attendance, and goal achievement.

Finances. Although it's probably the least reliable barometer of ministry effectiveness, a simple cost analysis can help youth workers evaluate their ministries. This is not some kind of lengthy accounting process that requires banking experience (my expertise in bookkeeping extends to tracking on a ledger my payment of my daughters' allowances). Cost analysis is a process of looking at each element of the youth program to see what it actually costs. This allows the youth worker to compare the cost of a specific program to its value for the youth group.

My most vivid experience in cost analysis was when we evaluated our youth program's involvement in a church basketball league. After accounting for all expenses entailed in our participation (league membership fees, gym rental fees, uniform expenses, insurance, transportation costs), I divided the total cost of the program by the number of basketball-team members. With only eight or nine regulars, the cost came to over five dollars per student per game. That may not sound like much at first, but we began discussing as a ministry team if we really wanted to spend five dollars per student per week to get them to play basketball. It seemed a bit ridiculous. We started to realize, "This is not a basketball league, it's a part-time job!"

As we measured the expense of the basketball program against other elements of the program towards which we could direct the money, we decided on three options: a) require students to pay all costs associated with the program; b) require students involved with the program to assume some of the costs, and in addition require them to fulfill certain homework requirements that might contribute to their personal spiritual growth; or c) cancel the program. We knew the students wouldn't cough up five bucks a game; and after trying option "b" for one season, we found students did not support that alternative either. That left us only option "c." We simply couldn't justify the money and time that the basketball team was costing us.

What does it cost to reach a kid? There are other kinds of information available to us by using the same basic method. For example, if we want to find out how much is being spent per student per year in the youth program, we would simply divide the number of active students into the amount of the total youth-ministry budget. Let's say the total youth-ministry budget is forty-five hundred dollars and there are eighty-five youths active in the program. We can see it is costing the church approximately fifty-two dollars per year—or one dollar per week per student in the youth program. Not a bad investment!

It is important to remember that finances are the least reliable criterion of evaluation. Some activities will be consistently self-sustaining in terms of finances, while others will consistently lose money. But let's remember that our goal is to make a prophet, not a profit. I'll fund a Bible study over a beer blast any time, although the latter might predictably draw a bigger crowd. A youth ministry shall not live by "bread" alone.

Attendance. The one eternal truth in youth ministry is that kids vote with their feet. If they don't like a program, they won't come to it. To that extent, attendance is a good criterion for evaluating a youth program. But attendance is only a slightly more reliable indicator than finances. Evaluating on the basis of attendance generally measures wants, not needs.

The Meirs Park Church, a large church in North Carolina, was one of those churches in which numbers were used to evaluate almost everything: "How many members did we gain?" "Do we have as many in Sunday School as we did last year?" The youth workers at Meirs Park were so preoccupied with numerical growth that they began to forget why they were there. Programs that might have helped students to grow spiritually were replaced by programs that offered fewer opportunities for growth, but drew larger crowds.

A weekly drop-in center in which any Christian witness was somewhere between low-key and nonexistent replaced the weekly Bible study. The Christian music was dropped for music that the students said they liked better. Leaders ceased to be youth ministers and became chaperons. After about a year, attendance at the drop-in center leveled off at around a hundred kids a night, and the church board decided to discontinue the program in the face of growing complaints about drugs, drinking, and fighting in the church parking lot.

As churches become more interested in building programs than in building disciples, they forget the fundamental principle that "as commitment increases, attendance decreases." The more we ask of students spiritually, the fewer there will be who are willing to make that kind of commitment. That means that if we evaluate a program strictly on the basis of numbers, we will have a program that is high on crowds and low on discipleship. On the other side of the coin, it's impossible to do youth ministry without youths. We're only kidding ourselves if we offer "quality programs" that we can't get students to take part in.

Goal achievement. Woody Phillips, executive minister of a large church in suburban Philadelphia, explains that every year each of the ten senior staff members present to the elders a list of their goals for the upcoming year. Then periodically throughout the year, Woody and his staff reflect on how well they are meeting these goals. It is a process of evaluation using goal achievement as the major criterion of evaluation. Probably some of us read about a huge congregation with a senior staff of ten and say, "Who needs to evaluate? They must be doing something right! We don't have as many kids in our youth group as they have on their senior staff!" That, of course, is precisely the point. The more a youth ministry grows in attendance, the more important it is that it not be driven by numerical growth, but by asking ourselves, "Are we accomplishing anything? Are we moving in the direction of our vision?"

Larry Richards recommends evaluating a youth ministry by a model that defines goals in three key areas of the youth-ministry program: Bible, life, and body.[1] Using Richards' approach, we evaluate group needs and design program goals based on three key questions: Where are our students weak in understanding biblical truth? Are our students able to work biblical truth into the fabric of their everyday lives? Are our students living out kingdom relationships—are they being the body of Christ? Designing specific objectives based on these questions, youth leaders can evaluate how effectively their youth program is moving the group in the desired direction.

Adapting a concept popularized by Dennis Miller,[2] our ministry team began to think of our overall youth program as being shaped like a funnel—wide enough at the top to bring students in, but intentional enough at the bottom to accomplish our objectives. Using that funnel design, we evaluated goal achievement on the basis of our ability to move students through various levels of Christian growth.

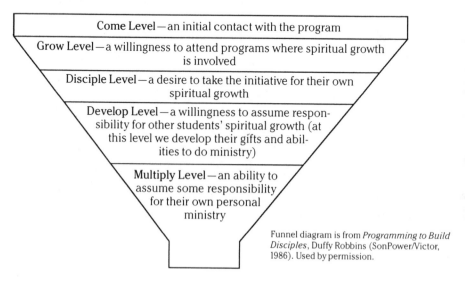

Come Level—an initial contact with the program

Grow Level—a willingness to attend programs where spiritual growth is involved

Disciple Level—a desire to take the initiative for their own spiritual growth

Develop Level—a willingness to assume responsibility for other students' spiritual growth (at this level we develop their gifts and abilities to do ministry)

Multiply Level—an ability to assume some responsibility for their own personal ministry

Funnel diagram is from *Programming to Build Disciples*, Duffy Robbins (SonPower/Victor, 1986). Used by permission.

We could evaluate our program by asking two questions in relationship to this funnel of commitment: Which of our activities minister to students at the various levels of commitment? Which students do we have at the various levels of commitment?

Mike Rowe, former youth pastor at Trinity Baptist Church in Nashua, New Hampshire, made use of the following weekly leader evaluation to get consistent input and evaluation of his ongoing work with students:

WEEKLY LEADER EVALUATION

NAME: _____ DATE: _____

Program Evaluation: Sunday

1. Please give your overall evaluation of our most recent Breakaway Sunday night.

   Music: _____

   Skit/Ice breaker: _____

   Devotion: _____

   Testimonies: _____

   Other: _____

2. Any suggestions concerning the program or the overall ministry. _____

   _____

3. Any prayer requests concerning people or situations in the ministry. __

   _____

4. Any praises concerning the ministry or things happening in the group. _

   _____

5. Any comments, suggestions, or evaluations concerning extra-curricular programs (parties, activities, Skyline, retreats, etc.) _____

   _____

Bible Study: Wednesday

☐ Sr. High I

☐ Sr. High II

1. Please give your overall evaluation of our most recent Bible study. _____

_____

2. What was the topic? _____

_____

3. Any ideas of suggested topics of study? _____

_____

Contact Ministry (time spent with youths outside of regular programs)

1. Who: _____

   How much time?_____

   What did you do? Where did you go? What happened? _____

_____

2. Any areas of concern with this young person? Any prayer requests or praises to share? _____

_____

3. What are your immediate and/or long-term goals or ideas in your ministry with this young person? _____

_____

4. Youths you are praying for specifically this week: _____

_____

5. What plans do you have for contact next week? _____

_____

Adult Sponsors

Do you know of any adults who would make great youth-team members? _

_____

Personal Evaluation

1. What is the strong point of your relationship with God right now? _____

   _____

2. What Scriptures have you been studying this week? _____

   _____

3. What other books, if any, have you been reading? _____

   _____

4. What have you done to keep quality time with your family this past
   week? _____

   _____

5. What have you done this week for your own enjoyment? _____

   _____

6. Any areas of concern regarding your job/school situation? _____

   _____

7. What are your personal goals for this week? _____

   _____

Additional Comments

_____

_____

_____

_____

While there are a number of different models for evaluation, there is essentially one basic strategy to evaluate our programs based on goal achievement: we first define our goals, then we identify specific objectives that will help us meet our goals. These objectives need to be *measurable*: we need to know whether we are meeting them or not. Example: "We plan to start two small discipleship groups for high school students by October first." They need to be *reachable*: it does no good to set goals for ourselves that we cannot possibly reach. Bad Example: "We plan to have Stryper play in our Sunday morning worship on Mother's Day, with the pastor singing lead and

111

his wife playing tambourine." The objectives must be *ownable*: it must be an objective that is embraced by enough of our leadership and students to accomplish the objective without destroying the youth group. Example: "We plan to do one mission outreach project every other month, and take one major mission trip this July."

Having formulated specific objectives, we're ready to measure each facet of the youth program by how it is helping to meet the prescribed goals and objectives. For example, rather than just spending time and money on programs because they are a matter of tradition or because they are well attended or because nobody has a better idea, we ask ourselves the following kinds of questions before and after each specific activity:

- What goal is reached by making use of it?
- Does it fit into our program and ministry objectives?
- Do I understand it? Can I visualize it?
- Do I like it?
- Would the kids like it?
- Can I trust the originator of this resource?
- How much time, effort, and cost is required to do it?
- Do we have the right talent to lead it?
- Do we have the right number of people for it?
- What kind of setup is required?
- Do I have the time to orient the other leaders to it?
- What risks are involved in doing it?
- If it fails, how bad will it be?
- If it works, how valuable will it be?
- What experiences have others had with it?[3]

Part of our sacred responsibility in youth ministry is careful evaluation and reevaluation to make sure that we are building programs that accomplish the purposes for which they were designed. We simply cannot afford power plants that can't light the darkness.

CHAPTER EIGHT
EVALUATING YOUR PEOPLE

Art Erickson, the veteran youth minister of Park Avenue United Methodist Church in Minneapolis, likes to say that one of the first steps in doing ministry is "exegeting your community." Basically, that means taking a good look at your community from different angles. Exegeting your community is the kind of examination that leads to a thorough evaluation of your youth ministry.

EVALUATING OUR KIDS

In evaluating a youth ministry, we want to ask three questions: What are our students' needs? How do they perceive the youth program? Are our students growing spiritually? Obviously, there will be some overlap from the kinds of questions we've already asked in evaluating the program, but our focus at this level of evaluation is not on the program. Our focus is on the people in the program.

WHAT ARE OUR
STUDENTS' NEEDS?

I will never forget the week I spent at a Bible conference in Florida one winter. I thoroughly enjoyed the in-depth teaching and preaching. I learned a lot. But I observed something about the culture of the average midwinter Bible conference in Florida the week I attended: ninety-five percent of the people in attendance were over the age of seventy. That's why I was so amused when during his series of in-depth Bible teachings one of the preachers devoted the bulk of his message to the issue "Why premarital sex is unbiblical." I thought a more appropriate title for his sermon might have been "Why premarital sex is impossible!"

We in the church have a bad habit of scratching where nobody itches. Youth workers sometimes fall into that same trap of doing youth ministry based more on programs, habits, expectations, or seasons than on student needs.

We can beat the tradition trap by using tools like those that follow to evaluate the actual needs of our kids.

Determining Needs In Your Youth Ministry by Dorothy Williams and Peter Benson.[1] With questions related to church, family, friends, school, lifestyles, values, and worries, this testing tool allows you to get a sketch of some of the needs of students in your group.

Search Institute Profiles of Student Life.[2] Recognized for years as one of the foremost sources of up-to-date research on youth culture, particularly youths within the church, Search Institute has prepared a comprehensive 117-item test to examine everything from student self-esteem to time use, from student attitudes about their families to the frequency with which they exhibit antisocial behavior.

Exhaustive tests, however, may be like killing a mosquito with a shotgun. For the average-sized youth group, the test sample (the size of the group tested) is too small. If one of your four kids is involved with his girlfriend, the survey will show that twenty-five percent of your students are sexually active!

Preparing your own surveys. Before doing a four-week series on sex and dating, for example, I surveyed my high school students to get some idea of their values and opinions. It was unscientific, but we hadn't planned to submit it to *National Geographic* anyway. We asked students to give us honest, anonymous responses to questions like

1. I want to marry someone who is a virgin. True or False.
2. It's okay to be involved with someone sexually if (check one):
   □ you really love them
   □ you like them a lot
   □ they will let you
   □ you have been dating for at least three months
   □ you can remember their name
3. At least three of my friends are currently dating someone seriously. True or False.

4. Define what you consider to be "serious dating."

WHAT DO THE
YOUTHS THINK?

Youth programs are for youths. That means our evaluation must include some reading of how the students perceive our ministry. We had two different kinds of small groups, one coed and one segregated by sex. I made the mistake of suggesting to one high school girl that we combine the two. It seemed like a good idea to me. I thought the students would be relieved by the cutback in scheduling. In response she gave me a look that fluctuated between outrage and confusion—as if I had just proposed filling the baptistry with jelly beans. That's one simple way to find out what students think—in the course of conversation, simply ask them. Students are remarkably responsive when they believe we sincerely want their opinions. We may not always hear what we like, but we may hear something we need to hear.

Another way to probe students' thoughts is to use surveys. The following survey, originally appearing in *Group* magazine, asks students to offer their input on the youth program using the imagery of weather.

OUR YOUTH-MINISTRY PROGRAMMING

	Sunny	Partly Cloudy	Cloudy	Stormy
Involves young people in the planning process	☐	☐	☐	☐
Uses surveys, needs assessments, and conversation to discover kids' needs	☐	☐	☐	☐
Meets young people's needs and is relevant to their lives	☐	☐	☐	☐
Publicizes well in advance so kids know what's coming	☐	☐	☐	☐
Communicates to whole congregation what young people are doing	☐	☐	☐	☐
Keeps parents informed	☐	☐	☐	☐

	Sunny	Partly Cloudy	Cloudy	Stormy
Follows detailed and organized planning process	☐	☐	☐	☐
Sets clear, specific goals and objectives	☐	☐	☐	☐
Anticipates problem areas in planning stage	☐	☐	☐	☐
Keeps backlog of ideas for emergency purposes	☐	☐	☐	☐
Sparks creative ideas for special seasons and church holidays	☐	☐	☐	☐
Offers something different each time	☐	☐	☐	☐
Varies format of meetings for element of surprise	☐	☐	☐	☐
Includes and involves other adults in various capacities	☐	☐	☐	☐
Collects all necessary supplies in advance	☐	☐	☐	☐
Checks out latest and most appropriate resources	☐	☐	☐	☐
Previews any resource (film, speaker, record)	☐	☐	☐	☐
Arranges meeting rooms to suit activity	☐	☐	☐	☐
Program flows smoothly from one segment to next	☐	☐	☐	☐
Involves students in leadership role	☐	☐	☐	☐
Takes time for one-on-one sharing	☐	☐	☐	☐
Plans for different group configurations (pairs, small groups, large groups)	☐	☐	☐	☐
Structures community-building activities	☐	☐	☐	☐
Is consistent with biblical truth	☐	☐	☐	☐
Approaches biblical truths in new, exciting ways	☐	☐	☐	☐
Combines experiences for all five senses	☐	☐	☐	☐
Does not embarrass people	☐	☐	☐	☐

	Sunny	Partly Cloudy	Cloudy	Stormy
Balances activities, discussion, input	☐	☐	☐	☐
Gives clear, understandable instructions	☐	☐	☐	☐
Creates inviting atmosphere as students arrive (music, greeters, involvement)	☐	☐	☐	☐
Incorporates, in some way, every student	☐	☐	☐	☐
Welcomes kids and makes them feel special	☐	☐	☐	☐
Christ-centered and different from other clubs	☐	☐	☐	☐
Allows time for announcements of upcoming events	☐	☐	☐	☐
Supplies song books or sheets for everyone	☐	☐	☐	☐
Begins with activities that get everyone involved (name tags, ice-breakers)	☐	☐	☐	☐
Closes with meaningful activity (prayer, hugs) to wrap up time together	☐	☐	☐	☐
Encourages individual and group prayer	☐	☐	☐	☐
Includes affirming words and actions toward each person	☐	☐	☐	☐
Unites all activities with theme	☐	☐	☐	☐
Sparks change or commitment in students	☐	☐	☐	☐
Stretches kids to think or act as Christians	☐	☐	☐	☐
Encourages students to bring friends	☐	☐	☐	☐
Welcomes newcomers	☐	☐	☐	☐
Is something kids proudly talk about—at home, school, or work	☐	☐	☐	☐
Grows and learns from mistakes	☐	☐	☐	☐
Starts on time	☐	☐	☐	☐

	Sunny	Partly Cloudy	Cloudy	Stormy
Ends on time	☐	☐	☐	☐
Evaluates successes and failures regularly	☐	☐	☐	☐

(Reprinted by permission from GROUP Publishing, Box 481, Loveland, CO 80539)

Evaluation of student response to this survey forecasts what changes need to be made in the youth program. A local survey is more accurate than consulting a denominational "farmer's almanac." To get even more specific, create your own survey about particular programs your church offers. This will arm you with critical information concerning proposed changes in sometimes deeply entrenched programs. You may feel sorry you asked, but you'll be glad you found out.

ARE OUR STUDENTS GROWING SPIRITUALLY?

Jesus said that the best way to learn something about the tree is to observe its fruit (Matt. 7:15-23). Paul lists some of the fruits of the spirit as "love, joy, peace, patience, kindness, goodness, faithfulness, gentleness and self-control" (Gal. 5:22, 23). As we evaluate the spiritual growth of our students, we look (and look and look) for evidences of these fruits. Try the following exercise to assess your students' progress:

• *Step One:* Each member of the leadership team (students and/or adults) lists all nine of the fruits Paul mentions in Galatians 5. Each leader then adds two to three other fruits of the spirit implied in other portions of Scripture. (Ephesians 4:29, for example, implies the fruit of encouragement—an ability to build others up. Philippians 2:5-7 implies the fruit of humility—a willingness to put others before oneself.)

• *Step Two:* Each leader writes out one practical way that this fruit might be manifested in a group of teenagers. (Self-control, for example. A student exhibiting this fruit is willing to be quiet when someone is speaking or sharing with the group.)

- *Step Three:* Combine the various lists of fruits and their manifestations, and allow students and leaders to grade the group using the various fruits described (perhaps using a scale of one to ten—one meaning "very evident," ten "nonexistent").

Several years ago I developed a test that students could use to help them evaluate their own spiritual growth. It is the kind of tool that a leader might use with a student to help that student do an inventory of his or her own personal walk with Christ.

A "SPIRITUAL" CHECKUP

Nobody likes going to the doctor. To begin with, sometimes they ask you to do things that make you feel a little uncomfortable like, "take off your clothes," "fill up this bottle," "bend over and cough." Not much fun. On the other hand, it's not much fun to be sick either. And an occasional checkup or physical done by a good doctor can help you keep your body in shape. Knowing that doesn't make the visit any more fun, but it does remind you why it's necessary.

You're getting ready to take a test that will provide a checkup of your spiritual life. We promise you can keep your clothes on, you won't have to bend over, and you won't have to fill any funny bottles. But it still may be a little uncomfortable. You may feel the pressure of some probing questions, or you may feel the pain of some areas that you don't like thinking about.

Your honesty is important in this examination. Nobody is going to see your answers but you and the person giving you this test.

Some Suggestions:

- Set aside at least forty-five minutes of quiet time to think through and write down your answers.
- Keep your answers between you and God, to be shared only with the one person giving you this test.
- Let's get together in about a week to go over the results of your examination.
- Jesus is the Great Physician. Try to keep an open mind about how he might want to use this checkup in your own life.

I. *Pulse:* Are you a Christian?
    A. Describe your relationship with Jesus Christ.
    B. On a scale of 1 to 10 (1 = potential ax murderer, 10 = the next Mother Teresa), how would you rate your relationship with Christ? Why?

II. *Red Blood Cells* (carry the oxygen that prevents anemia/sluggishness)
    A. Devotional life
        1. Do you spend any time during the week reading the Bible or praying on your own? Describe these times and about how often you do this.
        2. How would you like to see these times get better? And what do you think is keeping these devotions/quiet times from being all they could be?
    B. Relationships that keep the arteries open.
        1. In what ways do you feel that you and God have a friendship together?
        2. Do you have a church fellowship where you try to regularly take part in Sunday worship? Describe.

III. *White Blood Cells* (disease fighters for inner spiritual cleansing and renewing)
    A. How does your faith in Christ affect your ability to be accepting, loving, and forgiving?
    B. How do you deal with feelings of guilt?

IV. *Brain Scan:* Check out your mind
    A. What are three of the biggest doubts/questions that you seem to struggle with?
    B. What can you/are you doing to deal with those doubts and questions?
    C. How would you describe your understanding of the Bible? Pick one of the following phrases that best sums up your ability to find helpful answers in the Bible:
        1. Bible? What's a Bible?
        2. I can't ever find anything I need when I need it.

3. I'm okay with the New Testament, but the Old Testament is like an old "B" movie with blurry subtitles.
4. I think I'm beginning to get more out of the Bible when other people teach or speak from it.
5. I'm a regular Bible whiz kid: next stop is memorization of Leviticus.

D. How well do you feel you understand the basics of the gospel? Try to write a simple answer to the following questions:
1. What is sin?
2. What are the effects of sin?
3. Who is Jesus?
4. How does he deal with our sin?
5. Why does God offer us the gift of life with him?
6. How do you receive that gift?
7. Who is the Holy Spirit and how does he fit in all of this?
8. If you were a contestant on the TV game show "Serious Pursuit" and Vanna asked you to explain the following terms, which could you *not* explain? Circle them.

SANCTIFICATION	JUSTIFICATION	GRACE	FAITH
CONFESSION	REPENTANCE	FRUIT OF THE SPIRIT	

E. How would you describe your ability to fight off temptation? Choose the phrase below that best describes your approach.
1. Hot dog! This looks like fun!
2. Honk if you love Jesus!
3. Get the heck out of Dodge.
4. Pray.
5. Get with some people who are stronger than me.
6. Other.

F. How would you describe your self-image?

V. *Say "Ahhhhh"*: A look at the tongue
A. Would people who know you say that you spend more time encouraging people, competing with other people, or just ignoring other people?
B. What are some of the ways you build people up by what you say?

    C. What are the situations in which you are most tempted to sin by telling a lie?

    D. What types of situations trigger in you the temptation to cut someone down either in jest or in anger?

    E. Would your friends consider you a person who enjoys giving or receiving gossip?

VI. *Probing the Heart*

    A. Describe ways that you are trying to become more Christ-like in terms of pure thoughts/motives.

    B. What priorities in your life bring you closer to God?

    C. What priorities in your life might move you further away from God?

    D. How are your relationships with friends affected by your commitment to Christ?

    E. How are your relationships with your family affected by your commitment to Christ?

    F. How are relationships with the opposite sex affected by your commitment to Christ?

VII. *Reflex Check*

    A. How are you responding to some of the people around you who rub you the wrong way?

    B. How do you respond to some of the needs around you?
In your family?
Among your friends?
In other parts of the world?

    C. How do you tend to respond to failure?

    D. How do you tend to respond to success?

    E. How do you tend to respond to pressure (at home, school, work)?

VIII. *Eyes*

    A. What kind of vision do you have for how God might use your future?

    B. What are some of the blind spots in your life that seem to keep getting you in trouble?

C. What guidelines do you use in trying to think about what kinds of movies and TV shows are healthy for you to watch?

IX. *Hands*

A. In what ways are you involved in meeting the needs of others?

B. What kinds of pressures keep you from working against injustices and other wrongs that you see around you?

C. How willing are you to turn your financial decisions and choices over to God? How well is your Christian commitment expressed in your giving to the church or to those in need?

X. *Hearing*

A. At what times do you feel like you can really hear God speaking to you?

B. What kinds of things keep you from better hearing God's will in your life?

C. What other voices, sounds (music) in your life might be drowning out what God wants you to hear?

XI. *Feet*

A. If the Christian life is more of a marathon than a sprint, how would you describe your ability to go for the long haul?

B. What kinds of "weights" keep you from running full speed ahead for God? What is holding you back or tempting you to go off course?

C. Compared to where you were in your spiritual life one year ago, how would you describe your progress over the last year?

From Duffy Robbins, *Ministry of Nurture* (Youth Specialties/Zondervan, 1990). Used by permission.

EVALUATING OURSELVES

It was one of those books I had been saving for vacation, waiting to read it until I had time to "answer" the author as I read his book. By the time I had finished the first chapter, I was so captivated by the story that I finished the book in two days. *Dance, Children, Dance*[3] is the autobiography of Jim Rayburn, the founder of Young Life, both a legend and a pioneer in the field of youth ministry. It was a story that captured wonderfully the drama, the joy, and the high adventure of ministry with teenagers.

But, just as clearly, it gave a portrait of the grave danger stalking even the most gifted youth minister: the danger of an unbalanced life. His story of damaged health, a less-than-healthy marriage, and a family of people who both loved and resented their ever-absent father hit close to home. My wife and I took time for some stout, honest personal evaluation.

The third and final area of focus for a thorough evaluation of the youth program is the assessment of the leaders themselves. Unfortunately, this is both the most neglected and the most critical area of examination. It is far too easy to just "keep on keepin' on" week after week, stoking the fires of the program, neglecting the flame that kindles our hearts—until finally, something snaps. We stand up to pour and nothing comes out.

There are no quick tricks for self-examination. It requires the following:

• *Time*—Reflection takes time. Promise yourself at least one day every six weeks.

• *Accountability*—Follow-through is more likely to happen if we know that someone if going to follow up on us.

• *Openness*—David's prayer in Psalm 19 takes us right to the difficulty in this task. "Who can discern his errors? Forgive my hidden faults. ... " Our sins aren't usually hidden very well from those around us, but they evade our own discovery like rats in the basement. We need to pray for openness to the Spirit's enlightenment.

• *Contemplation*—Gordon MacDonald writes:

Isaiah is the contemplative man. He has learned that there are some things best heard in silence. ... The contemplative man has sensitive spiritual fingertips like the proverbial safecracker who can feel the slightest movement of the tumblers behind the dial on the vault. That sensitivity is jarred when God speaks in his ear, and it reacts, sometimes with pain, when it senses the hidden motives, the false assumptions. ... [4]

• *A Bible*—This living and active Word that judges the thoughts of the heart (Heb. 4:12) keeps us from wandering into self-persecution or navel-gazing.

WHAT AM I LOOKING FOR?

The work of self-evaluation takes place at several different levels.

Interpersonal support. Am I cultivating a group of people who hold me accountable and build me up in the faith? How do I relate to these people? Am I open to their input?

Leadership behavior. Am I the sort of leader who has to control everything? Am I a shepherd who pastors the students, encouraging them in their baby steps of growth, or am I a sheriff who pesters the students, always nagging them for what they aren't doing? How do I function within the leadership team? Am I developing and deploying the gifts of others? How do I handle decision making?

Family life. Do I ask my spouse to honestly evaluate my ministry to my family? In what ways do I celebrate my family? Am I making my family as special and fun an experience as I make my youth group? Am I as willing to be interrupted by a family member as I am by one of the youth group kids? Am I taking a consistent day off with my family? How are we as a family protecting our unique community so that we maintain our special identity and intimacy as family members?

Spiritual vitality. Is my heart still warm for Christ? Do I take time to develop a personal devotional life that is completely separate from my preparation time for youth group? Am I trying anything that really forces me to genuinely have to trust God to help me succeed? Am I reading books that deepen and enrich my understanding of the faith?

STAYING ON TRACK

When I first moved to Massachusetts from North Carolina, I was amused at the six-foot poles with flags attached that lined the roads near the seminary I attended. I couldn't imagine the purpose of those markers—until about two months into winter. I discovered that these markers were to guide the plows as the snow got deeper and deeper. No matter how many times the road was plowed, new snowfalls meant new confusion about where the road was and where the road was not. I can only assume that a few lawns were inadvertently snowplowed before someone realized the need for these markers.

In the same way, the work of evaluation is an ongoing process. The youth ministry that is thoroughly evaluated can stay on course through future blizzards of busyness only if consistent markers are put in place to keep that ministry on the right track. Having plowed through the evaluation process, here are some markers that will keep us on course.

• *Regular meetings.* Meet consistently with volunteers, student leaders, parents, and others who share the vision. Encourage and challenge each other to keep true to your common vision of discipling teenagers.

• *Frequent reevaluation.* Frequent evaluations with small corrections are not nearly as difficult as once-a-year evaluations that may reveal tumorous problems that can only be healed through major corrections and radical surgery.

• *Cold-blooded programming decisions.* If a program doesn't help to reach the prescribed goals, cut it. Be wed to the message, not to the method. There are always other ways to "skin a cat," and if Plan A seems to be ineffective, then it should be scrapped—cut off—neat and clean. When we experiment with new ways of solving problems, our attitude should be "Yes, and . . . " rather than "Yes, but. . . . "

• *Good records.* A clear picture of the youth ministry's past gives a much clearer picture of its future.

• *Long-range planning.* Long-range planning allows us to get a better idea of where a program is taking us. The long-range picture magnifies the program enough that we can actually see where it is presently and where it is going. It is easier to chart a westerly course by following the sunset than by rechecking the compass at every turn in the road.

Effective youth ministry means becoming careful diagnosticians. We are doing a work for Christ, and the impact of our ministry is felt directly in the lives of students. We simply cannot afford to be sloppy in our work. Frequent, ongoing evaluation is a part of our calling, part of caring. And caring is what youth ministry is about.

SECTION
THREE

SETTING OUT YOUR TOOLS

CHAPTER NINE

CARPENTER'S HELPERS: BUILDING A MINISTRY TEAM

Three weeks before I was scheduled to speak at a winter retreat for the youth group at Halverson Fields United Methodist Church, a suburban church in a large Ohio city, I received a letter from the youth minister telling me about his group. I wanted to learn about the group so I could tailor my ministry to the specific needs of his group, but I found out more than I wanted to know.

When I came to Halverson Fields, the youth group was about one hundred strong and had a group of twelve leaders. During a four-month interim between my arrival and my predecessor's leaving, the youth leaders formed a very close bond with each other and ran the program themselves—and they did it very well. They gave me the impression that they expected me to be responsible for the program and to take on much of the responsibility myself because they had jobs and families of their own. But when I did things my way—not theirs—we had constant conflict. If I planned a program they didn't like, they expected me to drop it. They were not aware that when there was a conflict it was almost always all of them against me—I was an outsider!

These volunteer leaders were very dedicated Christians, but they were not supportive of the church as a whole. The youth group had become a sanctuary for disgruntled adults; they did their own thing in the youth group, and weren't real happy with the church, which, in fact, supported the youth group strongly. The senior pastor wasn't very happy with these leaders because of their lack of support for the church, so there was some open antagonism between himself and our volunteer leaders. In times past, former leaders had even tried to continue as youth group leaders even though they had left our church to attend elsewhere. I was asked to make the youth group part of the church again—not a satellite on its own. I worked to that end.

My first year and a half was one of conflict. The conflict became open and obvious in February when I had a program that several of the leaders opposed. Those leaders moved to organize a counter-meeting in one of their homes where we were already having a midweek group meeting sponsored by the church. We were able to resolve the conflict before the counter-meeting so that it never happened, but the stage was set for an exit.

One of the volunteer leaders decided to leave the church, which meant that he would no longer be able to serve as a youth leader—my rule and the church's. When he insisted on continuing to be involved in our weeknight program as a leader, I asked him to stop. The Pastor-Parish Relations Committee backed me up on this. If he did not stop, we were going to cause the group to cease meeting.

In August/September we had a mass resignation of ten leaders and college students in protest against our not allowing this one person who left the church to continue serving as a youth leader. The whole group went to another United Methodist church a mile from us and set up shop, involving that minister in their planning, beginning a Sunday night youth program, and setting plans for a fall retreat that would take place two weeks before ours. They actively recruited youths from our youth program, sometimes coming into our own church to do so. It has caused a great deal of heartache and stress in the church, with the youths, the youth group, and for me personally.

It has been a time of rebuilding for the youth group, and right now we have about seventy attending on Sunday evenings. Some of the youths who left the church are starting to come back to our youth group. Many who were persuaded to leave go nowhere now—they have been lost. Presently those who left are starting to resurface with themes of reconciliation, but not really making any steps in that direction. We are not healed yet; it appears that they want to keep the wound open. Only two of the original volunteer youth leaders who were here when I came are still with the program, but they are both supportive and extremely hard working. This is a long way of telling you that things haven't been real rosy this fall.

Needless to say, as a veteran youth minister I knew exactly what to do in response to that letter. I quickly typed a note explaining that I thought I might have to be at a funeral or something that weekend and that it didn't look like I wasn't going to make it for the retreat after all.

Actually, I did the retreat as planned, but I have never forgotten the hurt and confusion I read in that letter. It remains in my files as a reminder of the vital importance of a volunteer ministry team— calling the right people and keeping the right people.

WHY TEAM MINISTRY?

No doubt the author of the above letter often asked himself if it wouldn't be much easier to lead the youth program without any ministry team. Unanimity and team harmony are easier to maintain when there is only one person on the team! The sailor on a solo voyage seldom has to deal with mutiny. Frustrations are normally part of any team effort: miscommunication, hurt feelings, botched plans, lack of dependability, lack of coordination, and too many coaches.

On the other hand, team ministry, with all its pitfalls and pains, is still the most common biblical pattern for ministry—Moses and Aaron, Elijah and Elisha, Jesus and the disciples, Paul and Silas, Paul and Luke, Paul and Barnabas, Paul and everybody. In fact, team ministry was one of the major themes of Paul's letters (1 Cor. 12; Eph. 4:1-7; Rom. 12:3-8).

Not only is team ministry biblical, it's just plain practical. Because each of us has different abilities and gifts, we can accomplish with a team what we cannot accomplish alone. A team ministry has varied personality types as well, giving our students opportunities to see what Christian commitment looks like on different types of personalities.

Team ministry also builds longevity into a youth program. Volunteers Mick and Caryn had been working with their church's senior high group for two years when the paid youth minister announced that he had accepted a call to a new position. Because Mick and Caryn had been equipped as part of a team ministry—trained to plan retreats, do Bible studies, and work closely with students—they ably sustained the work during the year-long search for a replacement. The paid youth minister could leave without taking the ministry with him.

Finally, team ministry is simply more reasonable. Anyone who has been doing youth ministry for more than three weeks knows that the quickest route to burnout is doing it all alone. Bob, a young youth worker with remarkable natural gifts and personal charisma, was ideally suited to a ministry with teenagers. But because he was unable or unwilling to nurture a ministry team, he survived in youth ministry for just under one year.

Through almost two decades of youth ministry, I have observed that the greatest guarantor of one's longevity in youth work is the ability to effectively recruit, equip, and keep a good team of coworkers. "A cord of three strands is not quickly broken" (Eccl. 4:9-12).

WHY IS IT TOUGH TO RECRUIT A TEAM?

How do we persuade normal, well-adjusted, contented adults that their lives will be more rewarding and pleasant if they agree to spend several hours a week with teenagers listening to music that is too loud, driving vans that break down too often, taking part in retreats on which they will get too little sleep, and working with teenagers who too often act as if they are totally ungrateful? Good question.

Calling the right people seems simple enough. The trick is getting them to answer. Most of the time they respond with an obvious "busy" signal. Mark Senter lists some of the reasons why it's so difficult to recruit good volunteer leaders.[1]

The movement away from volunteerism. The parents evaluating the last junior high ski retreat all nodded their heads and voiced their support of more adult supervision on the next such trip. But when I passed around a sign-up sheet for those who would be willing to work with the group (even though their own children were the direct recipients of the group's ministry), this strong gale of enthusiasm deteriorated into a small cloud of hot air. From the entire room we were able to muster only one name. Like Isaiah of old, the adults spoke with one voice, "Lord, here am I. Please, send someone else."

The "Me" orientation. We have huge Sunday school classes studying gifts of the Spirit like healing, prophecy, and speaking in tongues, but the group praying for the gift of helps can probably fit in the broom closet. In the church today, we lack a theology of service. Our culture has brainwashed us into thinking that we need and deserve long hours of leisure, lots of "space," time to "get our heads together." The fact that youth ministry isn't always rewarding, that kids and parents will be ungrateful, and that we will face lack of sleep, lack of decent vans, and lack of quiet music confirms to many that they simply can't fit service to others into their schedules. But Christ calls us to service. In the words of Francis Xavier, the gospel challenges us to "give up our small ambitions."

The social isolation of youth volunteers. The youth ministry is so demanding that we discover our commitment requires us to be voluntarily quarantined from the mainstream of adult fellowship in the congregation. We may not notice it until our first adult dinner party when we turn to the group and say, "Hey—let's shoot Cheerios out of our noses!" To counteract isolation, we need to create on our ministry team an atmosphere of fellowship and comradery, making the leadership team a nurturing community for the volunteers involved.

That has been the genius of Young Life through the years. They are able to recruit and retain volunteers because they typically have a Sunday night "Leadership" meeting in which they bring only the volunteer leaders together—no kids—for nurture, sharing, singing, and fellowship.

Working women. With more and more women working—by necessity and by choice—the pool of female volunteers is shrinking.

Apathy. Most of us don't even care about apathy any more, but judging from Ezekiel 22:30 it has been and always will be a problem.

Short-term orientation. Because we live such busy lives, most of us are unwilling to make any long-term volunteer commitments. We don't want to be "tied down." Research done by the YMCA found that people were more willing to work fifty hours over a four-week period than they were to work that same number of hours spread over a four or five month period. One youth minister, asking for parents to help out in Sunday school, found that the longest commitment the parents would generally agree to was six weeks.

That means that we need to find ways to use volunteers for short-term service. Obviously, in youth ministry, there will always be a need for a long-term commitment by some leaders. Short-term commitment simply is not the kind of soil that breeds a ministry of nurture and trust. But a wise youth leader will think of ways to use short-term leaders in such a way that their brief stints of service take some of the pressure off the long-term volunteers.

For example, one very effective way of doing this in the Sunday school is by dividing each quarter of the year into two segments: one segment for teaching a standard curriculum in which students are divided into age-graded classes. Then, a second four-week segment in which short-term volunteers are recruited to teach special elective courses. These courses can be based on student interest and can be offered in such a way that each elective is open to any junior or senior high student, regardless of age. That gives the long-term Sunday school teacher the option of attending the elective course or taking off the four-week segment. By using the short-term commitment of some volunteers, we are able to offer our long-term workers four four-week breaks each year.

The success of adult Sunday school classes. Twenty years ago adults were only too happy to bail on curricula they perceived to be outdated and irrelevant. Now, an adult volunteer may be passing up anything from a creative class on Christian financial management to a video by one of Christendom's greatest teachers. A growing number of adults are unwilling to forego the nurture and care of their own Sunday school classes to work with youths on Sunday mornings.

One way to assure them that we, too, want adult volunteers to grow in Christ is to use a staggered teaching schedule or elective format. At the very least, we can take the trouble to check out copies of video-tapes for leaders to take home and view on their own time.

Lack of prayer. Jesus started his recruiting drive not with potshots of guilt or rapid-fire pleading, but with prayer to the Lord of the harvest. "The harvest is plentiful but the workers are few. Ask the Lord of the harvest, therefore, to send out workers into his harvest field" (Luke 10:2).

Our own insecurity. Recruiting can rub our noses into some very uncomfortable questions: What if people see all of these volunteers and think I'm not doing my job? What if they're thinking "Aren't we paying you to do youth ministry?" What if people turn me down? Will that affect our relationship? What if my volunteers are better at youth work than I am? Can I effectively lead a group of adult peers in ministry? Will those volunteers who are ten years older than me accept my leadership?

Our volunteers' insecurities. The average adult generally man-ifests one of three clinical fears about doing youth ministry:

- *Intelligentsius snobus nerdus*—fearing that the kids will know more about the Bible than we do and we'll end up looking stupid when we can't answer one of their questions.

    Antidote:—We are working with students not because we're theological experts, but because we love students and Jesus.

    —Teenagers don't respond to Christ by listening for knowledge from our heads but by experiencing care and friendship from our hearts.

- *Nonterminus phobias*—fearing that if we volunteer for this position we'll never be able to quit without being considered AWOL. (Frankly, we all know there's truth to this fear.)

    Antidote:—Write into the job description a set length of ten-ure, assuring people they can dismiss themselves gracefully. This will also protect youth workers from being interminably teamed with volunteers who aren't working out. The only thing harder than getting workers on the team is gracefully getting them off the team.

- *Delinquitus barbarus phobias* — fearing that all teenagers are barbarians, incorrigible, and just a step above lower primates, and that going into a room or meeting alone with them is to risk being taken hostage.

  Antidote: — Experience. Invite prospective leaders to tag along for a weekend retreat or to sit in for a few weeks of youth group. They will gain a more realistic picture of both the challenges and the joys of ministry with students.

HOW CAN I
RECRUIT A TEAM?

Calling the right people for the right positions is perhaps the one area of youth ministry that causes the most frustration and headache. How do we find the people we want? How do we decide what kind of people we want to find? How do we avoid finding people we don't want?

Create a climate for recruiting. To raise up a crop of volunteers, we have to provide a climate of general congregational enthusiasm for the youth ministry. Showcase the youth group by encouraging student testimonies following retreats and by liberally using slides and videotapes to report to the congregation the momentum of the youth ministry.

Ask tough questions. In the average recruiting situation, we are so desperate for someone to take the job that we will settle for any person with a pulse. Whether recruiting for a paid position or a volunteer position, we simply cannot afford to cut any corners on the prescribed biblical guidelines for those in leadership. (Check out just these few samples: Lev. 21; 1 Tim. 3:1-13; Acts 6:3; Titus 1:5-9; 1 Peter 5:1-4.)

Any group of people responsible for recruiting youth-ministry workers should confront some of these tough questions:

- Will we allow divorced people to serve on the team?
- Do team members have to be active members of our church?
- Do our team leaders exhibit the evidence of spiritual leadership?
- What kind of standards will we have with regard to theological beliefs?
- What will be our stance toward team members who become pregnant outside of marriage?
- Do we want to establish any guidelines relative to age?
- Will we have any special expectations about team members' personal habits (smoking, using alcohol, etc.)?

These are not rhetorical questions with assumed answers. The major channel through which teenagers receive spiritual truth is the adult models they observe.

Recognize spiritual vitality. Paul writes to the church of Corinth that his life is an incarnation of the gospel, that he seeks to live his life as a living letter (2 Cor. 3:1-3). He encourages the Corinthians to imitate him as he seeks to imitate Christ (1 Cor. 11:1). The writer of Hebrews echoes the same idea: "Remember your leaders, who spoke the word of God to you. Consider the outcome of their way of life and imitate their faith" (Heb. 13:7). The number-one criterion for selecting prospects for a role on the youth-ministry team should be their competence as Christians.

Be aware of other pluses for youth ministry — things like an understanding of youth culture, interpersonal skills, the ability to communicate, a sense of humor, and, of course, patience. No research suggests that a volunteer must be young to be effective. Perhaps the best rule of thumb is that leaders need to be "old enough to be respected and young enough to keep up."[2]

Make recruiting everyone's job. Although we are called to "fish for men," most of us spend a lot of our time fishing for fishermen. However, one person alone simply doesn't have adequate contacts or adequate knowledge of the congregation to do thorough scouting. If everyone assumes some responsibility for recruitment, however, the prospect pool can be significantly increased. When recruiting is everyone's job, we can tap several networks of relationships and avoid recruiting the same people over and over again. Instead, the standard creed of volunteer recruitment in most churches seems to be, "If they're breathing, recruit 'em; if they're willing, run 'em into the ground."

To sum it all up, the three essential qualities of any youth worker are these: a love for Christ, a love for students, and a love for the church. No matter how skilled or charismatic or cool or likeable an individual might be, if we are recruiting leaders who are weak in one of those three areas, we are recruiting trouble.

NEEDLES IN A HAYSTACK

There are four basic approaches to recruiting youth volunteers, all of them helpful at times.

©1990 Leadership

"Maybe I shouldn't wait for Mr. Peterson to volunteer to sponsor the junior-high youth group."

The public appeal method. The most common method for finding the necessary volunteers for a youth program is the public appeal method. Typically the way this approach works is that the pastor or youth pastor stands in front of the congregation on Sunday morning and publicly pleads and bleeds until some poor, unknowing soul is driven by guilt to respond. Usually it sounds something like this: "Maybe you folks don't care if our youths are getting pregnant or using drugs, but if you do, we have a wonderful opportunity for you downstairs with our junior high Sunday school program."

For obvious reasons, this is the least effective means of recruitment. To begin with, it is the precise opposite of the approach Jesus took. Nowhere are we given any record that Jesus went into Jericho and announced, "If anyone is willing to be a fisher of men, please sign up over near the well or see me after the service." Nor do we have any record of Jesus putting an ad in the synagogue bulletin asking for "volunteers to help perform miracles and cast out demons." The root problem of this approach is that it often recruits people we do not want. Recruiting should be specific rather than general.

Kids recruiting leaders. Think of how the following invitation would melt some of the initial resistance of a potential volunteer youth worker: "You know, we asked the kids whom they would like to have working with them in their youth group, and sure enough, with one voice they began chanting your name." Granted, students will not always be attracted to volunteer leaders for reasons that might actually make someone a strong leader, but presumably any adult recommended by the students will possess basic interpersonal skills and at least some ability to relate to students. That's a major hurdle.

Volunteers recruiting volunteers. Volunteers recruiting volunteers are much more believable than youth pastors recruiting volunteers. I'm more likely to invest in my broker's recommended stock when I know he has already invested in that same stock. Active volunteers can pass on a realistic idea of the challenges and rewards of answering the call of youth work plus being a mom or dad, working full time, not having seminary training, and so on.

The one-to-one call. Jesus assembled his team by praying thoroughly, seeking the people he wanted, and then calling them individually by name. The strength of this method is that it allows us personally to meet and get to know each person who is considering joining the ministry team. And, just as important, it affords them the opportunity to meet and get to know us as well.

CLOSE ENCOUNTERS

The recruitment of volunteers doesn't end when they accept the call to youth work. Marlene Wilson (*Effective Management of Church Volunteers*) describes recruitment as a process beginning with the initial contact and continuing through our efforts toward retention of volunteers. Let's take a closer look.

STEP ONE:
MAKING CONTACT

Mark and Carolyn were both working at Rhode Island State Library when I met them. As members of our congregation, they had recently taken part in a church-wide survey of gifts and interests. Among other things, they had expressed their interest in youth ministry. We followed up on their response with a personal interview. Eager to impress them with a foretaste of what they might expect in youth ministry, I invited them both to lunch at a fast food restaurant across from the capitol in downtown Providence. (If possible, it is best to talk to both spouses if the interested volunteer is a married couple.)

During the course of our lunch, they were interviewed carefully, thoroughly, and intentionally. One of the mistakes that we make in recruitment is that we seem to feel a sense of shame at interviewing candidates for the position of volunteer youth leader. We should not. An interview is neither a friendly chat, a sales pitch, an indoctrination, nor an inquisition. It is an honest attempt to discern what God is doing in people's lives, and to think together about how they might be best used in the work of his kingdom. There's nothing shameful or devious about that.

The key in an interview like this is not that I get all the vital statistics on Mark and Carolyn. In fact, to some degree, I'm not really concerned about their history—where they went to school, how much experience they've had in youth ministry, or what their denominational background is. If I am interviewing someone for this kind of ministry, I am less interested in history and more interested in "his (or her) story." I am going to ask questions that will give me more than information about them. I want to find out who they are.

Instead of asking how long they've been married, I might simply say, "Tell me about your family." Instead of asking what they think their gifts are, I'm going to ask, "What do you most enjoy doing? Describe for me what would be your ideal role in a youth ministry program like ours." Rather than ask about specific prior experience, I am going to ask Mark and Carolyn to tell me what gets them most excited about the prospect of working with students: "What gets you most worried?" "What were some of the high points and low points of your own teenage years?"

Rather than asking them to give me their testimony, I might say, "Describe for me your relationship with Jesus in terms that you feel a teenager would understand." Or, "Tell me about some of the people who have been significant in your own walk with Christ." It is in the course of this one-on-one interview that we can seek together to hear God's call in their lives.

STEP TWO:
AROUSE INTEREST

I already knew that Mark and Carolyn were interested in youth work because of their responses to the gift survey. The best way to help them further define their interest was to invite them to sit in on our activities. Being with the kids is the fun part, anyway. Although they would have no responsibilities at this point, this observation time would let both parties see if God blows on the spark and fans it into a flame.

STEP THREE:
SPECIFIC PROPOSAL

As Mark and Carolyn became familiar with our program and sensed where they perhaps would like to fit in, we offered them specific, written job descriptions based partly on what we needed and partly on who they were. The following is a sample job description:

Position Description: *Youth Ministry*
Barrington Baptist Church — Barrington, Rhode Island

POSITION:

Sunday school teacher

The Sunday school teachers are integral to the overall youth-ministry strategy at BBC. The task of the Sunday school teacher is unique in that Sunday school is the one time during the week that there are few schedule conflicts interrupting a teen's opportunity for consistent input; and Sunday school provides an opportunity to minister to some youths who have no other contact with the youth ministry.

GENERAL DESCRIPTION:

The Sunday school teacher leads students to observe, reflect upon, and apply the Word of God, with the goal of discipling teenage guys and girls. While the bulk of this ministry is in the formal context of the Sunday school hour on Sunday morning, the teacher's ministry extends to in-depth discipleship beyond the classroom setting.

EXPECTATIONS:

The BBC Sunday school department expects the following of any persons serving as Sunday school teachers:

- Basic accord with our stated philosophy of youth ministry (see attached).
- Willingness to attempt to extend their ministries beyond the Sunday school hour into a less formal life situation (not necessarily by means of a class party at someone's home, but through one-to-one contacts — having a Coke together, mailing a note to absentees, sending a birthday card, making a phone call, and so on).
- Willingness to actively participate in occasional training and planning meetings.
- Solid commitment to the values of learner-centered teaching, a style of teaching that seeks to emphasize mutual discovery as opposed to a teaching style that emphasizes "telling" and "spoon-feeding."

- Commitment to accountability for students.
- Commitment to spend two to three hours a week in the ministry, including preparation time, class time, and times of personal contact. Someone who is too busy for this time commitment is too busy to teach Sunday school.
- Willingness to commit oneself to the ministry for one full year on a consistent, dependable basis. At the end of the year, the teaching covenant may be renewed by both parties.

TEACHING COVENANT:

(To be signed and returned to Duffy Robbins; the signed sheet will be copied and returned to the teacher for his or her reference.)

I have read and fully understand the expectations and philosophy of the Youth-Ministry Sunday School Department and will work within these guidelines as God enables me.

Signed: _____

STEP FOUR:
SIGN ON THE LINE

After Mark and Carolyn received specific information about the position for which we were recruiting them, they were invited to sign up. Give recruits a definite span of time to think through (and discuss with their spouse) the decision—aweek is about enough time. If we leave the propositions too open-ended, we start playing cat and mouse. They duck behind the baptistry when they see us coming because they know we want an answer. We start to feel self-conscious because these otherwise nice people have developed a gestapo-like fear of us. Just make it clear that by a certain date, within a week or two, they will answer yes or no about the opportunity.

STEP FIVE:
RETENTION

Calling youth volunteers is only the beginning of building the team. Next we turn our attention to three other elements of team ministry that enable us to retain the volunteers. Our challenge at this point is to court them, counsel them, and cover them.

CHAPTER TEN

TURN-ON OR TURNOVER: HOW TO MOTIVATE YOUR MINISTRY TEAM

Several years ago, Ronald Wilson wrote an article for *Leadership* journal that ought to be required reading for any people recruiting volunteer leaders. Entitled "Letter From an Ex-Volunteer," this imaginary letter has an important message for us.

Dear Pastor Potter:

You and some others are down in Finney Hall in the church basement stuffing 20,000 envelopes for the Madison County Deeper Life Campaign at the fairground. I guess I should be there. You asked for volunteers last Sunday, and I had my hand halfway up when you announced hymn number 263, "Work, for the Night is Coming."

As you probably guessed, I'm feeling a little bad about that and about not getting to choir practice and dropping off the planning committee and canceling the literature distribution training session scheduled for our house last month.

For one thing, pastor, I think I'm burned out—spent, pooped, empty. I've been hearing about it lately, and they say that if you're not careful, it can lead to dropout. I always used to say I didn't mind burning out for the Lord, but lately, I've been afraid I might go up in one big poof.

Well, to close, pastor, like I said, I haven't dropped out. Maybe I just need to hear you say it once more: "Wilson, it's the ninth inning, and we're two runs behind. We've got two outs and no one on and you're up. We're counting on you to hit. So go get 'em!"

Your brother in the Lord,
Ronald Wilson[1]

Change a few of the activities in that letter, and it could have been written by almost any youth-ministry volunteer. It seems like most of us only volunteer in three speeds: cop out, help out, or burn out.

SERVICE AFTER
THE SALE

Les Christie, of Eastside Christian Church in Fullerton, California, estimates that the turnover rate among youth volunteers is about thirty percent every year.[2] That equals almost complete turnover every three years! With all of the effort that goes into recruiting qualified youth workers, we simply cannot afford to tolerate such high turnover. As the letter reminds us, it's only a few steps from burn out to dropout.

Our responsibility to volunteers goes beyond the sale. Calling forth those who would minister with teenagers is a critical part of the work. But effective team ministry includes strategies to not only court volunteers, but also to counsel and cover them.

COURT THEM

Marriage teaches us a lot of lessons about everyday life. Great truths like: "Don't always say exactly everything on your mind," and "He who insults the stew insults she who made the stew, and thus lands himself in a stew." One of the lessons that couples learn early in a marriage, if they're lucky, is that they should never stop courting. E. V. Hill, the great pastor and preacher from Mount Zion Missionary Baptist Church in Watts, California, told a crowd of a thousand youth ministers at the National Youthworkers Convention in Dallas, that they should "Never stop courting! Remember the flowers. Remember the phone calls. Remember the fun. Remember not to forget!" It's sound advice.

The average volunteer youth worker receives affirmation and encouragement for approximately the first week of their labors. It begins with the pulpit announcement: "Devlin and Carol have told the C.E. board that they are willing to start working with our youth group. We praise the Lord for their availability and openness to this vital work." After a congregational euphoria that lasts all of about ten minutes, there is a collective, almost audible sigh as pastor and people think to themselves, "Thank goodness. Now we don't have to think about the youth ministry any more until these two quit."

Good youth-ministry leadership courts volunteers, makes them feel appreciated, makes them feel wanted, lets them know that theirs is an important ministry. The average youth worker expects to be underappreciated by teenagers. Any sane person would be suspicious if the kids swarmed around him at the conclusion of the Bible study gushing, "Great Bible study, brother Devlin! That was a remarkable piece of exposition from the Word. God has wrought a deep work in my life tonight." But what a surprise when the congregation is not only apparently ungrateful but critical. "I thought you said you were going to have the kids back here at this church by 11:00 tonight. Do you realize I've been sitting in this church parking lot for the last half hour just waiting?" No wonder there is such turnover among volunteers. The wonder is that there isn't more. In Ronald Wilson's imaginary "Letter From an Ex-Volunteer," he underlines this point.

> Take Eddie Turner with his five kids, three of them teenagers. He's into everything. Practically eats and sleeps at the church. Now what if someone said to him, "Hey, Eddie, two kids in the youth group accepted the Lord this week. All that driving around you've done to take the kids to Camp Ocheewahbee and the roller rink and everyplace really helped. You had a part in it." Not that Eddie needs anyone to say thanks, you understand. But the way he's going, he's going to need a little encouragement.
>
> Or take the people down at the church tonight. They should be real thankful they can work for the Lord like that—and I imagine they are. But it may be a little hard, as someone put it, to see the eternal value in running a damp sponge over twenty thousand envelope flaps. It might help to get some of those folks back next time if someone stood up in church and gave a report on the Deeper Life Campaign, even said a word to all those envelope stuffers and workers. . . . [3]

If we are going to convince our youth-ministry volunteers that they are serving a vital role, we will have to go out of our way to make that known. We need to court them. Cheryl has been working with the eighth-grade Sunday school for four years. She's recently said she is thinking about "taking some time off." Although you agree that maybe all she needs is a little time off, you're concerned that there may be some other issues at stake. After all, she did make a point of saying, "I'm just not finding the job fits me the way I feel it used to."

Assuming that the problem is with the position, and not with some external problem (marriage, job), how can you keep this valuable veteran on your youth-ministry team? What do you do?

Let her go. A person like Cheryl is going to get plugged in somewhere, though, and it's a shame to lose someone with her skills, relationships, and experience. There must be a way to keep her involved.

Bribe her to stay. Forget it. There isn't enough money in the youth budget to bribe anybody!

Promise she'll never have to do lock-ins ever again. No way. That's a lie, and besides, you need experienced people like Cheryl at the lock-in so that you can leave the church at ten and go home to get some sleep.

Give her a one-year sabbatical from youth ministry. This is a good idea, but a year is a long time. People get interested in other areas of ministry, and we lose them.

Tell her scary stories about teenagers' problems, the need for willing volunteers, and the judgment of God. If Cheryl has been through four years of lock-ins, nothing is going to scare her!

Utilize some strategy of job design. Rather than working so hard to change Cheryl's mind, change the design of the ministry to better use Cheryl's gifts and help her feel satisfied and challenged in her ministry. People are more important than positions. We recruit people. We don't recruit positions. As we noted earlier, "Productivity comes through people."

TAILOR-MADE MINISTRY

There are three specific strategies we can use to better tailor a position to fit the volunteer: job enlargement, job enrichment, and job simplification.

Job enlargement. One way to court Cheryl's commitment may be to enlarge her ministry, increasing the breadth of her responsibilities. For example, we might offer a new assignment as a "troubleshooter"—a teacher who rotates among the various youth Sunday school classes. After four years with the eighth grade, she knows most of the students up through the senior class and has gained some valuable insights through her experience.

Another way to affirm Cheryl's ability and make constructive use of her experience is to ask her to present teacher-training workshops for the other volunteers. Or maybe she would feel challenged by teaching a larger, combined junior high Sunday school, working with a team of volunteer helpers. She might feel motivated by leading a small discipleship group one afternoon a week in addition to her Sunday school responsibilities, or she might even prefer one-on-one discipleship of two or three of the students in her class.

Caution: When using job enlargement, assign jobs that really need to be done. Three meaningless tasks will not add up to one meaningful task.

Job enrichment. It may be that the better way to court Cheryl's commitment is not by changing the breadth of her ministry, but by changing the depth of her ministry. Most tasks have three main components: planning (before), doing (during), and evaluation (after). Thus far, Cheryl's input in the youth program has been at the *doing* level. She has faithfully taught her class every week for four years, but someone else has told her what material to use, where the class will meet, when it will meet, whether it will include just eighth graders, and whether or not it will include both guys and girls. Job enrichment is a strategy of redesigning Cheryl's ministry so that she becomes more involved in *planning* and *evaluation*, keeping her fresh, fulfilled, and on the growing edge.

The kind of job enrichment we offer depends on the volunteer's unique gifts. Sheila had been playing guitar for the youth choir; now she is asked to lead it. Joel had been teaching Sunday school; now he is asked to train other teachers. Jenny's dad had been the unofficial driver of the bus for all youth outings; now the church asks him to head a committee overseeing the service and maintenance of the bus, and the possible purchase of a new bus. Charles and Marie had been leading a weekly Bible study group; now the Council on Ministry asks them to head up a youth committee. All of these are examples of job enrichment.

Job simplification. Of course, the issue with Cheryl may not be that she is looking for broader or deeper responsibilities at all. It may be that she is simply groaning under the burden of her many responsibilities as mom, wife, and part-time employee at the local bookstore. Like many of our volunteers, she's looking for less to do, not more. Thus, the third strategy of job redesign is simplification—the process of taking a difficult task and breaking it down into more manageable responsibilities.

Among Cheryl's responsibilities in an average week as Sunday school teacher, for example, are the following:

- Preparing her own curriculum
- Calling or visiting at least two of her students
- Sending a handwritten note to any students who were absent
- Picking up doughnuts before she comes to Sunday school
- Teaching her class during Sunday school
- Making announcements pertaining to the overall youth program
- Securing all necessary A-V supplies for her lessons
- Making sure the classroom is cleaned up before she leaves
- Attending the C.E. board meeting once a month

To simplify her job we eliminate tasks, delegates tasks, or design a plan for sharing her tasks. In a team-teaching role, Cheryl could cut her load almost in half just by sharing some of the ongoing tasks of teaching, visitation, and curriculum preparation. Perhaps we could recruit one person whose job is to tend to the A-V needs of all the youth teachers, freeing Cheryl of her weekly rummage through the A-V closet looking for an extension cord. Cheryl could delegate to students the responsibilities of buying doughnuts and cleaning up the classroom. Maybe all of the teachers could be represented at the C.E. board meeting by the youth minister or the chair of the youth committee or by one of the teachers each month on a rotating basis.

What so often burns out the average volunteer is not jobs that are too challenging, but that they are too trivial. Are we asking our volunteers to fill out detailed reports that no one ever reads or heeds? Do we ask them to be at extra meetings that neither train them nor inspire them, just so we can say we have had our departmental meeting this week? This kind of "administrivia" exasperates good leaders.

LIGHT UP A LIFE

In an article entitled "How to Light a Fire Under People Without Burning Them Up," Ed Dayton and Ted Engstrom identified several means[4] by which we can effectively show our appreciation for those who serve with us:

Begin together. Make sure that everyone shares a common vision for the ministry. People are more enthusiastic when the group's goals are their goals.

Build community. Our volunteers need to perceive those on the ministry team as friends, not just as coworkers. Some of the best experiences I have had with volunteer teams have happened when we were out together (with no students) for a day of white-water rafting. Those afternoons paddling the Big South Fork of the Cumberland River melded our volunteer team into a fellowship of friends who laughed together, helped each other, sweat together, faced death together (!), and reminisced together. It's hard to leave teams like that. It's like leaving friends and family. Whether it's a potluck or a yearly backpacking trip, volunteers experience team-building, praying together, dreaming, and bonding that shows them they are important, even when no adolescents are around.

Keep good lines of communication. Most volunteers fear that the last words they'll hear from a youth worker will be, "Well, we're certainly glad that you decided to take this position." Professional youth workers can indeed be aloof and hard to contact. Some youth-ministry professionals have incorporated basic report sheets so that the volunteers are not haunted by the fear of the phantom youth worker.

Youth-Ministry Report Sheet
Please submit to Shelly after each ministry activity. Thanks.
Class/study group: _____
Leader's name: _____
Topic of study: _____
Total attendance: _____ Regulars: _____ Visitors: _____
Comments: _____
Materials you need: _____
Shelly, please get in touch with me this week. Yes _____

Practice accountability. Some youth workers find it effective to ask volunteers to turn in weekly reports of contacts they've had with students. But beware of administrivia. The point is to follow-up on assignments and requests in a prompt manner, affirming to volunteers that their efforts are important.

Keep motivating over the long haul. The best recruiting work we can do is among those who have already signed on. These people know the job, know the kids, and know the ministry. It's almost impossible to find green recruits with that kind of résumé.

Give attention to supervision and administration. If we say we're going to have the materials in their hands one month before they are to teach, let's make sure we do. If we ask them to prepare a presentation for this Sunday, let's not show up with our own prepared lesson and ask them to wait until next Sunday. One of the greatest frustrations of volunteer leaders is professional youth ministers who operate by the seat of their pants.

Give them a chance to succeed. A wise leader creates for volunteers working conditions that say, "We take your ministry seriously." That means well-lit rooms, clean blackboards with functional chalk, markers that actually mark, and projectors that really do project.

Be generous with affirmation. Use notes, phone calls, public recognition. If a student shares something with me about how a leader has been helpful to them, I pass it on to that leader in a note within the week. Part of the task of leader is being a cheerleader for the volunteers.

The two keys to effective affirmation are recognizing effort as well as results and being specific in our praise. Rather than saying, "You did a good job Sunday night," we should be saying, "The game where you had the kids chew silly putty was really ingenious. What a creative idea! I've never seen the kids that quiet. How long did it take the EMT to get Jimmy breathing again?" The one affirmation that is never appropriate is comparing leaders to each other so that one's praise is at the same time another's putdown. Wise youth workers will be intentional in affirmation and take every opportunity to "consider how [they] may spur one another on toward love and good deeds" (Heb. 10:24).

Special T-shirts or hats for the leaders, appreciation dinners, notes, phone calls, free baby-sitting from youth group kids—all of these are ways of saying "Thanks for doing what you do." One creative youth minister wrote periodic profiles in the church bulletin—"What kind of person hangs around teenagers in their spare time, surrounded by loud music, junk food, and screaming people? [Name] does—here's her story."

COUNSEL THEM

Luke tells us that Jesus appointed seventy-two people to serve as his advance team in coministry. They were sent out "two by two ahead of him to every town and place where he was about to go" (Luke 10:1). What is especially intriguing about Jesus' method with these folks is not that he sent them out, but that he called them back. In Luke 10:17-20, we see Jesus with the seventy-two, sharing and celebrating what has happened in their travels. It's halftime and the coach brings the team back to the locker room to discuss strategy and give them critical instruction.

The Master's model reminds us to give our volunteers the instruction and counsel necessary for them to complete their missions. The great fear of most volunteers is that they will be thrust into a small dungeon-dim classroom with a room full of adolescents and given absolutely no training on how to survive. Unfortunately, this happens more than we would like to admit.

We sometimes neglect to train people to do that which we've asked them to do because we don't want to take the time to train them.

Other times we fail to do so because we don't know which facets of youth ministry require training. And ironically, we sometimes neglect training of volunteers because we're so naturally gifted at youth ministry that we don't really understand why what we are doing with kids is working, and therefore, we can't tell someone else how to do it.

Volunteers can only travel so far on God-given talents. Even the best of us needs to have our abilities honed and sharpened. We need leaders who send us out to do ministry, but then call us back in so that we can discuss what worked and why, what bombed and why. People need to be trained gradually, at a pace that neither insults them nor threatens them.

Effective training of youth volunteers requires both preservice training (before they start the work) and in-service training (after they've started the work). Although training procedures vary, certain basic training applies to any program. The following are sample topics that might be covered at the preservice and in-service levels:

Preservice Training

A look at youth culture

Understanding our philosophy of youth ministry.

Understanding how the youth program works (why we do what we do and why we've chosen to use certain programs).

Procedural Issues

What happens in an emergency?

What happens in case of fire?

Where do I get materials?

Who are the people I'm working with?

What is my role within the team?

How am I reimbursed for supplies I purchase?

Youth Group 101

- Student-centered learning—teaching the Bible in a way that puts students in the heart of the investigation process instead of using a teacher-centered lecture approach.
- How to discipline in a youth group.
- How to get close to kids (contact work).

In-Service Training

How to use questions effectively.

154

Counseling kids who are hurting.

Discipling students/one-on-one ministry.

Stretching muscles of creativity.

TRAINING THAT STAYS ON TRACK

Meredith is an admissions counselor at Eastern College. Her background is in business, but she is naturally skilled in getting along with teenagers. A few years ago she didn't know what a Young Life club was. When I spoke with her recently, she was seriously considering going on Young Life staff! How did she go from green recruit to capable leader?

Youth worker and writer David Stone describes the training process as the Four Phases of Ease:

"I do it—you watch." The volunteer simply observes the job being done. Allow new volunteers to attend youth group for a few months before asking them to lead anything. Help them to get used to the stage before they are expected to take part in the play.

"We do it together." At this point, the volunteer still isn't pedaling his own bike, but he is riding tandem. He's getting a feel for how this new role handles and turns, and what it takes to keep everything in balance. In practical terms, a leader might suggest to the volunteer something like this: "Look, next week's Bible study has four sections to it. You've watched me do Bible study now for about four months. You know most of the kids. Why don't we share responsibility for next week's Bible study? I'll do the opening and the closing, and you do the two middle portions of the study."

"You do it—I'll watch." In this critical phase of the training process, volunteers take steps independent of our help, but we are walking beside them in case they fall. Students in my youth-ministry class serve as interns in church youth groups. Then in class Monday mornings, we evaluate what happened and, in some cases, what didn't happen so they learn how to sharpen their work.

"You do it—I'll go train someone else." At this stage the volunteers graduate with a level of competence that allows them to exercise their own ministries within the context of the youth group. No one has to constantly tell them what to do or how to do it. They have

developed some instincts for what will and won't work in youth ministry. We don't desert them, however. We update them on new resources and strategies and sit in on their classes occasionally to help them continue to sharpen their skills.

We like doing most what we feel we do best. People don't enjoy doing those things which they do poorly. If we want our volunteers to enjoy their work, we need to counsel them on how to do youth ministry well. Our biblical mandate as leaders is to "prepare God's people for works of service, so that the body of Christ may be built up" (Eph. 4:12).

COVER THEM

By the time we have gone to all the trouble of recruiting, affirming, and training volunteers, we want to protect our investment. That's why our ongoing priority is to cover our volunteers. Youth ministry is legendary for its abysmal record of retention. We go through leaders so fast that students can scarcely learn their names, let alone build with them any kind of in-depth relationships. Covering volunteers is protecting them for long-term involvement—protecting them from themselves, from the parents, and from the students.

Themselves. It's not the people who do not like youth ministry who burn themselves out. It's the people who so enjoy their work with students that other parts of their lives get out of balance. One way to protect our volunteers from unbalanced priorities is to develop a pool of backups so that volunteers can have occasional days off. Even if the youth group is run by one couple, without any backup or support people, there is no reason why that couple shouldn't take off one Sunday night in eight to stay home.

Parents. Nothing discourages volunteers as much as discovering how unappreciated they are by many of the parents of students with whom they're working. Except for volunteers who are also parents, I don't believe that volunteer team members should attend parents' briefings. When I have permitted volunteers to attend, I have generally been embarrassed for the parents and resentful for the volunteers. Honest criticism can always be passed along to volunteers through gentler, more sensitive channels.

Students. Ironically, the more effective we are with students, the more apt we are to be smothered by them.

Bill naturally drew students to himself. He was always spending time with kids, leading a Bible study with kids, or preparing to lead a Bible study for kids. He was one of those dream volunteers who was always ready. Over the course of time, however, it became evident that he was spending time with the youth group kids at the expense of time with his family. It was beginning to affect his marriage. Finally, at his wife's request, I took him to lunch and told him that he would have to step down from the ministry team for at least a month or so to spend more time at home; that he needed to regain some balance in his life. It was a difficult conversation and a painful step to take, but it made more sense to release Bill in the short term so that we could protect him and retain him over the long haul.

Although spending time with the students earns volunteers the right to be heard, we must also be watching that volunteers aren't neglecting family time, personal time, or other kinds of responsibilities at work or in school. If we care for our volunteers, we owe them that.

SHARING THE LOAD

Trying to do youth ministry without a team, or with a team that we don't use, burns us out. The four men who took to the roof that day in Mark 2 to get their friend to the feet of Jesus demonstrated a classic example of team ministry. The healing that day might never have happened if someone had not recruited others and trained them to do their work. The load was too heavy. One man could not have borne it alone.

No subject in this book is more important than team ministry. Call them, court them, counsel them, and cover them. For most youth ministers, their successes in all four of these dimensions of team ministry spell the difference between youth ministries that go the distance and youth ministries that wear themselves out.

CHAPTER ELEVEN

THE SECRET OF ANNOUNCING: PUBLICIZING YOUR YOUTH MINISTRY

Dale (not his real name) was excited about reaching out into the community of the upper midwest church that had recently hired him as youth minister. In his previous South Carolina church, he had lifted up Christ through monthly concerts given by various contemporary Christian musicians. Within six months of accepting his new position, Dale had a committed group of praying kids and a network of area youth ministers laying plans for a major concert at the local high school auditorium.

As the concert night drew closer, Dale could sense the excitement. The local Christian radio station agreed to send over one of their announcers to emcee the event. It looked as if the stage was set for a great night. Finally, the big night came. The band was great. The ministry was powerful. The only problem was that, in an auditorium that would comfortably seat four thousand people, only three hundred people came out.

The band graciously agreed to forgo the majority of its fee. The sound company and the auditorium management were not as understanding. The youth minister and his church went about three thousand dollars into debt.

As a result of this debacle, the church staff and congregation began to question Dale's credibility, the kids felt discouraged by this apparent failure, and the youth budget was swallowed by indebtedness. By the end of his first year at the church, Dale sensed that he should look for another job. Within eighteen months he was gone, leaving behind a debt of just over twenty-two-hundred dollars. The other youth ministers in the area canceled their plans for a follow-up concert, assuming that there just wasn't enough interest in the area to support that kind of ministry.

* * *

There may have been a number of mistakes and mishaps that led to this true scenario, but one of the major factors that foreshadowed this disaster was that this youth minister, for all of his zeal, enthusiasm, and faith, had neglected to adequately and effectively publicize and promote the event. A lack of promotion led to a tragic demotion.

What this means for us in youth ministry is that effective promotion and publicity for an event is a significant part of our spiritual responsibility. We simply cannot embrace students with the gospel if we aren't able to bring them within our reach. No matter how powerful, how anointed, how fun or creative or positively blessed an event is, if teenagers do not attend it, they cannot directly benefit from it.

The average high school student is not intuitively aware of your youth calendar. He probably doesn't know your youth group even exists, and what's worse, he doesn't care. It's a rare non-Christian teenager who spends time on a Friday afternoon calling around to different churches to see who is hosting an outreach event. If students are going to find out about our ministry to them, it will be because we have been aggressive in making contact.

WHY SHY?

Why are we so reluctant to publicize youth events? We claim to be dispatchers of the Good News of Christ, and yet our approach is so timid that one might well question whether we really believe in the vitality of our message at all. For hours a day the average American is torpedoed by important announcements about critical matters like "Kibbles and Bits," "1000 Flushes," "Obsession," and the new, commemorative "Rice Krispies." Between the ages of six and eighteen the average child watches approximately seven hundred and fifty thousand of these commercial announcements. Why are we reluctant to enter the marketplace with news about the one matter that really does matter?

For one thing, some of us are uncomfortable with all of the hype that surrounds us. We feel it's inappropriate to out-glitz and out-shout the voices vying for attention. It's unseemly. Too worldly. We feel a flashy campaign does dishonor to the gospel of Christ, as if those of us in ministry were sideshow hucksters. For another thing, some of us are uneasy with aggressive promotion because it could be interpreted as an attempt to muster through the flesh what only God can accomplish by his Spirit. Perhaps we are trying to have a successful event because it's on our calendar, not because it's on God's.

Although there is wisdom behind these concerns, the gospel certainly must be proclaimed in the arena of everyday life where most kids will hear it. There's a lot of room between out-shouting and being completely mute. We have too long used the "Little Bo Peep" approach to outreach and publicity: "Leave them alone and they'll come home dragging their tails behind them." It's not working. The sheep are scattering and looking for other shepherds. Our youths are being brainwashed and exploited by people who are willing to be robust and aggressive with their messages.

Perhaps in honesty we should admit that part of the problem is we're just plain lazy. While painting over the real picture by using spiritual excuses, we neglect to do effective publicity mostly because it's hard to do. It's much easier to request a public service announcement by post card than it is to brainstorm what creative promotion can best get our message to the audience of students that most needs to hear it. If we're going to go fishing for men, we better be prepared to use a lure.

SEVEN KEYS FOR PROMOTION AND PUBLICITY

We don't have to hire some New York ad agency to do effective publicity and promotion for our youth activities. And fortunately for those of us who are artistically impaired, we don't have to be especially gifted in that area, either. What we do need is a desire to reach kids and a willingness to do the hard work of creativity. Here are seven guidelines for designing a more effective promotional strategy.

THE "EYES" HAVE IT

My favorite compliment from a student was when Keith told me one day that he had saved every single youth-group mailing that had been sent to him. I felt that rare sense of accomplishment that I get when I have actually succeeded in doing something for which I have no training whatsoever (replacing toilet hardware, wallpapering a room, and hanging a ceiling fan are in this same category). When I remembered how as a high schooler I was never even remotely tempted to open anything my church sent me, I realized the magnitude of Keith's compliment.

The purpose of doing publicity is to capture someone's attention long enough to give them the desired message. That means it is to our advantage to make every flyer, handout, or letter from the youth group as attractive and interesting as possible. Unfortunately, we more often send out notices about wonderful, fun, life-changing events in letters and envelopes that have all the appeal of dog food coupons. Grabbing the attention is everything in publicity, and if we are willing to do some creative thinking and hustling, it is possible to make collector's items of youth-group mail.

Geoff Kohler, youth pastor of Paoli Presbyterian Church, begins every fall with a special kickoff mailing. One year he sent out a book of tickets for each youth group event. Packaged in a special "Youth Stuff" brochure, he called his promotion "Passports to Adventure."

The youth-ministry team at First Baptist Church of Cleveland, Tennessee, sent out a postcard "guaranteed to put a smile on your face." On the flip side of the postcard was a mirror-image note. The only way it could be read was to hold it up in front of a mirror. Right in the middle of the postcard was a big red pair of lips forming a huge smile. If a student held the card in front of the mirror to decipher it, the obnoxious smile would look as if it were on the reader's face.

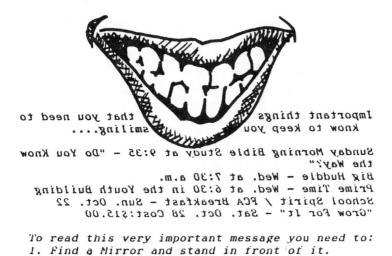

To read this very important message you need to:
1. Find a Mirror and stand in front of it.
2. Place card under your nose for best effect.
3. Read !!!!!

Our youth ministry once promoted a backpacking trip by printing an actual boot print on every envelope we mailed out. We simply put the envelopes on the floor, donned one hiking boot, stepped into a wide pan of brown tempera paint and stamped (stomped?) each envelope and letter.

With all of the clip art products on the market today, there is simply no excuse for posters and mailers that are boring.

One of the great undiscovered sources of creative clip art is a series of nineteenth-century "pictographs" available from Dover Publications.[1] Each book in the series includes several hundred copyright-free illustrations reproduced from such periodicals as *Illustrated*

London News and *Harper's*. Titles in the series include *Food and Drink* (edited by Jim Harter), *Women* (Harter), *Men* (Harter), and *Children* (edited by Carol Grafton). Tip: When using these pictures for posters or mailings, add a caption referring to students or activities of the group.

Special tip for cheapskates: Collecting promotional materials from clip art companies is a great source of free clip art! Also, as long as the clip art is strictly for promoting activities within your youth group, you may use portions of ads, words, pictures, and graphics from magazines and newspapers. Some of the best artwork is when you replace the faces of celebrities or world figures with pictures of students' faces. Mark Cannister, at Shadyside Presbyterian Church in Pittsburgh, has made this an art form, using pictures of U2, Gorbachev, and others to promote various youth activities.

DO LONG-RANGE PROMOTION

Today's students are very busy. They won't wait around keeping their calendars open until we plan something. School calendars are usually set a year in advance. Band camps, football practices, and cheerleading camps fill up late summer months of the following year before most of us have planned our fall retreats. If we hope to involve these students, we need to do long-range promotion, giving students the word about events three to six months in advance — even earlier in the case of projects that require extra planning and money.

Of course, knowing the teenage mind, we also realize that an event announced in late December will probably be forgotten if it doesn't happen in early January. That means we have to send out early promotion with enough information so that students and their families can block out important dates and weekends, but not so much information that there's nothing left with which to tantalize students later on.

A great way to accomplish this and make some points with parents is to sell Youth Group Gift Certificates. These advance-payment coupons cover upcoming youth events, like the winter retreat, summer camp, or a work project. At our late fall parents' briefing, we inform parents of our schedule for the next eight months through August. Then we give them a chance to buy a Youth Group Gift

Certificate to give to their kids for Christmas or a birthday. That provides us with early registration for events, and gives parents advance knowledge of our youth group schedule, along with the chance to make two purchases (a Christmas gift and a retreat registration) with one check.

Whether it's poster-size, a three-color brochure, or done in a *National Enquirer* format, the youth group calendar is a consistently popular way of doing long-range promotion. An effective calendar gives students a long-range and (hopefully) eye-catching peek at upcoming events, giving them a sense that this group is going somewhere.

While some of the calendars we've pictured here are pretty incredible productions, that doesn't mean this kind of promotion is out of reach for small youth groups. Following are some tips:

• *The busier the better.* Lots of graffiti mixed in with kids' names and pictures makes a calendar more interesting to look at and read.

• *Make use of clip art and stickers* to add eye appeal. (Stickers can be purchased at most drug stores for under two dollars.)

• *Find a good source of weird facts* with which to pepper your calendar. For example, *Cosmic Mind-Boggling Book*[2] or *The Experts Speak: The Definitive Compendium of Authoritative Misinformation.*[3]

• *Leave out days for which there are no youth activities planned.* This makes it possible to get three months of calendar on one standard page of paper, and it makes the group look unbelievably busy! Why document all the days when your group is not doing anything?

• *Don't include all of the information on a particular event.* Calendars are basically a tool for announcing dates. Specific promotion and registration materials for each event show up later.

• *Make it excellent.* The printing should be clear and readable. (Perhaps solicit a professional printer to help with printing and layout.) Check the piece for correct spelling, too. I remember a brochure from a New Hampshire church announcing a summer preaching series entitled "How to Survive the Twentieth Century." Below the series title the flyer was to read, "Worship at Old South Baptist Church." Somebody goofed in the proofreading, however, and what the flyer actually promised was a series entitled "How to Survive the Twentieth Century Worship"—an intriguing question, but not the one they hoped to pose.

RUN A PROMOTIONAL CAMPAIGN

The days are over when we could send out an announcement about "a fellowship supper and singspiration in the church basement" and expect students to come. Too many more enticing options beg for our students' attention. Effective promotion grabs a reader's attention, arouses interest, and seeks a commitment (signing up, paying a preregistration fee, turning in a registration form).

A "teaser campaign" might kick off the promotional strategy. Prior to my arrival to speak at a Youth Week in Pascagoula, Mississippi, a few years ago, the kids in the sponsoring youth group produced an effective teaser campaign with subversive blackboard graffiti. Every morning before school started, student volunteers wrote in the corner of every blackboard in every classroom, "Duffy is coming!!" No dates—just that message. A few weeks before Youth Week, they kicked into gear with stickers, hundreds of stickers, that simply said, "Who's Duffy?" By the time they finally got around to putting up posters about the event, people were discussing it all over the high school.

Another effective promotional strategy is to use one event to promote another. At the large Saturday night outreach in January, promote the upcoming winter retreat by showing a fun video of the previous year's winter retreat and distributing flyers to everyone in attendance. Or at the close of the outreach retreat, give the kickoff announcement about the new small-group discipleship program. Promoting an event that appeals to the constituency of the present event gives us the best chance at reaching the audience we want to reach.

Other elements of a good promotional strategy might include using a sign-up poster. The theory is that students want to sign up for an event, but they don't want to be the only ones who do. Or, what's worse is when you sign up first, and no one else signs up because they realize you're going to be there. Teenagers have nightmares about stuff like this.

So, we can encourage quick sign-ups by offering an early-bird discount on all major events that have a registration fee. For example, the first ten students who sign up for the fall retreat get ten dollars off the cost of registration. Then, we put up a creative poster with pictures and clip art with those ten names that says: "These people are going to be a part of the action for 'The Rise of Fall.' Get your name on the list!!" As students register for the retreat, they are allowed to write their names on the poster. The idea is that once ten students are signed up, it's a lot easier to get the next ten signed up. And with twenty signed up, you've got the makings of a stampede!

Along those same lines, one youth group sponsored a Beach Party Dance for middle schoolers. They did the usual—charging four dollars for advance tickets and five dollars at the door—but on the back of the advance tickets was a coupon for a free drink at the dance. That encouraged students to buy the tickets in advance and started "good gossip" around campus about the dance.

HAVE FUN WITH PUBLICITY

It's amazing how often we betray ourselves by publicizing really great events in really boring ways. We should not forget Marshall McLuhan's adage that "the medium is the message." The publicity for the event is the first and best hint students have of what the event will be like.

We once promoted a Halloween event with an "Identify the Scream" contest. We recorded several different youth group kids giving loud, long screams (each student was recorded separately so they wouldn't know the identities of their fellow screamers). Then one of our leaders recorded an announcement about the event, punctuating it at proper intervals with the mystery screamers.

For two weeks before the event, we played the tape twice in Sunday school, each time without any introduction except to turn out the lights. After listening, the students attempted to identify, in the correct order, the phantom screamers. The contest not only built interest in the event, but guaranteed that every student listened carefully to the announcement when it was played.

Mike Yaconelli tells about a time he used videotaped, man-on-the-street interviews to promote a Bible study on Hosea. The week prior to his Bible study, he and three of his students asked shoppers this question: "If you were a prophet, would you marry a whore named Gomer?" He also sent a postcard to all the students posing this same question and adding, "Come to Bible study this week and find out." Mike usually jokes that no students showed up, but about a hundred parents turned out!

One ingenious group of youth workers promoted a cookout and beach party with a whole, uncooked chicken. They cut a hole in the back of the chicken to use it as a puppet. They tied pieces of string to the tips of both wings so an off-camera assistant could make the wings flap, and then taped a fantastically fun video in which the headless chicken describes the beach party, gesturing with its wings and moving its body around for expression.

We promoted our winter retreat one year by making an instructional movie with this fictional skier, Robin Van Duffyswart. The opening scene showed a little doll-like figure perched at the top of a smooth slope. The narrator announced, "There's nothing that gets an avid skier more excited than the feeling of being at the top of a steep bald." At that point, the camera pulled back to show that this smooth bald was actually my head! (That's not funny.)

Another youth group generated student interest in an upcoming series of Bible studies on sex and dating by developing their own Sex and Dating Poll (that was already enough to get people interested). They credited Dr. Alexander Tenfoot with designing the poll. The poll consisted of questions like these:

- If sex is so dirty, why are we supposed to "save it for the one we love"?
- Does the Bible say anything about French kissing?
- Is it okay to exchange chewing gum during a kiss?
- Who sets the limits: the guy dating the girl, the girl, the girl's dad, the girl's steady boyfriend, the school counselor?

At the bottom of the poll were these words: "If you answered 'yes' to three or more of these questions, you didn't understand the questions. To find out about all of this stuff, come to Cornerstone this Wednesday night . . . and be careful with this document. There are certain things you don't want to touch with a Tenfoot poll."

A group of youth ministers in Knoxville, Tennessee, were hosting the "World's Largest Lock-in" to which they were hoping to attract about two thousand high school students. To get their message out, they produced a rapid-fire, thirty-second video and received permission from the local cable company to run their spot on MTV. All it cost them was effort.

Sometimes making publicity fun is as simple as using music in the background while making the announcement in the youth meeting, using crazy overhead transparencies, or rapping the announcement. I recall one Sunday night promotion of a skating party—one of the youth group girls skated through the room with a placard announcing the event.

Can you help Matt find his way to Bible Study?

June 9, 1982

UMYF

Encounter 82

205 Banta Ln.
near Killian's
Shawn's House
and Gunther's house

AFTER THE STUDY: We will pile in the church bus and be further enriched by the watching of Star Trek II. Bring money for snacks. Study starts at 7:00.

People with Record Loan albums out please return, so we can inventory!

REACH OUT AND TOUCH

The reason students come to an event is almost never because of the event—they come because of who else is going to be at the event. The best publicity is friend to friend, kid to kid. Remind students that all of the posters and flyers are simply to provide a context in which they can personally invite friends to an event. One of the ways to facilitate this kind of interaction is by using "bring a friend" discounts, by which students can get a lesser admission if they bring a visitor. Obviously, a system like this can be abused and won't always be appropriate, but in some cases, it's a good way to encourage students to reach out to their peers.

TELL THE WHOLE TRUTH

One of the mistakes we make in promoting events is getting so cute that we do not make the information clear. In doing promotion, keep these realities in mind:

• Parents need to have enough information about the event to assure them that their child will be properly supervised and safe. Students may love it when we say, "We're going to raft a stretch of the canyon that no youth group has ever dared to raft before!" but parents get squeamish.

• Give the students enough information to assure them that they're not going to feel like jerks when they arrive: "Hey, I thought this was a costume party. Why am I the only one here dressed like a biblical character?" "How come you didn't tell me that this event was for seventh graders?"

• If the event requires any special abilities or know-how, make that clear to the students. Most of the time this will not be the case, and we need to make that clear also. For example, the average student hears about a rafting trip or a backpacking trip and automatically discounts himself because he isn't Nanook of the North. Somehow, the publicity material needs to assure students that no experience is necessary.

• If it is an outreach event, call it that, and program for that. But if the event is for leadership development or deeper spiritual growth, make that clear up front and from square one. In our zeal to attract big numbers, we are dishonest with students about what they should expect of an event, and, just as important, what will be expected of them. This is one of the most common errors in youth ministry.

DON'T SAY TOO MUCH
OR TOO LITTLE

Remember that in doing promotion, we are only trying to give students enough information to say "yes." The more information we give them, the more likely they are to hear something that sparks superfluous questions. Students need to hear a lot about an event, but they don't need to know a lot about it.

Another common error is to call every event a "special event." This habit usually runs in one of two directions: the students either start ignoring the word "special," assuming that if everything is special, then nothing is; or we fall into the trap of having to make every event more special than the last event—"Okay kids, we're going to ride to the beach on live elephants led by a presidential motorcade with Elvis in the lead car!!"

LET 'EM KNOW
YOU'RE THERE

I was speaking recently at a conference in a small Virginia town. The event was about an hour from the nearest major airport, so when I hit town I pulled up to the drive-through window of a local fast-food restaurant for something to drink. While waiting for my order, I asked the woman at the window for specific directions to the church. She didn't know of the church and neither did any of her coworkers. No one in that restaurant had ever heard of this church. And it was a huge downtown church!

When I finally found this massive church, occupying one entire downtown block just three streets down from the restaurant, I was amazed. How can a church hope to reach out to the community when the community doesn't even know it exists? Too many youth programs are precisely like that church, quietly minding their own business when God has called us to aggressively mind his.

Part of the business of promotion is simply making our presence felt in the community, letting kids know we're around. It's the same idea as Nike getting basketball players to wear their shoes, or Bollé getting skiers to wear their goggles. These athletes never come out and make a direct pitch, but there is a very subtle and powerful message of presence.

There are several good strategies by which we can maintain this kind of ongoing publicity.

Booster placards. Some youth groups print the youth group calendar and church phone number on one side of the placard and some kind of school spirit message on the other side. They give these placards away by the hundreds at school sporting events, and every student wants to have one.

School newspaper and yearbook ads. Buying space for a carefully designed and not-too-heavy-handed ad makes our presence felt on campus. Perhaps include some comments from students about what the group has meant to them.

Youth group brochure. Introduce the youth ministry to visitors and new kids by creating a brochure/information packet. The Vineyard youth ministry of Bethel Full Gospel Church in Rochester, New York, has put together a first-class packet, including a sketch of the various programs, a flyer about upcoming events, a visitor's card, a three-month calendar, and a recording made by the youth minister and some of the students in the group! A student sees this material and can't help but be impressed.

THE VINEYARD VISION	"FUSION"
BRANCHES	BASIC TRAINING
SUPERTRIPS	"ROCK OF REFUGE"
PUBLICATIONS	YOUTH SOCIAL ACTIVITIES
OUTREACHES	VINEYARD LEADERSHIP MINISTRIES

a look at the youth ministry of BETHEL FULL GOSPEL CHURCH Rochester, New York

THE SKY IS THE LIMIT
SCHEDULE OF VINEYARD MEETINGS

SERVICE	DAY	TIME
VINEYARD Youth Meeting	Wednesday	7:00 PM
PROJECT TIMOTHY		
Youth Leadership Training	Tuesday	7:00 PM
GENESIS BRANCH	Saturday	10:00 AM
Youth Discipleship Training	Sunday	5:00 PM
YOUTH PRAYER GATHERING	3rd Sunday Each Month	5:00 PM
"ROCK OF REFUGE" SKATE NIGHT	4th Monday Each Month	7:00 PM
YOUTH WORKERS MEETINGS	1st Tuesday Each Month	7:00 PM
HEIRBORN Rehearsals	Thursday	6:00 PM
P.A.R.T. Parent Aid & Resource Team Fellowship	Tuesday	7:00 PM

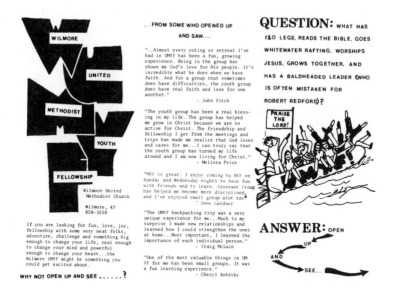

Youth group T-shirts. One of the great things about T-shirts is that students can wear them on campus, where our posters and flyers may not be as welcome. One of my favorite youth group T-shirts was designed for the junior high group at First Broad Street United Methodist Church in Kingsport, Tennessee.

The Top Ten List of What R.A.D. Stands For:
1. Radically Aware Disciple
2. Rocks Are Dead
3. Romantic and Debonair
4. Research and Development
5. Rockin' Awesome Doors
6. Royal Academy of Dolphins
7. Retired Albino Dobermans
8. Real Active Dudes
9. Really Angry Democrats
10. Race Against Drugs

Youth group newsletter. A quarterly or monthly publication can keep students' interest by printing news of the ongoing program. At

Gospel Lighthouse Church in Dallas, "Ozone" is published every month. Youth minister Link Warde, in his column "Link's Lingo," previews the weekly programs for the month and highlights rallies, fun stuff, trivia, special interest stories, and other announcements about upcoming activities.

The youth newsletter of First United Methodist Church in Lakeland, Florida, *ACTS of the Youth Group*, includes articles and music reviews written by students in the youth group. Martin Barker, youth pastor of First Church of the Nazarene in Bradenton, Florida, includes a monthly feature in his group's *Youth News*, spotlighting one of the students in the youth fellowship.

Newsletters not only make great handouts around school, but they initiate visitors into the group and enhance the sense of community. They don't have to be *USA Today* quality to be effective. Start small, and let the newsletter develop as students get more involved with it. It could also include student poetry, volunteer leader profiles, interviews, and news stories about achievements of youth group members. This kind of promotion doesn't publicize a specific event, but it does a wonderful job of publicizing the group.

Doorknob notices. Speaking of presence, Dave White, a youth pastor in Anchorage, Alaska, came up with an idea for letting students know that he had been by for a visit even if they weren't home. His group printed up the following flyer that hangs on doorknobs:

Dear:
- ☐ To whom it may concern
- ☐ Friend

_____

SORRY I MISSED YOU!!!!!!
I just came by
- ☐ to chat   ☐ to rap   ☐ to chew the fat
- ☐ to shoot the breeze
- ☐ to take you out for a Coke
- ☐ to try to get you to take me out for a Coke
- ☐ to see if you were still alive
- ☐ because I didn't have anything better to do
- ☐ to borrow a cup of sugar
- ☐ other _____

I will
- ☐ come by again at _____ o'clock
  a.m. ☐   p.m. ☐ _____ , 19___
- ☐ phone you soon!
- ☐ see you at church
- ☐ see you in court
- ☐ see you at the grocery store
- ☐ see you around
- ☐ pay you the money I owe you

Please
- ☐ give me a call
- ☐ come see me
- ☐ pay me the money you owe me
- ☐ other _____
  - ☐ Love,
  - ☐ Sincerely,
  - ☐ Yours Truly,
    David White
    5007 Cambridge Dr, 769-2240

Locker posters and book covers. While an increasing number of schools are getting stricter about what posters can be placed on school bulletin boards, students can get away with almost anything in their lockers. Print up information about the youth group on posters that fit on the inside of the locker door. And while you're at it, print book covers sporting the youth group calendar and some student quotations. Book covers go everywhere students go.

LEST WE LOSE
OUR PERSPECTIVE . . .

The best promotion in the world won't do any good if the event stinks. We need to make sure that the product lives up to the packaging. Nothing succeeds like success. The best publicity is God changing lives. When people see the oil flowing from previously empty jars, they'll start wondering what's going on over at the prophet's house (see 2 Kings 4:1-7).

We need to remember also that what we win them *with* is what we win them *to*. If we win the attention and allegiance of students solely on the basis of fun, we can't expect them to suddenly be willing to shoulder the demands of the Cross. When we reshape the packaging, we must take care not to reshape the contents of the gospel to make it more appealing.

Finally, from all appearances, God has never been very astute at marketing. Isaiah describes the coming Messiah as One who

> had no beauty or majesty to attract us to him, nothing in his appearance that we should desire him. He was despised and rejected by men, a man of sorrows, and familiar with suffering. Like one from whom men hide their faces he was despised, and we esteemed him not (Isa. 53:2, 3).

This first-class PR disaster reminds us that substance is more important than appearance. Advertisements in the storefront mean nothing if we don't have it in stockroom. As Paul wrote, "The kingdom of God is not a matter of talk but of power" (1 Cor. 4:20).

CHAPTER TWELVE

SQUEEZING BLOOD OUT OF A TURNIP: BUDGETING AND FINANCE

Whether he is writing a letter to the brethren in Thessalonica (1 Thess. 2:3-6, 9) or saying a final farewell to the church in Ephesus (Acts 20), the apostle Paul is quick to recall his financial responsibility as proof of his love and of the sincerity of his calling. It's as if Paul recognized that the management of his personal finances and the manner in which he conducted his ministry finances were two of the major ways that people would judge the integrity of his ministry.

If this was true for Paul, how much more true is it for those of us involved in youth ministry? I was once in an audience of pastors and youth workers who were warned by evangelist Billy Graham: "The two main pitfalls of people in the ministry are abuse of sex and abuse of money." Not that money is evil in and of itself. Anyone involved in the nuts and bolts of youth ministry knows that both nuts and bolts cost money. What it does mean is that our handling of personal and ministry finances affects the way people view our ministries.

FISCAL FUNDAMENTALS

Our handling of personal and ministry finances takes on even more importance in light of the following five basic facts:

Fact #1: Most youth ministers are not highly trained handlers of money. Our natural interests don't typically include budgeting and quarterly reports. If we're paid youth ministers, we have probably discovered that handling our salaries has never required that we spend much time working through investment portfolios. We would rather focus on people than pennies. The average Bible college or seminary training is heavy on theology and light on financial management—which is unfortunate because of fact number two.

Fact #2: It's not unusual for youth ministers to deal with a heavy cash flow. A work project overseas can easily generate a budget of up to fifteen thousand dollars. With a youth group of fifty students, summer camp fees generate a cash flow of as much as five thousand dollars. Even monthly roller-skating trips add up. A lot of cash passes through our hands. (Sad to say, it usually passes through without stopping for a visit.) The frightening part is that we can hang ourselves decisively with five thousand dollars worth of rope!

Fact #3: Ironically, money management is one of the main criteria by which the average congregation judges our ministry. Typically, they won't know about the great retreats, the growing turnouts for Bible study, or the incredible ministry of one-on-one discipleship. But they will hear how the youth program overspent its funds or wants to increase its budget.

Fact #4: Authority equals the power to spend funds. A youth worker who is allowed to drive the van over to the garage, find out what's wrong, get an estimate, but must stop short of actually getting the vehicle repaired until he reports to the C.E. board, doesn't really have authority for maintenance and upkeep of the van. The committee to whom he must report is the party really responsible for van upkeep. The youth minister is only doing the committee's leg work. I don't mean to sound cynical or negative; it's simply a fact of life. If a youth worker assumes responsibility for maintenance of the church bus or van, that should mean he receives permission to authorize spending on repairs and upkeep (within a reasonable range of cost).

I once worked for a church that, at my request, divided the annual youth budget by twelve and then gave us that amount on a monthly basis. We deposited the funds in a youth-group bank account to spend at our discretion. It was great—we could buy balloons without having to requisition three committees, get a presidential order, and cast lots. On the other hand, we had to be very careful to document how and why we spent every dollar, because we were well aware of the potential abuses in the system. That much freedom gives almost anybody enough ammunition to shoot themselves in the foot. There needs to be a balance between authority to spend and accountability for spending, but we don't really have authority for a program unless we have authority to spend.

Fact #5: Youth ministry is an expensive proposition. Part of the nature of the beast is that it costs more per person involved than any other ministry in the average local church. When the five-year-olds finish a week of vacation Bible school, they are each given little combs or key rings as prizes — total cost to the budget: three dollars. But at the graduation banquet for high school seniors, a comb or key ring just doesn't elicit the same excitement.

To some degree, the high cost of youth ministry is caused by students having their own money. They aren't dependent on the church for recreation and leisure activities. In a sense, the youth program is competing for the attention of students. Recognizing that the youths can access enough money to choose from many options beyond the church forces us to allocate more money for attractive, quality programming. And of course, this is complicated further since students don't expect to pay for church activities. Their unspoken assumption is that they are doing us a favor by being there.

PLANNING A BUDGET

When some of us hear about planning a budget, we feel a smirk coming on. It isn't hard to develop a plan for spending the zero dollars a year that many youth programs are offered. Most of us hope that the budgeting process would be a little more difficult. Yet far too few of us could budget with enough care, foresight, and precision to enable responsible stewards of God's resources to effectively allocate the funds needed.

Paul Borthwick, youth-ministry veteran of Grace Chapel in Lexington, Massachusetts, suggests that we begin the budgeting process by asking two questions.[1]

WHAT IS THE BUDGET HISTORY
OF OUR CHURCH OR ORGANIZATION?

According to previous budgets, how much money has been allocated to the youth program in the last five years? *What is the average percentage of increase (if any) in the budget over that span of time?*

Flo had only been able to get her budget increased once over the preceding four years, but the increase in that one year was almost eight percent. By averaging out that single eight percent increase over the four-year period, she was able to go before the board and justify an annual increase of two percent.

According to previous budgets, what is the budgeted money supposed to cover? For example, in one church, the youth budget had never included expenses associated with the Sunday school program. Monies for purchasing Sunday school curricula had always come out of the Christian education budget. When the Christian education committee decided it didn't want responsibility for funding the youth Sunday school program, the youth minister had to request a sizeable increase in the youth budget. Had he not made it clear to the finance committee that the youth budget had never been used previously for funding Sunday school programming, he could not have justified such a disproportionate increase.

According to previous budgets, who controls the purse, and how does one gain access to budgeted funds? I laugh about it now (sort of), but I can still remember in my first full-time youth pastorate playing tug-of-war with the church treasurer to access money budgeted to the youth ministry. Making any purchase above my petty cash allotment of fifty dollars—ordering curricula or arranging for retreat deposits—was a tedious process, requiring several signed requisitions, committee approval, shameless pleading (which I was willing to do if necessary), and the promise of my firstborn child. I was reminded of the basic principle I learned playing Monopoly as a little boy—it is not always the banker but the one sitting closest to the bank who controls the flow of money. When evaluating an organization's budgeting process, find out who is sitting closest to the money.

WHAT ARE WE PLANNING TO DO WITH OUR PROGRAM OVER THE LONG TERM?

How many retreats will there be? What other major projects need we be planning for? What electronic equipment, sports gear, transportation, or ministry resource books do we need? To find out, we must discipline ourselves to plan ahead, to do some careful research, and to prioritize.

For a lot of youth workers, "advance planning" means thinking four to ten weeks ahead. Good budget planning, however, usually requires a minimum of eighteen months advance planning. If, for example, the budget for the next calendar year is voted on in September, then the youth-leadership team must decide in broad terms by August what it plans to accomplish through December of the following year.

To make wise planning decisions about our ministries, we need accurate information gathered through careful research. Winging it is a good way to crash. A five-year figure gives a picture broad enough to encompass the typical fluctuations of any youth ministry. We can begin with enrollment projections: If our group continues to grow or decrease at its present rate, how many students are we apt to be working with? If we plan for no growth, we'll probably achieve it. How much has the group typically been able to count on through fundraising? How much has the group been spending per active student?

Gary Shirk, when he served as youth pastor at Christ United Methodist Church in Jackson, Mississippi, was able to demonstrate to his church board that even though he was increasing his budget, he would actually be spending less money (good trick!). He thoroughly researched how much money was currently being spent per active student and then divided his total proposed budget by the projected attendance increase, based on the past history of his group. He showed that even with the budget increase, he would actually be spending less money per active student than he had in the previous year. His argument for the increase must have been convincing — he got the money.

Prioritizing is the discipline of deciding which budget items are most important to our ongoing program. If the budget has to be cut back, which items will be erased first? If we can only take two retreats next year instead of four, which two will they be? If we must choose between sports gear and a mission-trip scholarship, which will we choose? Can we operate safely if we put off overhauling the van for another year? Prioritizing requires that we go back through the budget and tag certain items as more important than others. It's coming up with a plan B, C, and D, in case we can't afford plan A.

SQUEEZING BLOOD
OUT OF A TURNIP

After we've come up with credible projections about financial needs and goals for our programs, we are ready to ask how we are going to come up with this money. In a traditional congregational ministry, we may have access to funds allocated through the overall budget, and that's seldom enough.

Money Magazine reported in the early eighties that a congregation generally needs to have at least two hundred members to sustain its ministry without the church having to look for a financial bargain either in facilities, program, or pastor's salary. And there are a lot of churches out there with less than two hundred people.

So where does the money come from? There are several alternative sources of funding.

GET THE STUDENTS TO PAY

One of the obvious ways to fund the youth program is to have the students help fund it. They are, after all, the direct beneficiaries . . . and many of them have the money. The average American teenager in the 1990s brings home somewhere in the neighborhood of twenty to thirty dollars a week. That's a lot of cash, and most of these students are not buying groceries, paying utilities, insurance, or making housing payments. Most of the money is being used for discretionary spending. In 1989, American teenage girls spent approximately twenty-eight hundred dollars each!

The Student Body, the youth group at Wheaton (Illinois) Bible Church, came together to raise seven hundred and fifty dollars a month so that they could rent an apartment for their sidewalk Sunday school program. That works out to nine thousand dollars a year, but they did it. For most students, the money is there if they choose to use it for church activities.

The advantages of having students support the program are readily apparent. First of all, paying for the program gives students more ownership in the program. They are apt to more responsibly care for equipment and property if they know that their money has been used to purchase them. Holding the students responsible for paying their

184

own way also helps them learn the value of work and the discipline of earning money. Heavily subsidizing the program through the church budget or another source may be underwriting bad spending habits instead of helping teenagers out. We've all watched the kid with the camp scholarship bound off with cash in hand every time the van stops.

On the other hand, what about the few students who can't come up with the money for the ski retreat? Are they cut out of the ministry? And what does student-subsidized funding do to evangelistic ministry or a ministry of nurture? Common sense and experience tells us that students won't be willing to fund the program until they have a more mature commitment to Christ, and they won't develop a more mature commitment to Christ without the program. Which comes first? Typical teenagers are willing, perhaps, to pay for something they want. It may be more difficult to get them to pay for something they need.

SUBSIDIES FROM OTHER SOURCES

Art Erickson, of Park Avenue United Methodist Church in Minneapolis, presides over an inner-city youth ministry that has an annual budget in excess of one hundred thousand dollars a year, and only a small percentage of the money comes from his moderately sized urban congregation. That's because Art Erickson is one of the best in the country when it comes to soliciting outside funding for his youth program. He taps corporate sponsors for cash and materials, applying for foundation grants and raising several thousands of dollars yearly over and above what his church allocates to the youth program.

Although the money is available, it takes some experience to learn how to write the kind of grant proposals that will move foundations to support a youth program. The whole process begins by knocking on doors. Start with major corporations or large businesses in the area. The local businessman sometimes feels he has more to gain by supporting a local service project than an international charity. We needn't always ask for money either. Sometimes a car dealer will donate a van or mark it down drastically. Park Avenue was able to get several free computers from the Apple Corporation to use in the after-school tutoring program.

The main warning printed on the label of this box of money is that it can be habit forming; it may even bring an unhealthy dependency. Ministries of all kinds have compromised their vision because they were too indebted to some sugar daddy who started using money as leverage to control their ministries. Look carefully for strings attached to corporate gifts.

LOW-COST, NO-COST ACTIVITIES

It's a fallacy that youth ministries need to be ultra-expensive. Sometimes budget increases are just an excuse for thoughtless spending. Dennis and Marilyn Benson have written a book that lists youth-ministry activities and teaching tools that are available for low cost or no cost.[2] The real cost-cutter, though, is the mind-set that there's more than one way to "skin a cat." Ingenuity and hard work can provide what hundreds of budgeted dollars cannot.

FUND-RAISERS

Doing fund-raisers doesn't mean we have to be involved in selling gift-wrapping paper, broomsticks, or ginzu knives. In place of selling a product of some kind, another popular genre of fund-raiser is selling a service—"slave auctions," car washes, and the like. Then, of course, there are the myriad of "-athons," the basic scheme of which is to get people to pledge on the basis of some activity: rocking (waste of time), walking (good exercise), running (too good an exercise!), picking up trash (neat idea), shaving (sexist), biking (best in areas where there are no hills), burping (not recommended).

When John Hall served at Hope Presbyterian Church in Minneapolis, his students sold "stock" to raise funds for the youth missions program. Students in the group invited church members to invest in the lives of student missionaries. Students corresponded with their shareholders before, during, and after the mission trip. Following the trip, everyone was invited to a shareholder's dinner to enjoy slides, videos, and testimonies of the project.

Youth ministry and fund-raising are not synonymous, however. I still have occasional nightmares of the day I opened my office closet to start my new youth-ministry position and found myself knee-deep in candy bars, light bulbs, and greeting cards. I told the board unequivocally that I felt the youth ministry of the church was worth the support of the congregation and that if I had wanted to get into retail work I would have applied for a job at K-Mart. Much to the relief of our youth (the sales force) and their parents (the consumer force), we got out of the retail business.

Perhaps most disconcerting is the amount of time that some youth workers must devote to raising money. I grew up in a large, wealthy church with a nonexistent youth budget. We held retreats so that we could plan fund-raisers, and we held fund-raisers so that we could have retreats. Unbalanced fund-raising takes too much time and energy away from the youth worker—time that should be allocated toward making disciples and not making money.

FAVORITE FUND-RAISING IDEAS

The best fund-raisers are quick (three weeks or less), involve a maximum number of students doing something useful or fun, and make lots of money! The following are some ideas that, for the most part, live up to this standard:

Door-to-Door Car Wash
Sidestepping the obstacle of getting people to bring their cars in for cleaning, a door-to-door car wash sends teams of students to bring the car wash to the neighborhood. Students working their way down both sides of the street ring doorbells and ask people if they would like their cars washed. The customer then pays whatever they wish. Instead of washing twenty cars in the church parking lot over a five hour period, a group that moves well can wash three times as many cars going door-to-door.[3]

Free Car Wash
One of the all-time great fund-raisers, the Free Car Wash involves a three-phase strategy.

Phase one: Students canvas the town to collect names, addresses, and pledges based on how many cars the group washes on the day appointed for the car wash. To help pledgers decide how much they are willing to pledge, give them a ballpark figure of how many cars the group might wash. If, for example, twenty students get ten pledges of ten cents per washed car, the youth group will earn twenty dollars every time they wash a car.

Phase two: Host a *free* car wash for all comers. Ask local merchants to provide food for working students, bring the tape player out to the parking lot, and make it a party! Post a student in the street with a sign that says "Free Car Wash." As cars enter the lot, a student requests the driver's name and address to verify the final total of cars washed and gives each driver a letter telling how the youth group will use the money received from the pledgers.

Phase three: Collect the money from those who pledged.

We had eighty-five students active in our youth ministry. We felt we could reasonably assume that at least thirty students would be able to collect twenty pledges of five cents each. We knew from experience that we could use two hoses from two different buildings and, using "Y adapters," run two hoses from each source. That gave us four washing stations, which were staffed by six students each. There were two students on each side of the car, plus one in front and one in back. There was one adult leader at each washing station for "quality control."

When we held our annual free car wash, cars were backed up in both directions on the street in front of our church. They would turn into our parking lot, get washed at one of the four stations, and pull on through the church lot, departing by the other entrance. We were able to wash about four cars every five minutes, earning approximately thirty dollars per car. That meant we were able to bring in about one hundred and twenty dollars every five minutes. That's what I call a fund-raiser! And that's why I dropped out of youth ministry to franchise this idea (not true).

Scripturathon

One "-athon" strategy solicits pledges on the basis of how many verses of Scripture can be memorized by kids in the youth group. The more Scripture students memorize, the more pledge money they collect. It may not be the best way to initiate interest in Scripture memorization, but it seems a better use of time than having kids spend twelve hours in a rocking chair, rocking for pledges.[4]

Shave-athon

The idea here is to invite everyone in the congregation to grow a beard (especially the women). Then, on an auction night, people bid for the right to shave a certain person's beard. This may not provide a useful service (except in some cases!), but it would probably be a fun family-night activity.[5]

BMX Competition

Ridge Burns, formerly youth minister at a church in San Juan Capistrano, California, has raised money by hosting a BMX biking competition in the church parking lot. Contestants pay to enter the competition in exchange for T-shirts, trophies, and a quality event in which to compete. This event not only raises some money, but introduces the church to some students who might never otherwise come on the church property.

Home Building

Another ingenious fund-raising strategy was developed by Young Life of Kansas City. They recruited ten adults from their local support committee to volunteer to build a house with a team from Habitat for Humanity. Then they asked each of those ten people to raise from acquaintances some donations for their work, all of which went to Young Life. The Young Life construction volunteers worked a combined total of 240 hours building homes for the homeless, raising sixteen thousand dollars for the local budget of Young Life as a side benefit.

Bake Sale

Young Life in Owatonna, Minnesota (a community of twenty thousand), has made use of an old idea with some new twists, and for the past twelve years has cosponsored with radio station KRFO an annual cake auction. The strategy of the project is to sell cakes marketed in different ways. For example, one hundred cakes are auctioned off to the highest bidder, and another forty sell for a donation of twenty dollars each. About one-third of the cakes have hidden inside of them gift certificates donated by local merchants. That boosts the bidding significantly. The whole affair, well supported by the community, takes place on a Saturday in the lobby of a local bank. Last year alone they raised thirteen thousand dollars.

BUDGET TIME

Back to budget planning. Now that we know our budget history, our long-term plan, and from where we'll get our money, we've got to draw up a readable, usable budget. The following sample models the layout and format of a possible youth-ministry budget:

Proposed Budget: Student Ministry
Wesley Baptist Church

CURRICULUM:
1. Cornerstone Bible Study:
   Junior High .... $ 200
   Senior High .... $ 200
2. Covenant Group:
   Quiet Time Diary................................ $ 200
   Study Materials .... $ 150
3. Summer Trips:
   Serendipity, IVP................................ $ 200
4. Sunday School (7-12)**
   Five classes .... $ 435
           TOTAL................................ $1,385

RETREATS:
1. Travel:
   Summatunga.................................... $ 200
   Winter... $ 200
   Cov. Group..................................... $ 100
   Backpacking .... $ 100
   Summer (Missions) — (from Mission Committee)
   Summer Trip .... $ 200
   Fall Retreat................................... $ 200
      Subtotal.................................. $1,000
2. Honoraria:
   Summatunga.................................... $ 100
   Winter... $ 100
   Summer .... $ 200
   Fall .... $ 200
      Subtotal.................................. $ 600

3. Scholarships:.....................................$ 500
4. Cov. Group Retreat Housing: ....$ 150
5. Ministry Team Expenses: ....$ 300
     Subtotal.......................................$ 950
     TOTAL.....................................$2,550

EQUIPMENT:
1. Maintenance:
     Shelving, Curtains for youth room, displays ....$ 100
     Sports Gear ....$ 200
     Office Equip.......................................$ 100
2. Resource Materials: ....$ 150
     TOTAL.....................................$ 550

INSURANCE:
1. Cov Group:
     Weekly Mtgs......................................$ 250
     Retreats (2) ....$ 100
2. Sunday School: Drinks and Doughnuts**.............$ 300
3. SPECIAL: Halloween, Summer program, etc..........$ 200
     TOTAL.....................................$ 850

     TOTAL (Excluding items noted below) $5,460
     Total if ** items (Sunday school related)
        are not added $4,725

Additional Items:
Youth Minister's Travel ....$ 900
Continuing Education ....$ 400
This does not include youth program related:
(a) postage expense
(b) printing costs
(c) telephone costs
The above information is respectfully submitted by David Williams,
Minister with Youth.

_____   _____

           Signature   Date

Most of the budget is self-explanatory, but three ideas deserve more attention.

Budget organization. This budget is broken down into five broad categories of expense: curriculum, retreats, equipment, insurance, and miscellaneous expenses (continuing education, postage, etc.). While it is possible to break down the budget in several different ways, what is important is breaking it down into components small enough to deal with.

Asterisks. Clarify in some way items not covered under the budget or items covered by another department's budget.

Appropriate information. Budgets should provide enough information so that readers can clearly understand what the money pays for, but not so much information that people easily get sidetracked by something they don't agree with (for example, specifying which curriculum, which speakers, where the retreats will be). People have a right to take potshots at your budget, but why take pains to provide them with ammunition?

THE JUDAS EXAMPLE

Money is a fact of life. Even Jesus and the disciples worked with some kind of treasury because we read that Judas kept the purse. We also read that the last chapter in Judas' life was one of betrayal and tragedy. Whether it was the money that finally got to Judas, no one knows. We know only that his betrayal earned him thirty pieces of silver.

Any wise youth worker will recognize that the spirit of Judas is alive in all of us. No heart is incapable of betrayal, and no one is so spiritual as to be beyond financial temptation. The opportunity is there for the youth worker who betrays his Lord to pull down a few pieces of silver. It doesn't take but a few instances of unwise or unthoughtful financial mismanagement to tarnish a youth ministry and damage credibility. We should walk cautiously here, at the same time being industrious to meet our own needs and being faithful to realize that it is God who supplies our needs.

In the words of the apostle Paul, "Now he who supplies seed to the sower and bread for food will also supply and increase your store of seed and will enlarge the harvest of your righteousness. You will be made rich in every way so that you can be generous on every occasion, and through us . . . generosity will result in thanksgiving to God" (2 Cor. 9:10, 11).

SECTION
FOUR

DELICATE
ADJUSTMENTS

CHAPTER THIRTEEN

TRANS-PARENT MINISTRY: WORKING WITH FAMILIES

We have finally come to the point in youth ministry where we are willing to admit that youth ministry is more than simply working with youth, that the kind of narrow-minded programming that focuses only on the students leaves out of the formula one of the most important catalysts for healthy personhood, and that is a healthy family. Look inside any effective youth ministry, and there will be some attention being given to effective family ministry.

Youth workers have historically defined their role as people who work with youth, not people who work with families. Why? Mostly because we are already busier than we should be. What we don't need is another whole realm of ministry and responsibility. And besides, family ministry intimidates us. We know how to act around kids. But parents? Plus, what if we're crossing into someone else's realm of responsibility? The professional youth minister may meet resistance from the senior pastor, who perceives family ministry to be more his own role.

THE PROBLEM OF PARENTAL RESISTANCE

Ironically, much of the time the greatest resistance to a ministry that includes parents is the parents themselves. Parents are reluctant to trust a youth minister because so many of them are younger than the parents of the students. As one father put it, "What do you know? Both of your children are still under ten years old."

In some cases, parents are reluctant to be involved with us in family ministry because they feel we already have enough inside information to make them squirm. The last thing they want is to air out any more dirty laundry on our line. I can distinctly remember a Tuesday morning sharing group when one of our girl students began sharing through her tears that she was worried about her parents' marriage, and that her dad had gotten "kind of violent" with her mom. I was stunned at her honesty in front of about twelve of her peers around the table. But I'm sure I wasn't nearly as stunned as her parents would have been if they had known what their daughter was saying in Covenant Group.

Then too, parents have a different focus than youth workers. They tend to look at the youth group only through the eyes of their own teens. If the program is not working well for their kids, then it doesn't matter how helpful it is to other students — it's a bad youth program. I vividly recall a conversation with a mother who wanted me to start a Bible study series on sex and dating within the next week. I told her that we had just completed a series on sex and dating four months earlier, but she persisted. When I asked her why, she blurted back, "Because Rachel has her first date this Saturday night!"

Because they have a different perspective, parents tend to evaluate our programs differently than we do. We get back from a mission trip on which three students got saved, one decided to be a career missionary, and five others decided they want to do short-term mission work, and we're ecstatic. The parents, on the other hand, are not impressed: "Sure, my kid will paint an orphanage down in Haiti, but I can't get him to clean up his room." Sometimes after an awesome weekend retreat where God really worked, we're ready to be named youth minister of the year. Instead, the mother of the kid who got a sore throat calls Monday morning to complain that her son couldn't go to school. As far as that parent is concerned, it was a bad retreat.

A STRATEGIC ALLIANCE

Youth workers and parents need each other. In most cases, the task of raising healthy, well-adjusted teenagers who are growing in Christ is just too big and too complex for either parents or youth workers to pull off alone. In-depth youth ministry demands that we reach beyond Sunday school to transcend the imaginary boundaries between church and home. Merton Strommen's classic survey of church youths[1] indicates that one-third of them are "much bothered" about the lack of understanding and communication in their relationships with parents. Thirty-nine percent of those students reported being distressed "very much" by the strictness of their parents. A remarkably high fifty-eight percent of the teenagers who admitted being sexually active also reported that they felt an absence of any real relationship with their fathers. A strong parent-teen relationship is just too critical to be ignored.

The parental role serves at least three important functions in the life of a maturing teenager. First, it provides a laboratory in which the teens learn how to make and live with responsible decisions—a process that best occurs in an atmosphere of grace and support. Second, a teenager's family also serves as a testing ground for interpersonal skills, an arena in which the students learn ways of relating to people effectively. Finally, the family helps teenagers identify with a set of values—to develop and refine their moral consciences. As one youth pastor commented, "The simple truth is that, spiritually, most young people will grow no faster and no further than their parents."

Youth workers, though, can bring to this volatile equation some significant skills. To begin with, we can talk to students. Our familiarity with youth culture gives us a different perspective on adolescent issues. We're not as apt to freak out when we see an earring through the nose. Plus, we know a side of the kids that their parents may never know. We see them with their friends, on their own. Over the years, teenagers have offered me the privilege of stepping into their world by talking with me about their doubts, concerns, worries, hopes, and fears. Sometimes they talk with me just because I'm available and willing to listen. For the most part, it's simply because I'm not their parent.

Parents, on the other hand, know their children in the context of their everyday lives, which we seldom see. The pictures of teenagers that their parents see may be shaded quite differently from the ones we view in youth group. Plus, parents love their children more than we do. No matter how deeply committed we are to our youths, their parents have at least thirteen years on us. And when we graduate a class or move on to other churches, parents still hang in with their kids.

Most importantly, parents can balance the influence of the church. Ironically, at times our perspective as youth ministers keeps us from ministering to youths in all the ways that are essential for their holistic development. If they are active in youth group and have signed up for the retreat, we generally feel as if their lives are well balanced. Only parents can offer the broader perspective of the students' growth — their educational progress in school, their ability to play a constructive and cooperative role in the family, the status of their physical well-being.

Bill McNabb tells of a time when a mother barged into his Bible study to take her son out of the meeting because he had promised to mow the lawn before he came to youth group. At first, Bill was really angry that this mother had intimidated her son in this way. He couldn't believe how insensitive she had been, reprimanding her son in front of the whole group. But as he thought about it, the more it made sense. His final verdict: "More power to her. She's trying to teach her son responsibility and accountability. She did the right thing."

STRATEGIES FOR TEAMWORK

Strengthening ties between parents and teens hasn't been a youth worker's forte. More often than not, the teamwork of the teenager, the youth worker, and the parents has come off looking like an episode of the Three Stooges trying to hang wallpaper. In our efforts at family ministry, the majority of us assume the role of *commentator*, giving scriptural teaching and describing problems from a safe distance. Others of us take on the role of *dictator*, threatening kids with Bible passages guaranteed to scare them into loving and communicating with their parents (see Prov. 30:17). The approach that will probably be most successful, however, is the role of *facilitator*, one who opens lines of communication and does whatever possible to assist parents and teens in understanding each other. Four strategies can help us fulfill our role as facilitators so that our youth ministries are rooted in family ministry.

INFORMING PARENTS

Keeping parents informed builds their trust in us. It will allow them to know and better understand what we are doing. This can be done in any number of ways.

Parent briefings. Host quarterly (at least) meetings for just the parents of students in the group. These meetings can be utilized for everything from announcing the schedule of upcoming events, to getting parental feedback on youth activities, to simply explaining how a certain activity fits into the overall scheme of programming. One can even use an evening like this to take the parents through a simulated youth group meeting, complete with songs, skits, Bible study, and food! I have had parents who became more cooperative simply because they came to a parent briefing and found out why we were doing what we were doing.

Parent newsletter. Once a month, John Hall and his team at Hope Presbyterian Church in Minneapolis put out a newsletter written and designed expressly for the parents of students in the youth group. "Parents With Hope" changes with every issue, but it typically includes any combination of the following: the youth group calendar, a column by John Hall, book reviews, recaps of recent youth events, and factual articles informing parents about youth culture.

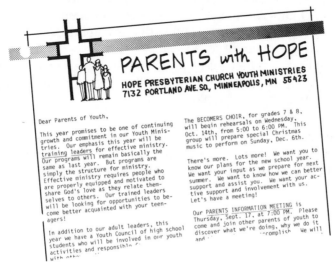

PARENTS with HOPE

HOPE PRESBYTERIAN CHURCH YOUTH MINISTRIES
7132 PORTLAND AVE. SO., MINNEAPOLIS, MN 55423

Dear Parents of Youth,

This year promises to be one of continuing growth and commitment in our Youth Ministries. Our emphasis this year will be training leaders for effective ministry. Our programs will remain basically the same as last year. But programs are simply the structure for ministry. Effective ministry requires people who are properly equipped and motivated to share God's love as they relate themselves to others. Our trained leaders will be looking for opportunities to become better acquainted with your teenagers!

In addition to our adult leaders, this year we have a Youth Council of high school students who will be involved in our youth activities and responsible for with other

The BECOMERS CHOIR, for grades 7 & 8, will begin rehearsals on Wednesday, Oct. 14th, from 5:00 to 6:00 PM. This group will prepare special Christmas music to perform on Sunday, Dec. 6th.

There's more. Lots more! We want you to know our plans for the new school year. We want your input as we prepare for next summer. We want to know how we can better support and assist you. We want your active support and involvement with us. Let's have a meeting!

Our PARENTS INFORMATION MEETING is Thursday, Sept. 17, at 7:00 PM. Please come and join other parents of youth to discover what we're doing, why we do it and   accomplish   We will

Youth group hot line. It's now a simple matter to arrange a hot line number that parents (or students) can call to get up-to-date information about the youth group schedule. The hot line with a brief recorded answer can prevent the all-too-common scenario of little Johnny charging away from the dinner table with the explanation that he's just remembered there's "ayouthgroupactivitytonightand-momanddadIneedtohavetwentydollarsorDuffysaysI'llbekickedout ofyouthgroup!!" Parents can just call the hot line and get the full scoop well in advance.

In-home visits with families. As one youth counselor put it, "You don't really know a teenager until you've eaten with him, met his family, and seen the walls of his bedroom." One youth minister I know has a business card on which he has printed underneath his name this phrase: "Available most nights of the week for dinner."

Keep parents informed of community resources. Wise youth workers find that one of their greatest gifts to parents is a brochure announcing a helpful parenting workshop or a phone number parents can call to request help when they have children dealing with pregnancies, suicidal tendencies, or substance abuse.

ASSISTING PARENTS

Parenting teenagers today can be scary. The average parent of an adolescent is worried—worried about the child's welfare, moral choices, friends, education, complexion, not to mention the fungus that's growing on the walls of the teen's bedroom. It's usually while parenting adolescents that we learn what it means to pray unceasingly! I always explain to parents of adolescents that we go through labor twice with every child; it's just that this second time, the pains can last for about seven years.

It's for that reason that we in youth ministry need to sensitively assist parents in their task of nurturing their teens. Here are some suggestions for assisting parents.

Seminars. Hosting parent seminars about issues related to raising healthy teens can build bridges between parents of students in our youth group or even be a means of outreach to the community at large. Invite a noted speaker to address a specific topic, or show one of the video seminars on the market. Christian bookstores often have these available for rental.

Here's a sampling of topics that one might use:

"How to Pay for Your Child's College Education"
"How to Keep Your Kids Free From Drugs"
"Adolescent Suicide and Teenage Depression"
"Family Traditions—the Gift of Memories"
"Lava Lamps—Making a House a Home"

Support groups. A group of youth workers met at a Denver hotel to discuss parent-teen ministry. Following their enthusiastic interaction, one of the women servers on the hotel staff approached the youth worker who chaired the session. With tears in her eyes she said, "I couldn't help but overhear your discussions today. Please, when you do your seminars, tell people how lonely it can be to be the parent of a teenager." Her remark reminds us how important it is to assist parents by organizing support groups. These occasional get-togethers or ongoing forums allow parents to discuss with each other issues and questions or to share some of the difficulties they face. The support groups may be specialized groups like single parents or parents dealing with one particular concern (substance abuse, teen pregnancy, runaways).

Some parent support groups have found that these kinds of gatherings allow them to develop common ground rules for curfew, in-house parties, and the like. If a group of parents agree that they expect their teens to be in by 11:30 p.m., their solidarity can cut down on the dissension that begins with remarks like, "Well, Shari's mom lets her stay out later."

Opportunities for guided interaction. At occasional parent-teen gatherings, youth workers actively assume the role of facilitator, reaching across the communication gap and encouraging both sides to communicate. Guided interaction takes different forms. For example, it might be as simple as a Sunday school class interviewing parents—not about being parents, but about the pressures of being adults, husbands, wives, breadwinners. An exercise like this can help students appreciate the world in which their parents function. What are my parents' concerns? What pressures do they face?

For another approach, turn the interview around and allow some adults to interview teenagers about their lives: What's it really like at the high school? Why do they like that music? What do they expect from their parents? How can their parents best support them? Although it's naive to expect total candor on the part of either the parents or the teens, parents can get a feel for teenagers' attitudes about music, styles, fads, and so forth. Teenagers are surprisingly willing to talk if they feel adults are interested.

An excellent communication exercise is to show both parents and teens a picture of an adult and an adolescent obviously having an argument, and then invite everyone to suggest what the argument is about. Allow the parents and the youths to come up with their scenarios independent of each other, then bring them back together for dialogue. Ask questions about how the parent and teenager in the picture are feeling. How could they have avoided this argument?

Also, we can use role plays of teenagers facing their parents in various familiar situations—asking for the car, for example, or coming home after curfew, wanting money, getting caught telling lies. When doing these kinds of role plays, put the parents in the roles of the teens and the students in the roles of the parents. Then talk about the role play as a group.

Ask students to write letters from their parents about why their parents are running away from home. Ask parents to write letters from their children about why they're running away from home. Allow both parties to read and discuss their letters. Encourage students to reflect on what would it be like to be in their parents' roles. What would be good about it? What wouldn't be so good? Pose the same questions to the parents—"What would it be like to be my teenage son or daughter?"

Lead adults through an exercise of remembering "the way we were," journeying with parents back into their teenage years to recall everything from which songs were popular and which clothes were in fashion, to what the major areas of dispute were between them and their parents. One youth group has an annual "Back to the Future" night when parents bring in their old yearbooks and are asked to show and explain five pictures from their yearbook. These kinds of communication and interaction exercises facilitate parent-teen communication by giving everyone a chance to laugh together, listen to each other, and see each other as real people. There are a lot of teenagers who think their parents were born at the age of forty. Guided interaction can be a way of breaking through some of the stereotypes.

Family counseling. Despite all our efforts, there will be times when we need to intervene in difficult situations by guiding the whole family through a counseling session. Our role here is not to act like amateur psychiatrists, but simply to be a third party who listens, interprets, keeps everybody honest, and perhaps referees. Although there will be times when the most appropriate response will be to refer the family to professional counseling, sometimes families just need someone who will help them to fight fair.

Offer occasional Sunday electives for parents of adolescents. Merton Strommen notes five basic concerns that are shared by parents of teenagers: a cry for understanding; the cry for a closer family; how to communicate values to teenage children; help in learning how to share their faith; additional parenting resources and outside help.[2] An elective series on parenting adolescents might meet some of these felt needs. For relatively young youth workers who are intimidated by the thought of teaching a class on raising teenagers when they are themselves not yet married, the best strategy might be to help the parents find some appropriate material (a book, video, tape series) and simply agree to moderate and facilitate class discussions.

Big aunt/big uncle. In the teenage years, there are times when a girl from a divorced family needs a "mom," even if it's not her real mom, or when a boy needs someone for one-on-one basketball and informal guidance. The church can assist single parents by initiating a big aunt/big uncle program through which other adult church members are invited to "adopt" one of the youth group kids.

Parents' resource library. Begin collecting tapes, videos, and books relevant to the parents of adolescent children. I personally have found that parents genuinely appreciate this kind of help from us. They can receive help without having to actually tell us everything.

ENCOURAGING PARENTS

Parenting teenagers can be discouraging. For one thing, no one talks to you about your teenager unless your child has done something wrong. Youth workers can build strong friendships with parents by affirming and encouraging them regarding their kids.

Parent-appreciation events. Parent Sunday, thank-you dinners, mother-daughter occasions—there are lots of ways to affirm parents. One fun approach is to allow the students to host a dinner for their parents, preparing and serving the food, performing a skit or some kind of entertainment, and then letting several kids talk about what they appreciate about their parents.

Thank you notes/phone calls. Parents always open a note from someone working with their teenager with a tinge of dread. What did they do wrong this time? Adults who work with the youth group should be encouraged to utilize the Character Trait ID strategy. The strategy begins when an adult catches one of the students in the act of doing something good. The adult identifies a character trait demonstrated by the student's behavior and then calls or writes the mom or dad to relate the incident. The youth worker describes the positive trait by saying, "It reminded me of something you would do."

Dear Mr. Jones,
I was crossing the church parking lot just prior to worship on Sunday and I saw your son, Billy, run over Mrs. Slateside. I just want you to know that when he stopped to say how sorry he was, it reminded me of your compassion.

Attending special events in the life of the student. It seems as if everybody finds out when kids get in trouble, but no one hears when they succeed at something. One way to encourage parents is to attend special events, concerts, recitals, and award ceremonies of the students in the youth group. When we show up at the oboe recital or the Eagle Scout ceremony, the parents realize that there are about a hundred other places we would probably rather be. Our voluntary presence represents a special vote of encouragement.

INVOLVING PARENTS

Youth ministry is a shared ministry. At its best, it incorporates the efforts of teenagers, their parents, and the youth workers. Sometimes we are shy about parents ministering with their students, but there are some significant strategies for parental involvement with youths.

Care through prayer. At St. Thomas More Catholic Church in Denver, a group of parents meet weekly to pray for the youth ministry. Prayer marshals support for the youth group from people who "don't know what to do" or "don't know how to help." People are not as quick to complain about a ministry they have been consistently praying for. Another added benefit: God answers prayer!

Organize a parents' council. Scott Clifton, the junior high minister at Church of the Savior in Wayne, Pennsylvania, meets regularly with several parents who advise him about the junior high ministry. Sharing ownership of the ministry with the parents equips him to better handle parental complaints. He can always say, "Well, we discussed this matter with the Parents' Council first, and they felt that it wouldn't be any problem." For the gung ho youth worker, twenty-three years old and itching to make kids radical for Jesus, the "Urban Plunge" solo overnight for junior highers on the city streets seems like a great idea. But parental perspective has a way of putting a different spin on opportunities.

Involve parents in the meetings. One of our most memorable youth meetings was the night we brought three pairs of parents in for a discussion of dating. Utilizing a "Newlywed Game" format, we interviewed each of the moms and dads separately, and then brought their spouses back into the room to compare their answers to various questions. Parents were asked questions about their dating patterns: Who was the first to say "I love you?" "Where was your first kiss?" "How did the actual marriage proposal happen?" Students began to see their parents as real people who really did know what it was like to be in love and date. The students thought it was a riot. We had some great laughs, a few decent arguments, and one divorce (just kidding).

Utilize parents in short-term service. Walt Mueller of Headfirst Ministries (Glenside, Pennsylvania), helps youth groups better integrate family ministries into their programs. One of his strategies is to periodically distribute parental involvement sheets that parents can use to volunteer their services to the group.

Breakaway Parental Involvement Sheet

Your name: _____

Phone number: _____

Please fill out and return to Walt Mueller by January 4th.

Check any boxes which apply to you.

I WILL HELP WITH THE FOLLOWING EVENTS:

January 11th: Family Potluck/Multimedia
- ☐ Set Up
- ☐ Kitchen Help

January 19th: Randy Stonehill concert
- ☐ Drive Bus
- ☐ Drive Van
- ☐ Chaperon

January 23: Ski Trip
- ☐ Drive Bus
- ☐ Drive Van
- ☐ Chaperon

January 30: Family Fun Night at Lakeside
- ☐ Drive Bus

February 13th: Ski Trip
- ☐ Drive Bus
- ☐ Drive Van
- ☐ Chaperon

February 20: Petra concert
- ☐ Drive Bus
- ☐ Drive Van
- ☐ Chaperon

March 6: Senior High Spaghetti Lock-In
- ☐ Drive Bus
- ☐ Drive Van
- ☐ Chaperon
- ☐ Cooking Help

MINISTRY IN THE
CROSS FIRE

Our Lord described the role of the peacemaker as "blessed," but it has its ups and downs. One of the pitfalls for a youth worker who intervenes in parent-teen conflicts is the temptation to manipulate or side against one party to gain the approval and admiration of the other party. A similar error is for a youth worker to begin usurping the God-given role of the parents. At a certain point, protecting confidences and remaining quiet about a problem steals a parent's role from them. We dare not take this liberty. To be sure, we have a sacred responsibility to maintain strictest confidence when students share with us their secrets, but certain kinds of information must be shared with parents or we hinder their ability to carry out their God-ordained responsibilies.

Finally, we must resist the temptation to give up on a family. Although a family may appear so dysfunctional that healing is impossible, God *can* intervene. We are all aware that some parents don't want anything to do with their children, whether it involves the church, the school, or any other area of their teens' lives. But even then, God can work his purposes in young people. In spite of all we've said about the vital roles parents play in the spiritual development of teenagers, we must never forget that God himself is the sole essential.

The ministry of the youth worker is that of facilitator—involving, informing, assisting, and encouraging. Without question, this can be one of the more delicate tasks of youth ministry. Everybody wants to "kill the umpire." But in the long run, facilitating may be one of our most effective forms of outreach and ministry.

CHAPTER FOURTEEN

BLESSED BE THE TIE: STAFF RELATIONSHIPS

Over and over in the Scriptures we glimpse people of God working together: Moses and Aaron, Jesus and the disciples, Apollos and Aquila, Paul and Barnabas, Peter and John, Paul and Timothy, Paul and Luke, Peter and Paul, Peter, Paul, and Mary, and so on. Since the Bible reports on real life, we also glimpse some of the challenging dynamics of these relationships—passing the buck, overcoming failures, handling conflict.

The following excerpt from the "YOUTHWORKER Roundtable" vividly articulates this point. Among the church professionals interviewed were Brent Bromstrup, youth pastor at Brooklyn Park Covenant Church, Brooklyn Park, Minnesota; John Hall, formerly youth minister at Hope Presbyterian Church, Minneapolis, Minnesota; Alexia Newman, youth minister at Calvary Church, Abbeville, South Carolina; Gary Flanders, youth minister at Westminster Presbyterian Church, Waterloo, Iowa; Earl Palmer, senior pastor of First Presbyterian Church, Berkeley, California; and Mark Senter, assistant professor of Christian Education at Trinity Divinity School, Deerfield, Illinois.

SENTER: Many youth workers feel brutalized by their staff relationships, but most of them think it's worthwhile to stick with their ministries, anyway.

FLANDERS: Nonetheless, we all need to have a support system. I've been reevaluating whether or not my senior pastor can be part of that system, or if it's realistic to think that a supervisor can be part of a support team. My conclusion is no.

HALL: That's an overgeneralization. I represent the whole church, and my goal is to involve my young people in the life of the whole church. It's important for the entire church to see that I have a good relationship with my senior pastor and the other pastors on my staff. The kids need to know that I haven't built a youth-ministry "fortress." It would damage my ministry if I didn't have a good relationship with my senior pastor. Of course, I have to earn it.

FLANDERS: Maybe it's my own failing, but I feel that my senior pastor isn't supporting me while I'm slogging it out in the trenches. It's easy to become bitter . . . I believe my senior pastor should be interested in not only what I'm doing, but who I am. Yet my pastor doesn't know what's important to me . . . I feel—maybe due to my own failing—that the atmosphere for that kind of relationship building doesn't exist with him. To be honest, I think it's his fault. He hasn't created the atmosphere. Maybe that's laying too much responsibility on him, but as senior pastor, he's got to set the tone for the staff.

HALL: I disagree. We've got to take the initiative. It's a big burden to pastor a multiple staff. At times my senior pastor probably feels I don't care about his pressures and how hard he's gutting it out in his trench. If I can communicate to him that I care about what he's going through, the attitude will be reciprocated.

PALMER: So much depends on the personalities involved. If we have a staff of strong, competent entrepreneurs able to get on with their work, they won't need as much support. What can then happen, however, is "empire building," where each of us builds our own constituency, and that constituency becomes a ghetto within a large fellowship.

The church may even applaud this approach. And we may feel it's only fair. After all, we've built our constituency—the kids. For a while we may thrive in that Lone Ranger role. (It happened to me in my own career at one point.) But this staff model will only work for so long. It's an invitation to burnout: the empire builds and builds without the accountability necessary for resolving conflicts and healing hurts. Resentments begin to build among the members of the staff.

[We can avoid these ghettos] by developing a sense of mutual support in a staff where we endorse each other's visions. I tell my staff that I want them to build a constituency, because we've all got to have people who look to us. That doesn't threaten me, and it shouldn't threaten other members of the team.[1]

THREATS, GHETTOS, AND MUTUAL SUPPORTS

In an unpublished survey of 103 youth workers prepared by Mark Lamport of Gordon College, twenty-seven percent of those questioned said that they would consider leaving (or had already left) their youth-ministry position because of frustrations over staff relationships.[2] On the other hand, two-thirds of those surveyed disagreed with the statement, "I feel as though I do my job alone without any support." In fact, a remarkably high fifty-five percent said that they receive "support and helpful evaluation from board members." An even higher seventy-eight percent affirm that their supervisors are supportive of their leadership.

For the most part, youth workers apparently feel moderate satisfaction about their relationships with ministry coworkers. There's nothing quite like the comradery and community of joining together with like-minded men and women who share our vision for ministry. The psalmist was right: "How good and pleasant it is when brothers live together in unity!" (Ps. 133:1). On the other hand, few frustrations are more nagging and draining than negative team relationships.

LIKE IT OR NOT, WE'RE A TEAM

Fact #1: If we are feeling frustrated about staff relationships, any initiative for improvement will probably have to come from our end of the equation, not the top person or the senior pastor.

According to author Kenneth Mitchell, the senior minister usually grades the quality of staff relationships more highly than do other members of the same staff.[3] In one sample of eighty-eight churches, Mitchell found that while 61.2 percent of the senior pastors graded the staff relationships as "basically good," seventy-four percent of the assistant pastors on the same staffs rated their relationships with the other ministers as "basically poor." When asked to rate on a scale of one to five the quality of staff relationships in their churches, ninety-five of 136 assistant pastors gave a grade of one or two. When the senior pastors on the same staff were asked for their assessment, however, forty-two of the eighty senior pastors rated their staff relationships as a grade of four or five.

In other words, if we are waiting until the pastor realizes something's wrong, we may be waiting a long time. Not that senior pastors don't care. But if asked, "How long can you stand together like this?" it's the people on the top of the pyramid who are most optimistic. The people on the bottom of the pile are the ones feeling the pain. Any suggestions about reshuffling the structure are apt to come from the bottom up.

Fact #2: Nearly a third of all associate ministers are in their first pastoral position, involved in an internship program, and/or are under thirty-two years of age.

This means that by virtue of their positions on the staff, most youth workers are perceived as the stereotypical rookies, short-term young people hoping to learn the ropes of ministry so that they can move on up to more weighty, long-term positions. Youth workers who have seminary educations, ten years of youth-ministry experience, and are over thirty-five, may therefore be treated as if they have just gotten out of college, with no graduate degree, no experience, and no long-term commitment to youth ministry.

"I wouldn't go in there if I were you."

214

Fact #3: The more we enjoy our coworkers, the more likely we are to enjoy our work.

MODELS OF
STAFF RELATIONSHIPS

The staff of Grace Church is top-notch: professional people who play out their roles on the ministry team with commendable commitment and a sense of excellence. Known for its strong pulpit ministry and varied programs for all ages, the church is growing and the ministry flourishing. From all appearances, Grace Church is an oasis of vibrant ministry. And in many ways that's true. But for the person who needs or enjoys close working relationships shaped by a sense of community and mutuality, Grace Church is more of a desert than an oasis—a wasteland of organizational charts, interoffice memos, and staff meetings that are ninety-eight percent business and less than two percent nurture.

Bannerside Presbyterian Church is almost the exact opposite. To begin with, the staff is much smaller, and the organizational chart is something someone drew up on a napkin one night after the staff had eaten dinner together. Off-hours, the staff gets together for recreation, cutting firewood, or some kind of fellowship. Staff meetings, held during the daily morning coffee break, are an informal mixture of ministry business, personal sharing, and chitchat.

Grace and Bannerside represent the two models of staff relationships that youth workers are likely to find: the functional model and the fellowship model. Let's take a look at the strengths and weaknesses of each.

THE FUNCTIONAL MODEL:
THE CHURCH AS CORPORATION

At Grace Church, staff relationships are on functional lines—everyone, from the senior pastor to the youth pastor, has a role to play, and the lines dividing jobs are clearly drawn. Members of the staff are courteous to each other and willing to work together, but typically are uninvolved with each other at a deep relational level.

The major advantage of shaping staff relationships on the functional model is that it is more efficient. Particularly in a large church, the emphasis may need to be on accountability rather than community. If community receives the emphasis, the staff may discover jobs that are falling between the cracks. The staffers will be in love with each other and having a big time, but the work won't be getting done!

The functional model is most effective when each staff member has a clearly written, explicit job description, thus avoiding the turf battles that break down staff relationships. Typically, this model is best led by a strong, directive, hard-working senior pastor who can manage a staff of people working in different areas while moving them towards a common goal. Because the lines of responsibility are clearly drawn, only a strong senior minister can prevent staff members from building their own little fiefdoms. If the senior pastor is detached, preoccupied, disinterested, or weak, the staffers may busily develop their own pet projects and neglect working for unity in the overall ministry of the church.

The staff that operates along functional lines is usually operating a ministry organized by specific programs and policies as opposed to a ministry based on personalities or areas of giftedness. In other words, the youth pastor would typically be responsible for all areas of youth ministry, and only the areas of youth ministry. It wouldn't matter that the youth worker is also a good preacher; that's not the purpose for which he was hired. The youth minister who is gifted musically and wants to start a youth choir will have to negotiate the idea with the music director, or her efforts might be construed as trespassing on the music director's turf.

When staff relationships are functional, staff members generally work with a committee that pushes for specific areas of responsibility. The children's minister, for instance, works with the children's committee, the youth minister with the youth committee, and so on. Staff members develop their own support constituencies through the committees. The difficulty is that when staff members leave, their committees tend to lose their clout, and the groups they represent may get short shrift until the staff member is replaced.

One advantage of the functional model is that jobs are clearly defined, making it easier for new staff members to move in and begin working without having to learn underground, informal networks of relationships. For that reason, the functional model tends to be more advantageous to women youth ministers. When the emphasis is on relationships, she is more apt to be unintentionally left out of decision making, not because someone wants to cut her out, but perhaps because she isn't playing racquetball at the club with the guys when one of them has some great idea.

The fatal flaw of the functional model of staff relationships is that it tends to breed little long-term tenure, particularly among people who have grown up in this postsixties era when we so emphasize the importance of relationships. Walking out of an organizational role is much easier than walking out on relationships. We build loyalty, not by giving out job descriptions and offices, but by giving of ourselves.

Both the positive and negative points of the functional approach to staff relationships are reflected in the following conversation from a YOUTHWORKER Roundtable:

HALL: Our staff moves in very different social circles. We're not likely to have each other over for dinner, but we're now going through a stress-management course together. We're talking about our particular stress points and how we can help each other through them. It's not recreational, but we're sharing who we really are and how we operate. It's been good for us. It's what a staff needs.

BROMSTRUP: That's not true in our case. We have a shallow "friendship" among our staff. We pray together, but we lack creative interaction; we just file facts with each other. We're not going anywhere as a staff, even though there is no personal animosity.

THE FELLOWSHIP MODEL:
ONE BIG, HAPPY FAMILY

The five staff members at Bannerside Presbyterian Church are not only coworkers, they are close friends. It's not that they are working without job descriptions; it's that they approach their work the way a family approaches weekly life together. Everyone works together to do what must be done. If that means the youth minister is needed for help with hospital visitation, it's no more a big problem than when the family member who usually takes out the garbage gets pressed for time and asks another family member to care for this chore.

An advantage of the fellowship model of staff relationships is that when we're working with friends, it's more fun to do the work. We trust other members of the staff to defend us if our work is attacked. We trust them to direct critics to come and speak to us personally, rather than allowing them to stew behind our backs. We're also not as likely to concern ourselves with turf battles and power struggles. If we are members of a family, at least in theory(!), what's good for you is what's good for me. Plus, the fellowship model tends to breed staff loyalty and longer tenures of commitment. People can walk into and out of functional positions without a lot of emotion, but when it comes to walking out on family, the cords are tougher to sever.

So why doesn't every staff operate this way? Who would pass up a chance to work with the Walton family? Because the reality doesn't always live up to the ideal. Sometimes it's strictly because of staff size. I spoke with a youth minister recently who is serving at a church in Colorado on a staff that numbers thirty-five people. Frankly, this makes it hard to genuinely flesh out the fellowship model. A household of thirty-five is a complex family to manage! Unless the staff approaches this fellowship model with seriousness and intentionality, it simply won't happen.

In addition, a staff that functions on the basis of strong relationships functions poorly if, for some reason, there is a breach in fellowship. Unlike the functional model where "getting the job done" carries staff members through tense relationships, a fellowship model withers or flourishes with people's moods. A breach in the fellowship can mean a breach in the operation of the ministry.

Another problem encountered in a fellowship model of staff relationships is that the close-knit feel that retains employees also tends to make it difficult for new staff members to get into the flow of relationships. We don't get that uptight about a new milkman or a new paperboy, but we're apt to be a little more cautious about someone who is going to join our household. The loyalty nurtured by the fellowship model can also nurture cliquishness.

Probably the biggest problem with the fellowship model of staff relationships is that good relationships take a lot of time and hard work. What are some of the barriers to genuine staff fellowship? Let's listen again to our YOUTHWORKER Roundtable:

NEWMAN: Dishonesty.

FLANDERS: And much of the responsibility for this lack of honesty is ours. Too many of us have not worked through the concept of submission. I've had to pray like David over and over, "Lord, search me and see if there are wicked ways in me." Why am I reluctant to be open with my senior pastor? Is it because I don't want to submit?

SENTER: There are two kinds of honesty, though. There's a dumping "honesty" where we just let things fly with no regard for the pastor's feelings. They may be true statements but he feels attacked by them.

Then there's the other kind of honesty that says, "What I feel about the situation may be a sign of immaturity on my part, but these are my honest feelings anyway." This allows the senior pastor the option to respond rather than react.

HALL: I know youth ministers who are frustrated with their senior man because deep down inside, they want his job. They're frustrated at being on the bottom of the ladder.

NEWMAN: Pride gets in the way, too. Our denomination is small, and I've worked in the presbytery so long that I know everyone. It hurts my pride now to have my pastor, the session, and the parents question things I do.

BROMSTRUP: Another problem, especially in small churches, is that the youth minister might be better read, a better speaker, and more energetic than the pastor. The youth worker may begin to think the pastor is incompetent.

Meanwhile, church members may be telling him or her, "I wish we could get rid of our pastor and put you in." People love to criticize the pastor to an associate. Sadly enough, the youth worker sometimes starts to believe the things people in the congregation are saying.

PALMER: In my conversations with youth pastors, one of the biggest stress points I hear about is pastors' jealousies. They're "punished" in direct proportion to the success they're having.

It's a real and very difficult problem that grows out of the insecurities of the senior pastor—but not just his. The jealousies can be worse from other colleagues on a multiple-member staff if their ministries aren't thriving as much as ours. There are no easy solutions for this problem. Sometimes we must simply have a confrontation.

I like to think I've never been jealous of my teammates. I have a philosophy that we're in this together but with different gifts, which means rejoicing with our colleagues when they rejoice. But the hardest thing in the Christian life is rejoicing with those who rejoice. It's much easier to weep with those who weep.

Confrontation is a risk, and we should be very cautious in our use of it; but it can be a good experience for a staff to have even a painful confrontation. Our staff has had that happen several times, and in each case it's been for the good of each of us.

"BEFORE I ACCEPT THIS JOB, DO YOU HAVE OLDER BROTHERS?"

Most of us would feel kind of funny asking a question like that in a job interview, and it is a bit bizarre. But research has shown that a person's place in the family constellation influences the relationships of seventy to eighty percent of the adult population. While it sounds like some kind of pop-psychology, Freudian gobbledygook, it's worth considering that birth order may play a part in the patterns we use in relating to other members of the ministry staff. Renowned parish-ministry expert, Lyle Schaller, puts it in proper prospective: "While it is only a minor consideration in the total context of staff relationships, the most widely neglected factor in building a model of staff relationships is birth order."[4]

Researchers who have explored this dynamic have found the following traits typically influence our relationships:

Firstborn: Firstborn people tend to be more conscientious, just as mom or dad were more cautious, serious parents with the firstborn than with the siblings. Firstborn people are often more task-oriented, persistent, and high-achieving. They always got lots of affirmation for achievement as children. If just going to the bathroom by oneself got rave reviews, one can imagine the child thinking, "This is going to be easy. Look out world. The sky's the limit!"

Firstborn people are generally comfortable giving orders, again not surprising given the fact that they probably spent their childhood ordering around their younger siblings. Likewise, it's no wonder that firstborn people are usually inclined to develop relationships defined by hierarchy. When you're the oldest and the biggest, you're less concerned with equality and parity in relationships. Any time favors are doled out on the basis of hierarchical factors (age, size, strength, grade in school) the oldest child usually comes out on top. They learn to like that system.

Middle-born: The middle-born person is typically more relationally oriented, relaxed, friendly, and more skilled with people. Since they have spent the better part of their childhood dealing with siblings who are bigger, older, better educated, and stronger, it's not surprising that middle-born people develop interpersonal and diplomatic skills. No wonder they are always saying, "I think we can talk this out without anybody getting hurt." Along the same lines, researchers found middle-born people are likely to smile more easily (again, an early learned survival skill).

Last-born: Last-born people like to have fun. They're more playful, more lighthearted, and it's no wonder. By the time they were born, there were people all over the place who wanted to hold this child, play with it, make faces, and tickle it. Basically, childhood was a nonstop party. Last-born people are usually more casual in dress and appearance, due, no doubt, in part to the fact that they have grown up wearing clothes that have probably already been through two generations of wear. Interestingly, one of the traits researchers found in last-borns is that they demonstrate the capacity to ignore that which does not interest them and concentrate on tasks and concerns that do. As one might expect, last-borns are generally more willing to accept subordinate positions (they've grown up taking orders), but they also tend to express great interest in change (they're tired of always taking orders!).

Does birth order make any difference? Lyle Schaller suggests on the basis of his interviews with the multiple staffs of some 296 large congregations that birth order is a significant factor in staff relationships. (Schaller doesn't make any distinction between the various roles on a multiple staff. I'm making the assumption that what is true for an associate minister in general would be true for the youth minister specifically.) In fact, Schaller makes these observations on the strength of his studies: First, a disproportionately large number of senior ministers are firstborns. Second, the least happy staff relationships usually involve two or more firstborn staff members or an only-born senior minister and only-born associate minister (Schaller found this combination to be so rare that it was virtually nonexistent. His assumption is that it is so rare simply because it almost never works out). Third, the most enjoyable staff combinations are typically those that include a middle-born senior minister and a middle-born associate minister. Finally, the most effective teams tend to be comprised of middle-born senior ministers and firstborn associate ministers involved.

> If all the factors used in selecting a candidate for a position on a multiple staff have a combined value of one hundred points, in perhaps three out of four cases the birth order factor should be given a weight of ten to twenty points. With the other one-fourth of the candidates, birth order probably deserves a weight of zero to five points in selecting members of a multiple staff team.[5]

For those of us in youth ministry, Schaller's observations are simply factors to consider. I personally wouldn't want to base my "yes" or "no" to a call on the birth order of other staff members. That seems a bit silly. On the other hand, it's information to feed into the equation.

EVOLUTION OF
STAFF RELATIONSHIPS

Another way of evaluating and understanding staff relationships in the context of youth ministry is to observe how relationships change over the course of time. Mark Senter, Assistant Professor of Christian Education at Trinity Evangelical Divinity School, discusses the normal evolution of staff relationships in terms of various stages. We can use three of these stages to assess the challenges we will meet at various mileposts on our journey with a ministry team.

STAGE ONE:
GETTING ACQUAINTED

When a youth worker takes a new position, a fog of euphoria generally covers the ministry landscape. The church or agency is pleased to be able to end their search successfully, and the youth worker feels that he or she has found a place to plug in for ministry. This honeymoon period is characterized by a sense of relief, discovery, and, most importantly, a sense of ignorance. At this point, staff members and constituents don't expect the newcomer to "know any better," so this forgiven ignorance should be used to the best advantage.

For example, this honeymoon period is a wonderful time to ask "stupid questions"—questions about jurisdiction, lines of responsibility, and expectations; questions that, if asked one year into the position, might give someone reason for offense. People are more gracious at this stage of the relationship—staff members are themselves adjusting to a new team member and are more likely to flex. The key at this stage is to remember the old adage that "As the work begins, so will it go." We should balance our desires to push, probe, and test the boundaries with the reminder that first impressions often leave lasting impressions.

Dan was in a new position at a church in South Carolina when he sought to hire an intern who was not of the same denomination as his church. It didn't seem like a big deal to Dan, and in some ways it probably wasn't. But it was to Dan's pastor. Dan wasn't allowed to hire the intern, and from that point on he never seemed to get back in step with the senior pastor. Dan left the position within a year.

STAGE TWO:
GETTING ESTABLISHED

Stage one in the evolution of staff relationships usually ends with some sort of crisis. The good will is spent, and the willingness to overlook has expired. This ushers the youth worker into a second stage in relationship to his colleagues—a stage in which the critical issue is between trust and mistrust, credibility and lack of credibility.

If youth workers have earned the trust of their colleagues, it will generally be made manifest in some of the following ways:

Greater vulnerability—staff members agree to admit that no one but Jesus walks on water.

Honest communication—staff members feel free to express disagreement.

Job refinement—there is some freedom to redefine the position now that you are in place and have seen up close the necessities of the situation.

Community—there is support among the staff. Even in failure there is loving rebuke.

If the youth worker has not gained this kind of trust, it may be manifested in some of these ways:

Gradual isolation—no one sits next to you at staff meetings.

Interpersonal conflict—philosophical differences are exposed, and people begin to deal with each other on the basis of categories rather than on the basis of specific concerns.

Big hints—the trustees pull out your phone and remove your desk to the dumpster.

If youth workers or staff members have not earned the trust of their fellow workers by stage two, they probably never will. Things won't get better; they'll get worse.

STAGE THREE:
GETTING ROLLING

By the time a youth worker has moved into stage three, the key issues professionally and relationally are growth versus stagnation. Having gained a certain amount of momentum thus far, will the youth worker be able to sustain it, or will he or she become stagnant?

Growth at this stage is characterized by

- Better time management
- Broader responsibility given by the staff and/or supervisor
- Growing honesty and loving confrontation among staff members
- Systems being developed by the youth worker that enhance efficiency and expediency.

Stagnation will be marked by some of the following:
- Exhaustion—physically, emotionally, and/or spiritually
- Feeling unchallenged by the job
- New priorities—usually something outside the church—detract from job performance
- Financial worries
- Withdrawal from staff relationships and an unwillingness to share honestly with others on staff.

SOME SUGGESTIONS FROM A PASTOR

Probably the best insight into the dynamics of staff relationships would come from someone who has been a youth worker and who also has the perspective of a senior pastor. Earl Palmer is just such a man. Drawing from his unique background, Palmer suggests four keys to more effective staff relationships.

Each staff member should have a mandate as important as every other member of the staff. In other words, staff members should feel and understand the vital significance of their own ministry roles to the whole mission of the church. For this to actually happen, the leadership of the congregation must free staff members to do most what they do best. If youth ministry is what I do best, then I am freed and affirmed by my coworkers to do youth ministry, with just as much credibility as the person who is preaching, leading Bible studies, or directing a choir.

Each staff member must have equal access to the senior leadership person (usually the pastor). That access should be direct and reasonably immediate. One of the major reasons for squabbles among staff members is the kind of professional jealousy that we observe in the disciples jockeying to be closest to Jesus (see Mark 9:34; Luke 9:46; Luke 22:24). When the pastor seems to be more available to one staff member than to another, the neglected staff member may begin to resent the extra attention, or suspect that his contribution isn't really valid. Equal access frees staff members to exercise real authority and experience real accountability.

Staff members must do what they have all promised to do—that is, act professionally. One of the major frustrations among coworkers in ministry is unpredictability: "Will they follow up on our conversation?" "Are they talking behind my back?" "Will their work be completed by the date assigned?" Nine times out of ten, a breach in staff relationships grows out of an instance in which someone acted unprofessionally.

Staff members should be allowed to develop their own constituencies. A lot of pastors feel threatened when they see staff members closely aligning with power blocks in the congregation. But these support constituencies are vital. They may be youth committees, youth groups, parents' support groups, or all of the above. One of the factors that leads to weak staff relationships is jealousy and insecurity. If staff members are encouraged to build support groups, those groups will give them the support they need to be vulnerable about mistakes, honest about concerns, and excited in the face of other staff members' successes.

A RESOURCE
FOR MINISTRY

Ridge Burns, currently the Director of the Center for Student Missions, made an entry in his journal several years ago when he was still the youth pastor at Wheaton Bible Church. It read:

Tuesday, March 18

Today, Rick Trautman asked me to come into his office for coffee. As we told jokes and talked about our ministry, I decided to risk a little more intimacy with Rick.

"Rick, I'm restless," I told him. "I've been here almost five years, and now I'm praying about whether or not to leave Wheaton Bible Church." After I told him I was thinking of leaving, Rick began to share with me how important I was in his life and ministry. We talked about the ministry ideas we have worked on together. It was exciting to remember all the things God has done through us.

I don't think Rick was cognizant that he helped me recall exactly what my position is here at Wheaton Bible—to pastor high school kids. God worked in my life today through Rick.[6]

The real reason for good, strong staff relationships is not a smoother operation. The real reason for good, strong staff relationships is that those of us in youth ministry need coworkers, and our coworkers need us. Some of the greatest times in my life have been when I have stood shoulder to shoulder with brothers and sisters on the staff, pooling gifts in an effort to glorify God. I will never forget the closeness I have felt in those times.

Likewise, I can still feel some of the pain of difficult encounters that have taken place over the years between myself and a colleague. Those scars are as slow to fade as the memories of the good times. Even as I write these words, some of those conversations are as vivid as if they happened yesterday—and that hurts.

But most of all, I have learned through various staff relationships that God is good. He works through people to make me into the person he wants me to be. On that one specific day, I thought I was discussing or arguing so that I could build a better youth ministry. Now as I look back, I realize God's intention was to use those people in my life, not to build a better youth ministry, but to build a better youth minister. When it all boils down, building a better youth minister is probably the best means and the best end of strong staff relationships. "As iron sharpens iron, so one man sharpens another" (Prov. 27:17).

CHAPTER FIFTEEN

WHEN THE TIE BINDS: DEALING WITH CONFLICT

Joe, the salaried youth minister at the First Church of Holy Baldness, has been faithfully working there for the last three years. His wife Jane has been a willing cominister with Joe, consistently serving the Lord, the church, and her husband. This spring, however, Joe is facing a problem that is growing into a major obstacle in his ministry.

For the past three years, the youth group has done an annual missions project—the part of his program that is most personally satisfying to Joe and most strategically effective in his work with the kids. The funds for the mission project have always been under the jurisdiction of the missions committee, chaired by fellow staff member, Napoleon Pickabone. This year, the missions committee wants Joe and the youth group to participate in a denominational missions project in South Dakota. Joe feels the project will not accomplish with the group what he has been able to accomplish in the past three years. And he's not even sure the project is valid.

Joe wants to see the funding system changed so that the youth mission project funds are directly under his supervision. He feels that the present system effectively puts this important part of his program under the control of Napoleon Pickabone and his committee. Aside from this particular missions trip, Joe feels that there is a principle at stake here.

The pastor of First Church is the Reverend Genghis Falter. He has told Joe to back off. He feels the issue is not worth getting Napoleon and his committee up in arms. Their committee's role in raising money for the church's mission outreach is critical, and if a problem erupts with them, it will be a serious problem indeed (read: "it will hurt giving"). Joe is disappointed that Pastor Falter is siding with the missions committee and Napoleon instead of trusting in his leadership. Joe sees the whole issue as being one of trust.

As emotions and tensions accelerate around this issue, Joe's wife feels hurt. She doesn't like what she sees happening to Joe. Two months after the issue emerged, with no resolution in sight, Jane is suggesting that maybe it's time to move on to another ministry. Jane's pain makes Joe even angrier.

THE "C" WORD

Most of us in the church don't like to talk about conflict. We don't like to experience it; we don't like to believe it happens among Spirit-filled Christians; we certainly wouldn't ever want to encourage it. As children we were instructed that if we couldn't say something nice, we shouldn't say anything. We were taught that nice people don't argue and that "niceness" is the cardinal virtue.

©1990 Mary Chambers

". . . and when the pastor cut down the bean stalk, the giant committee came tumbling down and the church lived happily ever after . . . "

Scripture teaches us, however, that at times conflict is appropriate. In fact, it comes right out and says that if we have something against a brother, or if we feel a brother has something against us, the last thing we should do is to sit on it and stew.

Therefore, if you are offering your gift at the altar and there remember that your brother has something against you, leave your gift there in front of the altar. First go and be reconciled to your brother, then come and offer your gift (Matt. 5:23, 24).

Therefore each of you must put off falsehood and speak truthfully to his neighbor, for we are all members of one body. "In your anger do not sin": Do not let the sun go down while you are still angry, and do not give the devil a foothold (Eph. 4:25-27).

Two spiritual titans from the New Testament demonstrate that believers are not immune to conflict.

Some time later Paul said to Barnabas, "Let us go back and visit the brothers in all the towns where we preached the word of the Lord and see how they are doing." Barnabas wanted to take John, also called Mark, with them, but Paul did not think it wise to take him, because he had deserted them in Pamphylia and had not continued with them in the work. They had such a sharp disagreement that they parted company. Barnabas took Mark and sailed for Cyprus, but Paul chose Silas and left, commended by the brothers to the grace of the Lord (Acts 15:36-41).

This isn't one of those passages you have embroidered on the hem of your ordination robe. We prefer to think that Paul and Barnabas (the "son of consolation," for heaven's sake) would never be involved in any kind of conflict—certainly not a conflict that they couldn't just pray through, talk out, and resolve.

Luke's intriguing glimpse into the working relationship of Paul and Barnabas, however, confirms that godly people who are walking in the Spirit, sensitive to God's Word and burdened for ministry, are quite capable of conflicting. There's no way to dismiss their "sharp disagreement" as a passing squabble. These two men, having faced unbelievable turmoil together, now, in the face of disagreement, are so divided that they decide to split up.

We also note that Luke's account gives no hint that the church was particularly uptight about the conflict, which is quite a paradox in light of how much Paul emphasizes in his letters the importance of unity among the brethren. It appears that the church accepted certain kinds of conflict as valid, normal, and a fact of community life. Indeed, we are told that Paul and Barnabas went off in their separate directions, "commended by the brothers to the grace of the Lord."

Finally, the story of this conflict confirms the accuracy of the biblical writers. One of the greatest proofs of the veracity of Scripture is the honest and often unflattering way in which the biblical writers paint the heroes of our faith. Had they been less concerned with accuracy, this would surely have been an episode to gloss over. The modern-day PR approach to the incident might have produced something like the following: "In an effort to double their impact, Paul and Barnabas felt led by God to split up and move out in two opposite directions, Barnabas taking Mark and Paul taking Silas."

MYTHS ABOUT CONFLICT

Youth ministers are not immune to conflict any more than lay Christians are. In a survey for *Group* magazine, Paul Woods reported that youth ministers cite some of the following (in no particular order) as being issues that bring on conflict: "The senior minister's abuse of power, families with money or influence seeking to control the church, gossip and rumors, the youth minister's lack of clout, power plays over the church budget, negative people on church boards, adult expectations overruling the youth group's needs, committee red tape and money-making ministries getting priority."[1] Very simply, conflict is what happens when "two or more people (or parties) perceive that what each one wants is incompatible with the other."[2] If we do youth ministry for very long, we will have to deal with conflict.

A number of misconceptions breed our fear of conflict.

Myth #1: Conflict can never lead to anything positive. "Confrontation is a risk," says senior pastor Earl Palmer.

We should be very cautious in our use of it; but it can be a good experience for a staff to have even a painful confrontation. Our staff has had that happen several times, and in each case it's been for the good of each of us. We never would choose confrontation gleefully. No one likes confrontation because it means admitting that we've failed each other somehow. But we ministers are in a prophetic tradition. We shouldn't run away from that positive heritage of confrontation, yet it has to be done with skill and love.[3]

Myth #2: Conflicts are the result of clashing personalities. Personalities do not conflict. Behaviors do. Two people, one of them wild and crazy, the other serious and thoughtful, can work together for years without having any trouble—until their behaviors conflict. Although people with certain personalities tend to exhibit behaviors that may rub people of different personalities the wrong way, conflict is not inevitable.

Differentiating personality from behavior makes conflict manageable. If conflict is based on personalities, we can do little else but bear it. We can hardly say, "Pastor, I've been having some struggles lately with our Christian education director. Would you be willing to ask her to change her personality?" Behaviors can be altered. It's a bit more difficult to change personalities.

Myth #3: Conflict and anger go together. We should not assume that conflicting with someone or some party means there is some enmity involved. The emotions generated in a conflict run the gamut from sadness to invigoration, from fearfulness to excitement. Understanding this allows us to put a different value on conflict, removing one more blockade to resolution.

CAUSES OF CONFLICT

Let's return to our case study about Joe and the missions project funds. Rank the characters in order according to your perception of the greatest to the least contributor to the conflict:

_____ Joe, the youth minister

_____ Jane, his wife
_____ Napoleon Pickabone, chair of missions committee
_____ Missions committee
_____ Genghis Falter, pastor

Here's a key question: What kinds of issues do you believe brought the saga of Joe and the mission trip to such a grim and murky threshold?

The first and best way to deal with negative conflicts that are draining and disruptive is to eliminate the circumstances that give rise to such conflict. If you don't want to breed rats in your house, you'd better deal carefully and completely with the garbage. The question for youth workers is, *What kinds of garbage cause conflicts in a youth program?*

AMBIGUOUS LINES OF RESPONSIBILITY

In our case study, Joe felt that, as youth pastor, all aspects of the youth ministry were his responsibility—particularly the part of the ministry that Joe identified as one of the most significant aspects of his work, the annual missions project. On the other hand, Napoleon and his committee were acting on a mandate the church had given them—to allocate funds for missions projects. The problem here is that both Joe and Napoleon are right. The conflict surfaced not because one person or one group was power hungry, but because no one ever made clear the limits of the power of either the committee or the youth worker. Ambiguous jurisdiction is one of the quickest ways to brew unproductive conflict.

Although it may feel uncomfortable to confront an interviewing committee with specific questions, direct and straightforward inquiry is the most loving and thoughtful way we can circumvent these problems. Before the issues arise to cause unproductive conflict, ask questions: Do I have control over monies budgeted for youth activities that are allocated by other committees? How do I access those funds? Who will make decisions about scheduling youth activities? What if the youth choir director plans an activity that conflicts with another youth group event? Who has the authority in a situation like that?

CONFLICT OF INTEREST

Conflict may grow out of competition for scarce resources. The youth committee wants to buy a new van. The worship committee wants a new sound system for the sanctuary. Both groups know that the pie is only so big. If the youth committee gets a bigger slice, the worship committee feels they're being starved.

COMMUNICATION BARRIERS

Joe made some assumptions about the money from the missions committee. The missions committee made some assumptions about their authority over monies designated for youth missions projects. Since neither group had carefully articulated their assumptions, a conflict erupted. Building in strong lines for honest and frequent communication among team members, staff members, youth group parents, and students is an essential for avoiding needless conflict.

BODY ODOR IN THE BODY OF CHRIST

Have you ever argued with a stranger who is in an elevator with you? Probably not. Why? Because even if our riding companion is whistling off-key or smoking a cigar or exhibiting some annoying habit with his nose, we simply won't be spending enough time with him to make it worth attempting honest dialogue about the areas of offense. On the other hand, coministers, staff members, or members of the youth-ministry team spend a lot of time together and must decide a lot of issues together. Even the most wonderful Christians in the world, if they spend enough time together and discuss enough issues together, will eventually find subjects about which they disagree— they start to notice that body odor troubles even the body of believers.

NEED FOR AGREEMENT

The more important it is that we agree on an issue, the less likely we are to do so. If it's a question of how to grill hot dogs, people are open to lots of different opinions. After all, complete agreement isn't really that important. But deciding where to hold the winter retreat, choosing a summer mission project, determining when to bring the sixth graders into the junior high group, or any concern related to budget expenditure—these more significant issues call forth strong opinions.

GENERATIONAL DIFFERENCES

Especially in youth ministry, the attitudes and attire of one generation conflict with those of another. Parents can't understand, for example, why the youth director shows up for Sunday school in jeans, long hair, and sporting an earring. The pastor can't understand why the younger members of the staff seem so interested in making staff meetings a time of honest sharing and openness when there is church business to be tended to. The choir director resents the fact that the youth group would rather go to the Petra concert than stay back at the church for the Easter cantata.

THEOLOGICAL DISAGREEMENT

The youth worker doesn't emphasize water baptism like the pastor feels she should. The pastor feels the youth group is too charismatic, and that "things are going to get out of hand." The youth minister, on the other hand, may feel like the congregational worship service is archaic and incapable of meeting the needs of teenagers. Or she may resent the use of church resources to underwrite the music ministry or the children's ministry because the youth group is forced to raise its own funds.

MISCOMMUNICATION

The youth worker forgets to inform the pastor of his plans to use the sanctuary for an all-nighter. The parents are angry that they weren't informed that the youth group is beginning a fairly in-depth study in sex education.

DIVERSITY IN PERSPECTIVE

One member of the youth staff feels we need to spend more time emphasizing personal holiness. Another feels that our students are weak in the area of service. Another feels that the kids get enough serious stuff at school: "Let's show them they can be Christians and still have fun."

MAJORING IN MINORS

Insisting that the youth minister be at every meeting; insisting that the youth pastor always wear a tie or a dress (or both); insisting that any youth ministry intern should be from the same denominational background; insisting that the Sunday school should always use the official curriculum of the denomination; insisting that the youth retreat always end on Saturday so students can be back for Sunday morning worship; getting uptight because someone spilled sugar in the kitchen during the recent lock-in, and so on, ad nauseam.

ENVIRONMENT

Sometimes conflict is born out of the organizational climate. Is it too rigid? too formal? too traditional? too restrictive?

LACK OF RELATIONSHIPS

The youth pastor speaks to the couple volunteering with the youth group about what he considers a minor area of weakness. Unfortunately, the result is anger and hurt feelings. The key is not really the criticism, but the fact that the youth pastor has not taken time to nurture a good relationship with these people.

Before we leave the discussion of causes of conflict, take a minute to read through the case study of Joe and Napoleon one more time and see how many of the above-mentioned causes of conflict can be identified somewhere in the scenario.

DEFINING YOUR CONFLICT

Effective conflict resolution requires understanding the issues at stake and defining the conflict that is being played out. Understanding these two factors helps us better strategize for positive resolution. Essentially, we can define the issues under dispute by thinking in terms of four different levels of conflict.

LEVEL I:
FACTS OR DATA

A Level-One conflict occurs when parties simply have different information. This is the easiest kind of conflict to resolve.

I do a weekly radio show in Philadelphia with my good friend and teaching colleague at Eastern College, Tony Campolo. Our show is entitled, "Let's Talk It Over," although we have jokingly referred to it as "Let's Over Talk It." For those who have listened to our show, it's obvious that Tony and I have different political leanings. Tony comes from a more liberal political perspective, and I come from a more Christian perspective (just kidding). Every now and then we quarrel over something that is simply a matter of fact—not interpretation, not viewpoint—just fact. He suggests, for instance, that unemployment rose under a certain president, and I insist that it decreased. This kind of conflict is easily resolved by going back to data from the Bureau of Labor Statistics and uncovering the actual facts.

Within the realm of youth ministry, a Level-One conflict might involve a dispute over which topics the students want us to study, how much the youth budget has increased over the last five years, or whether or not we have held our last four summer retreats in mountain locations. To resolve a Level-One conflict, we simply postpone further discussion until we have the accurate information on hand.

LEVEL II:
PROCESSES OR METHODS

A Level-Two conflict occurs when Joy, the youth worker, and Mark, the Christian education director, agree that there has been a decrease in attendance since the church began the new curriculum, but disagree on how to turn the trend around. Mark says to scrap the new curriculum. Joy says that the problem is not in the material itself, but that a better job needs to be done training the teachers to use the new curriculum.

Generally, the key to resolution of a Level-Two conflict is compromise. Since the issue is more a question of "how do we get there?" than "where should we go?" compromise is usually a realistic option. At this level, both Joy and Mark are in agreement that Sunday school attendance has decreased, and both agree that this is a negative trend that needs to be reversed. How they are to do so is negotiable. For example, Joy might suggest offering better teacher training over the course of the next four months, and if attendance does not improve, then dropping the curriculum.

LEVEL III:
GOALS OR PURPOSE

At this level, the parties in conflict cannot agree on a proper goal for their mission. Mark feels that attendance is not even a factor to be concerned about: "We should be discipling a few students and training them to reach their friends for Christ." Joy says, "Our kids aren't going to reach out to their friends until they're more spiritually mature, and they won't mature spiritually if we can't get them to nurturing activities like Sunday school."

Negotiations at this level take patience and skill. Typically, youth ministers retreat from this kind of conflict because they simply are not of the temperament to work through the hard issues and uncomfortable dialogues that often accompany resolution of a Level-Three conflict.

LEVEL IV:
VALUES

The deepest and most serious conflicts relate to values—the parties disagree about basic meanings. Joy and Mark feel burdened to "reach the students for Christ," but John and Marilyn, a married couple on the volunteer team, feel that what is called "reaching students for Christ" is nothing less than brainwashing, and they are uncomfortable with what they describe as "fundamentalist, fire-and-brimstone evangelism." Frankly, any resolution at this level is almost impossible.

OVERLAPPING LEVELS
OF CONFLICT

Defining the level of conflict can help us to choose appropriate, positive responses to conflict resolutions. Unfortunately, most of the time, conflicts aren't neat. As we dialogue, explore, and excavate conflicts, we may discover that a coworker's disagreement at one level is really a smoke screen for a real conflict of values. The following case study illustrates how one situation may include several different overlapping levels of conflict:

A designated gift had been given to benefit the church's mission program. At their next regular meeting, the church staff began to brainstorm about how the funds might be used. Some staff members felt the issue should be decided by the staff. One felt the finance committee, representing the entire congregation, should decide. Still another felt the congregation should ultimately be allowed to vote. The pastor felt the money should be used for their local radio ministry as a home-mission project. The youth pastor felt the money should be used for a mission trip to Haiti. The children's minister felt that the money would best be used to start a child care outreach in the community. One staff member felt that the matter should not even be discussed in staff meeting. He felt that the church was wrong to accept a designated gift in the first place. He felt that it would give a single individual too much control over the finances of the congregation.

As you reflect on this case study, identify an example of each of the four levels of conflict.

Level 1: _____

Level 2: _____

Level 3: _____

Level 4: _____

KEYS TO
CONFLICT RESOLUTION

Obviously, we need to move beyond conflict definition to conflict resolution. A doctor who is only able to diagnose the problem won't have many patients. People are not content to die, even if they're well informed about why. Marlene Wilson suggests some specific questions we can use to better understand and resolve specific conflicts. The following material is adapted from her very helpful Conflict Questionnaire:

The People Who Brought You This Book...

— invite you to discover MORE valuable youth-ministry resources. —

Youth Specialties offers an assortment of books, publications, tapes, and events, all designed to encourage and train youth workers and their kids. Just return this card, and we'll send you FREE information on our products and services.

Please send me the FREE Youth Specialties Catalog and information on upcoming Youth Specialties events.

Are you: ☐ An adult youth worker ☐ A youth

Name _____

Church/Org. _____

Address _____

City_____ State _____ Zip _____

Phone Number (_____) _____

Call toll-free to order:

(800) 776-8008

BUSINESS REPLY MAIL

Question 1: What is the difference between what is being done and what is being proposed?

Question 2: Where does the difference originate?

A. Disagreement over facts?

If so:

- Work together to gather data that both parties agree are valid.
- Begin with factual data that both sides are highly likely to agree on.
- Ask both parties what information would further help to bring about some resolution of the issues.

B. Disagreement over methods? procedures? policies? rules?

If so:

- Start with an analysis of the facts.
- Begin focusing both parties on objectives they have in common, emphasizing that the conflict is over means, not ends.
- With the help of both parties, begin developing a list of criteria that would describe a method or procedure mutually acceptable to both parties.
- Using the criteria developed by both parties, begin brainstorming about alternative methods or processes.

C. Disagreement over goals? aims? purposes?

If so:

D. Disagreement over values? philosophies? lifestyles?

If so:

- Start again with the analysis of the facts.
- With the help of both parties, try to get a clear working statement of the problem in behavioral or operating terms. Then follow the procedures above. This may require facilitation by a third party.

Question 3: At what stage of conflict are the disputing parties?

A. One or both sides anticipate a change which will probably lead to conflict.

B. A conflict already exists implicitly, but as yet, it has not been expressed.

C. Discussions have occurred which indicate that a conflict exists.

D. There has been already an open dispute or difference of opinion, which has highlighted the opposing points of view.

E. Open conflict exists and one or both parties have firmly committed themselves to opposing positions and are working to solidify those positions.

Question 4: At what stage of problem-solving effectiveness are the disputing parties?

A. (One side only) (Both sides) ignore or deny that a problem even exists.

B. (One side only) (Both sides) admit to a problem but are unwilling to meet.

C. (One side only) (Both sides) are willing to meet but are blaming the other.

D. (One side only) (Both sides) accept part of the responsibility for the problem.

E. (One side only) (Both sides) are willing to test new approaches and ideas to solve the problem.[4]

CONFLICT RESOLUTION IN THE REAL WORLD

In the real world, conflicts don't always fit the nice schemes and neat, clean questions. We find ourselves dealing with two groups who don't want to resolve their conflict. Or we discover that the issue at stake has been discussed and we weren't even invited to the meeting. Or we find ourselves confronted by an issue that is so hot that it threatens to divide the youth group down the middle, and we can see no route to resolution. Every situation dictates its own approach. The following are some general principles we can abide by when there aren't any obvious alternatives:

The "win-win" principle. Begin by looking for a solution that makes both parties the winner. It isn't always necessary for one party to lose for the other party to win.

The principle of involvement. Any time we can involve the disputing parties in the process of finding a solution, we are moving in the right direction. It is much easier for people to follow through on solutions they have initiated. A group of students complained that Sunday school was dry, boring, irrelevant, obtrusive, and a waste of time. The youth minister formed a cluster of students to survey the youth group and propose a Sunday morning program that would meet the goals of the youth group as well as meet the needs of the students. Almost immediately, the complaints dropped off. Our tendency in youth ministry is to always accept complaints as our problem. We zoom back to our programming kitchen to cook up some new idea we hope the kids and parents like. And when they complain, "No, this time it's overcooked," we rush back to try some other concoction. The better approach may be to show the parties the ingredients we are working with and allow them to come up with their own recipe.

The "nip-it-quick" principle. The sooner we deal with conflict, the more effective we will be. Our tendency is to hope it isn't happening, pray it will stop happening, and turn our heads the other way. But Scripture and experience urge us to action: "Get rid of all bitterness, rage and anger, brawling and slander, along with every form of malice" (Eph. 4:31). Pulling a sapling from the ground with one hand is a simple matter. But a full-grown oak tree cannot be pulled up with even a hundred pairs of hands.

The principle of positive assumptions. For conflict resolution to happen, both parties must agree to assume the best about the other. If the youth worker enters the process already convinced that the board doesn't really care about the youth program, he generally comes away with the same conviction. Negative assumptions trap us into being reactors instead of initiators.

The principle of the here and now. Historical baggage unrelated to the current issue under dispute hinders resolution. The trustees complain that the church van has been brought back from the last two youth retreats dirty enough to warrant health inspection. Rather than dealing with the issue under dispute, the youth minister responds, "Well, nobody made any big speech about the elementary Sunday school Christmas party that left the place looking like Rambo

Meets Santa's Workshop." In conflict, our best progress occurs when the parties focus on the problem at hand. Save other issues for a separate discussion.

The principle of first agreement. Always begin conflict resolution by having both parties focus on their areas of agreement. We usually "get down to business" by saying "here's the problem." We should begin instead at the other end of the equation by asking, "What do we agree on?" Beginning with agreement establishes common ground that allows us room to maneuver for a resolution.

The dangerous-opportunity principle. I am told that in Chinese script the figure used for the word "crisis" is a symbol that combines the two words "dangerous" and "opportunity." Seeing conflict as a "dangerous opportunity"—a chance to find new alternatives, stimulate new thinking, open new dialogue—we're more likely to approach the process with optimism, making resolution more probable.

BLESSED ARE
THE PEACEMAKERS?

I once heard Gordon MacDonald tell of an incident when he and his family were stopped on the highway by traffic backed up in both directions waiting to get under an overpass. He stepped out of the car to see what the holdup was. What he discovered was a bewildered skunk, dead center in the middle of the highway, struggling to get a Nestle's Quik container off of his head. MacDonald was intrigued by the notion that all of these people wanted to help this skunk get out of his predicament, and they all had the ability to do it. And yet nobody made a move because nobody wanted to risk the smell that might happen if they were to get involved.

That's the predicament we often face in dealing with conflicts in our youth programs. Sometimes being a peacemaker doesn't seem like much of a blessing. Even less of a blessing is being a wavemaker—the kind of person who realizes that regardless of how unpleasant, conflict is sometimes necessary.

When the apostle Paul describes our ministry as disciples, he calls us to be agents of reconciliation. Whether that means being reconciled to our fellow team member or staff member or even one of the students, that is a mandate we must take seriously. This doesn't mean we will always be ducking back into some turtle shell of martyrdom or accommodation. Nor does it mean that we should always charge into conflicts like Teenage Mutant Ninja Turtles. What it does mean is that as youth workers we must be prepared for the hard work of conflict.

Do not repay anyone evil for evil. Be careful to do what is right in the eyes of everybody. If it is possible, as far as it depends on you, live at peace with everyone. Do not take revenge, my friends, but leave room for God's wrath, for it is written: "It is mine to avenge; I will repay," says the Lord (Rom. 12:18, 19).

CHAPTER SIXTEEN

PACKING YOUR TOOLBOX: WHEN TO LEAVE A YOUTH MINISTRY

The following two youth workers both had within the last few months been through the pain, excitement, and questions that accompany the decision to leave a youth-ministry position. This forum of two is involved in dialogue with an upper-level youth-ministry class at Eastern College. The topic of the day is "When to Leave a Ministry."

PAUL'S STORY OF DEPARTURE

"After nine years of what I have considered to be effective youth work, I'm leaving my position at Church of the Holy Comforter—an Episcopal church—to accept a youth-ministry position with a growing and progressive Episcopal church in the Southwest. One of the reasons I'm leaving is because while I attempted to follow the steps in my five-year plan for reaching kids for Christ, the hierarchy of the church started throwing up roadblocks. Others in the church who didn't have any contact with the youth ministry followed the leadership's example.

"Now that's not necessarily a reason to leave. If my vision is not in tune with the vision of the church, I could bend my goals to fit what the church is doing. However, when it begins to affect the ministry— the relationships I have with students—then I need to sit up and say, 'Hey, what's going on here?'

"What happened was that we were experiencing tremendous growth in all three areas for which I had responsibility: junior high, senior high, and college. I needed help. So for the last five years I have submitted with my budget a proposal for a full time, salaried youth-ministry assistant. Every year they put it off. "Maybe next year," they said. For the last two years, though, my administrative work load skyrocketed, making it tough for me to get out from behind my desk. Obviously, this begins to affect your relationship with kids.

"This year I had a student, who accepted Christ through our program and later graduated from Syracuse, come back to me and say, 'I want to be involved in ministry.' So I brought him on as a part-time assistant, and the church, in a sense, told me and him that they would bring him on full time by the end of the year.

"Not only did they not hire him full time, but in the last two years my operating budget has gone from fifteen thousand nine hundred dollars to six thousand five hundred dollars. At the same time, the vestry—the board—says that our number-one priority is our youth. So I went twice before the board to ask, if youth ministry is our highest priority, why are we walking backward after we've built it up for so long? And why are we jerking this one kid around who wants to come back and get involved in ministry? I told them what we had with the ministry and what was keeping me behind a desk, hindering my work with kids, and they wouldn't see it.

"I have felt a tremendous amount of anger in the past two years— anger that affected my wife and my child, and my relationship with my students. Also by this point, I had been receiving offers for youth-ministry positions with different churches. Until last Christmas I would just toss them in the wastebasket because I really was committed to Holy Comforter and to the kids there and to the Episcopal church. But over Christmas, while my wife and I were praying, she said to me, 'You know, Paul, maybe you should listen to some of the offers of these other places, because if you just keep throwing them out, you may be limiting how the Holy Spirit wants to lead us.'

"So I said, 'Okay, I'll do that.' That week I received a second offer from this one church out west, and I said, 'I'll go down and take a look.'

"I told the senior pastor, the board, and my volunteer staff that I was beginning to look. I went down there and it was real exciting work. But at first I didn't trust my judgment. When you've poured yourself into a ministry for so long only see to your plans for it go haywire, another offer from another church is very seductive. Am I leaving because I'm angry? Am I leaving because of pain? Or am I leaving because this is truly God's call for me to leave Holy Comforter? So, I would say my leaving was a matter of vision.

"Another reason I'm leaving has to do with integrity. This year when I submitted my budget with the proposal to bring this younger guy on—and it wouldn't cost us a dime more in terms of total youth budget—they still turned it down. The message that comes back to me there is the church leaders aren't willing to listen any more to what Paul has to say about the ministry. We aren't going to listen to his needs. We aren't going to dialogue about that at all. And that's a question of integrity. When you lose credibility in a church, it's very difficult to get that back."

DAN'S PAINFUL EXIT

"I have been serving the same United Methodist congregation for about five years, so I'm not a short-term, fly-about youth worker whose idea of commitment is a one-year stint. I've faced tough situations and difficult decisions without losing my optimism about being a youth minister. I'm still committed to teenagers and excited about God's call. But I guess it came down to about four different clues that told me, 'It's time to leave.'

"The first was that both our senior pastor and associate pastor left the church. The new leadership ushered in a new vision and a new concept of our congregation's ministry that I didn't feel was as conducive to youth ministry. Another problem was that our church was going through a very difficult time with finances. My budget was cut from over twelve thousand dollars to around three thousand dollars, which is difficult to do with a growing youth ministry. The church leadership also decided they would cut my salary and the music minister's salary in half; but they weren't going to cut back our responsibilities. They still wanted us to be there full time. So . . . uh . . . we decided this might be a sign it was time to look around a bit!

"Another issue that arose, and this was probably the major issue, believe it or not, was an issue of integrity. In my ministry I have always made it my habit to put a welcome mat in front of my office door. It's a way of saying that all the kids are welcome into the church and into the youth group. I would say to the kids, 'No matter what we do, invite your friends'—referring to normal fun activities like bowling, miniature golfing, and things like that. We often reminded the kids that their friends were always welcome; and not just their 'good' friends who were Christians and carried their Bible to school, but all their friends. And the kids started doing that.

"The problem arose when the kids started bringing friends who were not the kind of friends parents wanted hanging around the youth group. We're talking about friends who wore earrings and chains in unusual places. I felt that since these kids needed Christ as much as anyone else, this was where they should be. But that was not the opinion shared by a small but powerful minority of parents.

"One night, just as one of these parents was dropping her son off at youth group, she saw another student getting out of the car with this kid that had long hair, earrings, chains, and black hair with blonde streaks. Let's just say this kid was out there on the cutting edge. It wasn't a good scene for this mother to see. She went to the board and said, 'This cannot be, because it's a bad influence on our kids.'

"Well, when both she and the board came back to me, I said, 'There are a lot of things we can compromise on: whether we serve hamburgers or hot dogs, whether we meet at 6:00 or 7:00, and all those kinds of things. But there are some issues on which I will not compromise, and one of those is my unwillingness to say to a kid, 'Because you are dressed like this, or because you look like this, you are not welcome in our youth group.' That is a no-discussion subject.

"They backed down a little bit, but it was in the back of their minds. And they watched, and they saw me going on campus, and they saw me bringing in kids who were 'undesirable.' This didn't happen overnight. My wife, Debbie, saw it too, which was fortunate because we really operate as a team, and it finally came down to the point where we both felt that God was leading us out of the church. So we decided to move on."

THE REVOLVING DOOR SYNDROME

For years, one of the favorite stereotypes of youth workers has been that they are fickle, undependable, slippery, and hard to hold on to. We've all heard the statistics, compiled by who knows who, that the average tenure of the professional youth worker in any one position averages between twelve and eighteen months. Is it true? Possibly. Are youth workers more professionally mobile than senior pastors? Probably. At Eastern College's Youth-Ministry Department, we receive a minimum of three to five requests a week from churches looking for youth ministers. In addition to that, we hear from probably one caller a week who is looking for a youth-ministry position. In the words of a great theologian: "There's a whole lot o' shakin' goin' on!"

WHY DO WE MOVE SO MUCH?

It's not the inherent personality of youth workers that leads to this game of professional hopscotch. Other factors lead the Dans and the Pauls to move on. My own experience has taught me that the high rate of youth-minister turnover could be blamed on the youth worker's role as much as on the youth worker. What are some factors that work against long-term youth ministry?

THE MARATHON FACTOR

Doing ministry, whether it be with youth or adults or munchkins, is like running a marathon. At the beginning of the race, when we first take the position, when people witness our ordination or installation, there's a lot of enthusiasm. The crowd is there, nodding their approval, showing their support. From the starting line, it's hard to see the hills on the horizon that will soon enough test our mettle.

Many people get into youth ministry thinking it will be all fun and games. They've seen a few sprints that looked like lots of fun. What's a marathon but just more of the same? Of course, when we get into anything full-time we discover that starting is much easier than continuing, that elements of the job that were fascinating when they were new become mundane with familiarity.

Youth ministry seems to be one of those occupations that looks easier from the sidelines than from out on the track. A high percentage of people who begin doing youth ministry counting on a sprint, a cruise, or a coast, begin dropping out by the second year when they discover there are sprains, curses, and costs. That's not really unique with youth ministry, except that youth ministry looks so deceptively easy when viewed from a distance.

GETAWAYS TO GET A RAISE

When Richard Nixon was president back in the late sixties and early seventies, our nation went through an inflation crisis. Facing rising prices and runaway inflationary rates, President Nixon instituted what became known as a voluntary wage and price freeze. The plan was that industry would voluntarily agree to freeze prices and wages at their current levels so that the rate of inflation could be slowed. In the long run, it would be better business for everyone. It seemed like a good idea.

About a year into the plan, however, *The Wall Street Journal* began running stories about executive mobility—the problem of people in top positions moving from job to job with discouraging frequency. What was happening, it turns out, was that with the wage freeze, the only way these people could get raises was if they changed jobs; if they stayed in their present positions, their salaries were frozen. If they moved to new jobs, they could negotiate for higher wages. In short, the executives were being penalized for being faithful and were being rewarded for being fickle.

Frankly, the same dynamic works in today's youth-ministry climate. While the rest of the country has moved beyond the wage and price freeze of the seventies, the church still holds to this principle. Although many churches increase salaries to keep pace with inflation, few churches give their youth ministers, or any other staff members, actual increases in spendable income. In short, that means that when financial burdens increase (due to a growing family or a crisis), we either tighten our belts or find new positions. A youth worker has to decide, "Do I stick it out here and let my family's income shrink, or do I move to the church down the street that is offering a few thousand dollars a year more?" We end up rewarding those who move and penalizing those who stay.

Because of the low professional regard most people have for youth ministry, youth workers are especially vulnerable to price freezing strategies. The average hiring committee views youth workers as desperate for a position, perhaps doing youth ministry because they are unable to do some other kind of more legitimate ministry. So the church pays incoming youth ministers enough to *get* them, but not enough to *keep* them. (The folly of this approach, by the way, is that the average search and relocation process for a new youth minister costs about three thousand dollars to forty-five hundred dollars. That means that the congregation could have increased the youth worker's salary by fifteen hundred dollars over a three-year period without even increasing their costs, AND they could have the advantage of keeping a seasoned youth minister.)

SELLER'S MARKET

In the youth-ministry offices at Eastern College is a notebook of job openings that have been sent to us. We list about sixty positions open for youth workers. We don't make those job descriptions available to any people other than those who have graduated from our youth-ministry program (so please don't call!), but we constantly have many more positions to fill than graduates to fill them.

Most youth ministers with any kind of track record get occasional offers from these organizations. They court youth workers, promising an increase in salary and offering a fresh start with a clean slate. Simply being wooed again makes that new offer very seductive. It's the same dynamic that leads men in mid-life to have an affair, or motivates women who feel neglected to seek out men who will treat them with respect: familiarity breeds contempt, or at least a lack of appreciation. In a climate where there are more youth-ministry positions than there are youth ministers, it is no wonder that many wander off looking for new relationships.

EMPTY BAG SYNDROME

A large contingent of youth workers approach youth ministry on the basis of new ideas, rather than on the basis of vision. As long as they are able to pull off activities that are bigger and better or do programs that are wilder and zanier, they maintain ministry momentum. But when the idea count runs low, their ministries become anemic. One of the reasons that youth ministers leave is simply that they have run out of new ideas. They've used all the old ideas once, all the new programs twice, and now that their bags of tricks are empty, they must move on to new audiences.

DISCOURAGEMENT

Even worse than running out of ideas is running out of hope—feeling that the soil isn't going to produce any harvest. That's when some youth workers decide to kick the dust off their feet and move on to other fields. In Mark Lamport's survey of youth workers,[1] seventy-six percent reported they would consider leaving a position or had already left a position due to burnout. Another forty-nine percent cited lack of results as motive enough for leaving a position.

The Lamport studies showed that about two-thirds (sixty-seven percent) of youth workers are "very pleased" with the progress made in their ministries. However, his studies go on to show that the amount of satisfaction diminishes with age. Of the eighteen-to-twenty-five-year-old age group, seventy-one percent express satisfaction with their work, while only sixty-eight percent of the twenty-six-to-forty-year olds expressed that same degree of satisfaction. For those youth workers in the over-forty group, the percentage of "very pleased" drops to thirty-three percent. Whether this downshift is caused by the dimming of optimism or the refining of goals is unclear. What is clear is that for many, discouragement becomes a more prominent factor the longer they stay in youth work.

LOSS OF NECESSARY SUPPORT

When asked why they stay in youth ministry, thirty-seven percent of youth workers say it's because they "feel needed," while twenty-six percent attribute it to "strong support from the church." One of the reasons that youth ministers most commonly cite for leaving positions is that they feel they lack the support of either the congregation, the leadership, the students, or all of the above. As we heard in the comments from the two youth workers at the opening of this chapter, one of the key issues in decisions about leaving is credibility.

"SHOULD I MOVE?"

Making a decision to leave a ministry is usually a gut-wrenching period of soul-searching and cross-examination, marked by a desire to seek the will of God, wrought by the fear that we may be misled by misconceptions and wrong motives. The following are some questions we can ask ourselves as we move through this process:

1. *Have I been here long enough to reach my most effective years?* According to the Institute for American Church Growth, the average tenure for pastors in the country's largest churches is twenty-one years. While there is a correlation between long tenure and large churches, no one is certain which causes which. Are the pastors apt to stick around for a longer time in larger churches because those churches can pay better and offer broader ministry opportunities? Or are we to infer that because pastors have stayed long-term in their churches that growth has resulted?

It is clear that surveys within the Lutheran, the Presbyterian, and the United Methodist churches show that long pastorates are more effective in attracting and holding members. Studies have shown that pastors tend to characterize their most effective years of ministry as beginning in their sixth or seventh year of tenure. One pastor put it this way: "In the first two years of a pastorate, everyone thinks you can do nothing wrong. In the second two years, it seems like you can do nothing right. By the fifth and sixth years of a pastorate, either you leave, or the people who think you can do nothing right leave, or you change, or they change, or you both change. By the seventh year, you start to really get productive."

This pastor wasn't referring specifically to youth ministry, but there's good reason to suggest that the same is true in the realm of youth work. No actual studies prove a correlation between youth workers with long tenure and large youth groups, but the anecdotal evidence points in that direction. Paul Borthwick, himself a prime example of long tenure in the same location, sums it up this way.

Sticking with youth ministry for a long time has many positive results:
- Effectiveness with young people will increase because the students trust you.
- Results (a hard-to-find commodity in youth work) will become more apparent as those who have graduated return to join the youth team.

- Parents will grow in their trust, which builds more continuity between family and youth ministry.
- Lay leaders will be trained over a period of time with one consistent philosophy and strategy of ministry.
- The youth minister will be a professional who is, in effect, the church's expert on adolescents.[2]

2. Do I have a dream for this ministry? Can you remember what it's like to be excited about your work? To dream about what God is going to do with your group? Only about two-thirds of youth ministers responding to one survey agreed with the statement, "I feel that my position is stimulating and challenging enough to meet my needs." About one out of ten disagree with the statement, and another two out of ten neither agreed nor disagreed.[3] When we lose the ability to dream for a ministry, it may be a good sign that it's time to move on. Not that every day should be "Raiders of the Lost Adolescent" or "Adventures in Youth Land," but beware of professional stagnation that comes from a lack of vision and a lack of challenge.

3. Do my spiritual gifts match the present needs of my ministry? In speaking to a group of youth-ministry students, Mike Fuguet, former youth pastor of Christ Community Church in West Chester, Pennsylvania, explained that he left his position at that church because he felt the ministry had grown to the point that it needed someone who was more of an administrator than he was. He felt that his gifts and call were more in the area of one-on-one discipleship. Rather than try to fit himself into a changing role, he resigned from the position and found an outside job to support his family while he continued to minister within the group.

Stories like Mike's are rare, but circumstances like Mike's are not. Ministries change and needs change. Almost two out of ten youth workers report that they could foresee circumstances in which they would leave a position because of an inability to adapt to the ministry setting or culture. A program that needed someone with a strong gift for outreach may develop into a program that has a strong need for someone with more of a discipling ministry. That doesn't always necessitate leaving a position. If we've built a genuine team ministry, it will be easier for us stretch and flex with the changing needs of a ministry. Nonetheless, there are times when we sense that even if we don't feel we need a change, we may feel the youth program does.

4. *Is my philosophy of ministry compatible with my church?* This is the kind of issue that Dan was dealing with in the opening pages of this chapter: could he continue to serve as youth minister of the church when the leadership and some of the parents were trying to restrict which students he could actually minister to? For Dan, that was a nonnegotiable. He decided to move on.

5. *Are people still willing to follow me?* Titles don't mean much in youth ministry. If the youths aren't willing to follow, then it's time to reassess whether we can really be their leaders. We're all familiar with the image of the solitary Old Testament prophet, standing alone and prodding an unwilling Israel to follow. That's a valid ministry, no doubt. On the other hand, it takes a certain amount of parental, youth, and board support to make any progress in ministry. When we've lost that support, it sometimes makes more sense to move on.

Bob is a youth pastor at a large church in North Carolina that has undergone painful upheaval over the last few years, resulting in the senior pastor being asked to leave. Although the turbulence had little to do with Bob's ministry, the support framework that he needs to do effective ministry in the church has been deeply eroded. In conversations with him, my recommendation has been to move on. We've only one life to live for Christ. Time is too short to waste it fighting to be a leader for people who don't want to follow.

"HOLD IT . . . DON'T TOUCH THAT RÉSUMÉ"

On the other hand, there are scenarios that usually give youth workers itchy feet, but do not constitute solid ground for walking out on a ministry.

Plateaus. The youth program has no appreciable growth numerically and we have lost the sense that something exciting is happening. The danger in this situation is that our walking out may be more a reflection of our needs than the needs of our youth group. Youth groups normally go through ebbs and flows in attendance, often solely due to demographic changes in the youth population. Even high schools experience these fluctuations in enrollment, and that's with compulsory attendance. Leaving a youth ministry just because it has reached some kind of growth plateau is probably more a reflection of our own need to run the biggest, "fastest growing" youth group in the area. We are not responsible before God to have groups that are always increasing enrollment. We are responsible to be faithful to Christ and entrust the results to him.

Problem people. A student, parent, parishioner, or board member is making us miserable.

David Seamands refers to these people as "Assistants to the Holy Spirit—people who are always there to convict us in case the Holy Spirit drops the ball." The problem with running from these people, of course, is that they are omnipresent. In the words of one veteran youth worker:

> One thing you're going to find in ministry is that there's always going to be somebody in the church who just rubs you the wrong way. Let's call him Tom Smith. No matter what you do, he's there giving you a hard time about it. So you say, "I'm sick of Tom Smith, I'm leaving," and you go to Church B . . . and guess what. It's "Tim Smith." And sometimes they even start to look alike! You will never be at a church where everybody agrees with you . . . it just will not happen.

Financial dissatisfaction. We have an offer for a higher paying youth-ministry position.

According to surveys of youth workers, fifty-nine percent don't think their salary adequately covers their expenses. If that's true (and who can doubt it?) almost six out of ten youth workers are dissatisfied with their pay at any one time. If they each moved on the basis of a better salary offer, there would be almost perpetual motion. Even more important to consider, however, is that many of that fifty-nine percent have probably already moved within the last two years, thinking that they would be happier with higher salaries. Whatever percentage moved on the basis of that motive have discovered that "enough" never seems like enough.

Finances are important. It takes money to support a family; and it's tough for us to do our best in youth ministry when we're worried about paying our mortgages. On the other hand, youth ministers who are baited from their posts by a hook with slightly higher salaries are going to be moving around the map faster than hummingbirds. There's always someone out there willing to pay us a thousand dollars more than we are making now. But is that the best way to operate? What about the added resettlement costs? What about uprooting the family? What about the will of God? Chasing a dollar to a new position is usually a poor way to discern God's leading.

Hurt feelings. We feel underappreciated, underaffirmed, under-supported, or just plain hurt.

Many times in ministry, others either knowingly or unknowingly hurt our feelings. Some respond to that deep hurt by deciding to change positions. But this knee-jerk response to hurt is usually misdirected and nonproductive. If someone hurts our feelings, it's understandable that we will be angry. What is not understandable is how our departure from the ministry is going to somehow make things right. It will hurt the students we're working with. We will hurt ourselves by putting our families through the trauma and trials of a move. We will hurt those in our congregations who support us. But how will all of this hurting make our pain any less?

And of course, after we've played this trump card once, we can't play it again very soon. It's the kind of ultimate statement we can only make once, and by making it we effectively disenfranchise ourselves from the process of change. Departure because of some hurt or offense usually brings the most pain and the least satisfaction. We will not find a ministry without pain.

WHEN IS A MOVE APPROPRIATE?

Some things, however, are more important than longevity. In my estimation the following four scenarios might justify a move:

When staying with the present church violates your integrity. Bill was working in a large United Methodist Church in the Southeast. Along with many members of the congregation, he became aware that the church's choir director was having a not-so-discreet affair with one of the choir members. He watched their smiles week after week during the services. His stomach turned when the choir director helped serve communion to the woman's husband. He listened as the matter was tabled in the board meeting awaiting further consultation with the pastor.

By the time Bill spoke with me about the situation, he was being eaten up on the inside. He felt he was somehow an accessory to the charade that was taking place in the choir on Sunday mornings. He had confronted the choir director and been strictly rebuffed, the choir director saying it was none of his business. When he went to the pastor about his concern, he was told there wasn't enough evidence to take any action.

My recommendation to Bill was straightforward and direct: "You've done all you can to confront and remedy the situation. If the church tolerates the situation, you must leave for the sake of your own conscience." Trying to make peace with a situation like that can damage our own integrity after a while.

When family needs would be ignored by staying. Family needs mean more than mere financial concerns. Family needs could include not enough time together, unfair expectations on the family, special health needs of a family member, or any number of other similar situations. Our first responsibility is to the ministry God gives us with our families. Obviously, departure is a last resort, but any job responsibility that effectively prevents us from carrying out that ministry gives us grounds to resign from our posts.

When your relationship with the congregation has deteriorated beyond reasonable hope of reconciliation. Whether due to bad decisions, interpersonal conflict, or other factors, when this occurs, a move might be justified.

When it is clearly the will of God that we move to a specific new ministry. This kind of call grows out of mostly positive circumstances—more an instance of being led to a position than of being driven from a position. This kind of leading is usually confirmed through three channels: prayer, brothers and sisters who know us and our gifts, and the surrounding circumstances. When weighing these three elements, prayer is the most important, the witness of the brethren comes second in importance, and surrounding circumstances are the least important.

Sometimes only the Spirit of God can explain why we are being led to a new work. It is beyond the understanding of the brethren, and from our human standpoint it makes no sense. But if God says move, we'd better move. The longer we live under the hand of God, the more we begin to trust that he wants us to know his will more than we want to know it. We don't have to fret and worry that God is trying to lead us and we are missing his point. If God wants us to move, he has ways of getting us to pay attention! My personal conviction is that God is not so concerned that we specifically work in this or that situation; his major concern is that we have faith in him (John 6:28, 29). God can use both positive and negative situations to nurture that faith—in fact, sometimes he can better use the negative situations to build our trust in him.

THE LEAVE PRINCIPLE

In my nineteen years of youth ministry, three or four times my family and I have had to go through the loneliness and dusk of moving to a new ministry. One pastor I was working with knew what we were going through, and rather than make me feel like a deserter, he gave me a guideline by which to judge my decision to leave one work and begin a new one. He called it the LEAVE principle:

Lack of personal growth
Expenses exceed income (not enough income to support my family)
A breakdown in relationships (among staff, students, parents)
Vision has ceased
Evidence that God is leading elsewhere

ENDNOTES

Chapter 1
1. Em Griffin, "What Motivates You?" *Leadership* (Summer 1985).
2. Dan Taylor, *Letters to My Children* (InterVarsity Press, 1989).

Chapter 2
1. Len Kageler, "Performance Reviews: Worth the Trouble?" *Leadership* (Summer 1985).
2. Thomas Peters and Robert Waterman, Jr., *In Search of Excellence* (Warner Books, 1982).
3. Ibid.
4. Ibid.
5. Ibid.
6. Ibid.
7. Ibid., quoting Thomas Watson, *A Business and Its Beliefs*.

Chapter 3
1. Robert Banks, *The Tyranny of Time* (InterVarsity Press, 1983).
2. G. M. Lebhar, *The Use of Time* (Chain Store, 1958).
3. Banks.
4. Fred Smith, *Learning to Lead* (Christianity Today, 1986).
5. Paul Borthwick, *Organizing Your Youth Ministry* (Youth Specialties/Zondervan, 1988).
6. Marlene Wilson, *Survival Skills for Managers* (Volunteer Management Associates, 1981), quoting Schwartz and Mackenzie, "Time Management Strategies for Women."
7. Ibid.
8. Ibid., quoting from *The Time Trap: Managing Your Way Out*.

Chapter 4
1. Marlene Wilson, *Survival Skills for Managers* (Volunteer Management Associates, 1981), quoting from *The Time Trap: Managing Your Way Out*.
2. Les Christie, *Getting a Grip on Time Management* (SonPower/Victor, 1984).
3. Fred Smith, *Learning to Lead* (Christianity Today, 1986).
4. Eugene Peterson, *Working the Angles* (Eerdmans, 1987).
5. Wilson, *Survival Skills for Managers*.

Chapter 5
1. Robert Moskowitz, *Creative Problem Solving Workbook* (AMACOM, 1978).

Chapter 6
1. Em Griffin, "Four Ways to Make Group Decisions," *Leadership* (Spring 1982).
2. Ibid.
3. Irving Janis, *Victims of Groupthink* (Houghton Mifflin, 1982).

Chapter 7
1. Larry Richards, *Youth Ministry: Its Renewal in the Local Church* (Zondervan, 1972).
2. Dennis Miller, *Changing Lives* (CD Publishing, 8434 Horizon Dr., Shakopee, MN 55379, 1988).
3. Doug Stevens, *Called to Care* (Youth Specialties/Zondervan, 1985).

Chapter 8
1. Dorothy Williams and Peter Benson, *Determining Needs in Your Youth Ministry* (Group Publishing, 1987).
2. *Search Institute Profiles of Student Life* (Search Institute, 122 West Franklin, Suite 525, Minneapolis, MN 55404).
3. Jim Rayburn III, *Dance, Children, Dance* (Tyndale House, 1984).
4. Gordon MacDonald, *Facing Turbulent Times* (Tyndale House, 1981).

Chapter 9
1. Mark Senter, *The Art of Recruiting Volunteers* (SonPower/Victor, 1983).
2. Les Christie, *Unsung Heroes: How to Recruit and Train Volunteers* (Youth Specialties/Zondervan, 1987).

Chapter 10
1. Ronald Wilson, "Letter from an Ex-Volunteer," *Leadership* (Summer 1982).
2. Les Christie, *Unsung Heroes: How to Recruit and Train Volunteers* (Youth Specialties/Zondervan, 1987).
3. Wilson, "Letter from an Ex-Volunteer."
4. Ed Dayton and Ted Engstrom, "How to Light a Fire Under People Without Burning Them Up," *Christian Leadership Letter* (May 1979).

Chapter 11
1. Jim Harter and others, *Men, Animals, Women, Children, Food*. These clip-art books and others are available from Dover Publications (180 Varick Street, New York, NY 10014, 1980).
2. Neil McAleer, *Cosmic Mind-Boggling Book* (Warner Books, 1982).
3. Christopher Cerf and Victor Navasky, *The Experts Speak: The Definitive Compendium of Authoritative Misinformation* (Pantheon, 1984).

Chapter 12
1. Paul Borthwick, "How to Design an Effective Youth Ministry Budget," *Youthworker* (Fall 1984).
2. Dennis and Marilyn Benson, *Hard Times Catalogue for Youth Ministry* (Group Books, 1982).
3. "Door-to-Door Car Wash," *Ideas 45* (Youth Specialties, 1988).
4. "Scripturathon," *Ideas 45*.
5. "Shave-athon" *Ideas 45*.

Chapter 13
1. Merton Strommen, *Five Cries of Youth* (Harper & Row, 1970).
2. Ibid.

Chapter 14
1. "Straight Talk on Staff Dynamics," *Youthworker* (Fall 1985).
2. Eugene C. Roehlkepartain, ed., *The Youth Ministry Resource Book* (Group Books, 1988).
3. Kenneth Mitchell, *Psychological and Theological Relationships in Multiple Staff Ministry* (Westminster Press, 1966).
4. Lyle E. Schaller, *The Multiple Staff and the Larger Church* (Abingdon Press, 1984).
5. Ibid.
6. Ridge Burns and Pam Campbell, *Create in Me a Youth Ministry* (Victor, 1986).

Chapter 15
1. Paul Woods, "Surviving Church Politics," *Group* (September 1986).
2. Marlene Wilson, *Survival Skills for Managers* (Volunteer Management Associates, 1981).
3. "Straight Talk on Staff Dynamics," *Youthworker* (Fall 1985).
4. Wilson, *Survival Skills for Managers*.

Chapter 16
1. Eugene C. Roehlkepartain, ed., *The Youth Ministry Resource Book* (Group Books, 1988).
2. Paul Borthwick, *Organizing Your Youth Ministry* (Youth Specialties/Zondervan, 1987).
3. Roehlkepartain.

A SELECTED BIBLIOGRAPHY FOR FURTHER STUDY

CONTEMPLATIVE THINKING

Borthwick, Paul. *Leading the Way*. Colorado Springs: NavPress, 1989.

Bratcher, Edward. *The Walk-On-Water Syndrome*. Waco, Texas: Word, 1984.

Carr, Jacquelyn B. *Communicating with Myself: A Journal*. Dubuque, Iowa: W. C. Brown, 1984.

Feldmeyer, Dean. *Beating Burnout in Youth Ministry*. Loveland, Colorado: Group Books, 1989.

Fernando, Ajith. *Leadership Lifestyle: A Study of 1 Timothy*. Wheaton: Tyndale House, 1985.

Kesler, Jay. *Being Holy, Being Human*. Carol Stream, Illinois: Christianity Today, Inc., 1988.

MacDonald, Gordon. *Facing Turbulent Times*. Wheaton: Tyndale House, 1981.

MacDonald, Gordon. *Ordering Your Private World*. Nashville: Oliver-Nelson, 1984.

Peterson, Eugene. *Working the Angles: A Trigonometry for Pastoral Work*. Grand Rapids, Michigan: Eerdmans, 1987.

Peterson, Eugene. *The Contemplative Pastor*. Carol Stream, Illinois: Christianity Today, Inc., 1989.

Rayburn, Jim III. *Dance, Children, Dance*. Wheaton: Tyndale House, 1984.

EVALUATION

Benson, Peter L., and Dorothy L. Williams. *Determining Needs in Your Youth Ministry*. Loveland, Colorado: Group Books, 1987.

Carr, Jacquelyn B. *Communicating with Myself: A Journal*. Dubuque, Iowa: W. C. Brown, 1984.

Miller, Dennis, with Amelia Hunt. *Changing Lives: A Practical Guide to Spiritually Powerful Youth Ministry*. Edina, Minnesota: Church Development, 1988.

FINANCES

Leadership (Winter 1987). (Entire issue is devoted to topic of finances.)

Hinchey, Margaret, et al. *Fund Raisers that Work*. Loveland, Colorado: Group Books, 1988.

Rust, Brian, and Barry McLeish. *The Support-Raising Handbook: A Guide for Christian Workers*. Downers Grove, Illinois: InterVarsity Press, 1984.

Willmer, Wesley K., ed. *Money for Ministries*. Wheaton: Victor, 1989.
Youthworker. (Fall 1984). (Entire issue is devoted to topic of money.)

GENERAL INFORMATION

Benson, Warren, and Mark Senter III, eds. *The Complete Book of Youth Ministry*. Chicago: Moody Press, 1987.

Borthwick, Paul. *Organizing Your Youth Ministry*. Grand Rapids, Michigan: Youth Specialties/Zondervan, 1987.

Burns, Jim. *Youth Builder: A Resource for Relational Youth Ministry*. Eugene, Oregon: Harvest House, 1988.

Roehlkepartain, Eugene C., ed. *The Youth Ministry Resource Book*. Loveland, Colorado: Group Books, 1988.

Sparks, Lee, ed. *Fast Forms for Youth Ministry*. Loveland, Colorado: Group Books, 1987.

Sparks, Lee. *The Youth Worker's Personal Management Handbook*. Loveland, Colorado: Group Books, 1985.

Stevens, Douglas. *Called to Care*. Grand Rapids, Michigan: Youth Specialties/Zondervan, 1985.

Wilson, Marlene. *Survival Skills for Managers*. Boulder, Colorado: Volunteer Management Associates, 1981.

LEADERSHIP

Borthwick, Paul. *Leading The Way*. Colorado Springs: NavPress, 1989.

Cavanagh, Michael E. *The Effective Minister: Psychological and Social Considerations*. Harper & Row, 1986.

Kesler, Jay. *Being Holy, Being Human*. Carol Stream, Illinois: Christianity Today, Inc., 1988.

Means, James E. *Leadership in Christian Ministry*. Grand Rapids, Michigan: Baker, 1989.

Richards, Lawrence O., and Clyde Hoeldtke. *A Theology of Church Leadership*. Grand Rapids, Michigan: Zondervan, 1980.

Richards, Lawrence O., and Gib Martin. *A Theology of Personal Ministry*. Grand Rapids, Michigan: Zondervan, 1981.

ORGANIZATION AND MANAGEMENT

Bratcher, Edward. *The Walk-On-Water Syndrome*. Waco, Texas: Word, 1984.

Dibbert, Michael T. *Spiritual Leadership, Responsible Management: A Guide for Leaders of the Church*. Grand Rapids, Michigan: Zondervan, 1988.

Gangel, Kenneth O. *Feeding and Leading*. Wheaton: Victor, 1989.

Kilinski, Kenneth K., and Jerry Wolfert. *Organization and Leadership in the Local Church*. Grand Rapids, Michigan: Zondervan, 1973.

MacDonald, Gordon. *Ordering Your Private World*. Nashville: Oliver-Nelson, 1984.

Peters, Thomas J., and Robert H. Waterman, Jr. *In Search of Excellence: Lessons from America's Best-Run Companies*. New York: Warner Books, 1984.

Rush, Myron D. *Management: A Biblical Approach*. Wheaton: Victor, 1983.

Smith, Fred. *Learning to Lead*. Carol Stream, Illinois: Christianity Today, Inc., 1986.

PARENTING

Arterburn, Stephen, and Jim Burns. *Drug-Proof Your Kids: . . . And Help Them Say No*. Waco, Texas: Focus on the Family/Word, 1989.

Borthwick, Paul. *But You Don't Understand*. Nashville: Oliver-Nelson, 1986.

Dobson, James. *Parenting Isn't for Cowards*. Waco, Texas: Focus on the Family/Word, 1987.

Elkind, David. *All Grown up and No Place to Go: Teenagers in Crisis*. Reading, Massachusetts: Addison-Wesley, 1984.

Glenn, H. Stephen, and Jane Nelson. *Raising Self-Reliant Children in a Self-Indulgent World*. Rocklin, California: Prima Publishing, 1988.

Huggins, Kevin. *Parenting Adolescents*. Colorado Springs: NavPress, 1989.

Kesler, Jay, ed. *Parents and Teenagers*. Wheaton: Victor, 1984.

Knorr, Dandi Daley. *Just One of Me: Confessions of a Less-Than-Perfect Single Parent*. Wheaton: Harold Shaw, 1989.

Rice, David. *Parents in Control*. Eugene, Oregon: Harvest House, 1987.

St. Clair, Barry and Carol. *Talking With Your Kids About Love, Sex, and Dating*. San Bernardino, California: Here's Life Publishing (Campus Crusade), 1989.

White, Jerry and Mary. *When Your Kids Aren't Kids Anymore*. Colorado Springs: NavPress, 1989.

PERSONAL CALL

Borthwick, Paul. *Feeding Your Forgotten Soul*. Grand Rapids, Michigan: Youth Specialties/Zondervan, 1990.

Burns, Ridge, and Pam Campbell. *Create in Me a Youth Ministry*. Wheaton: Victor, 1986.

Feldmeyer, Dean. *Beating Burnout in Youth Ministry*. Loveland, Colorado: Group Books, 1989.

Fernando, Ajith. *Leadership Lifestyle: A Study of 1 Timothy*. Wheaton: Tyndale House, 1985.

MacDonald, Gordon. *Facing Turbulent Times*. Wheaton: Tyndale House, 1981.

Peterson, Eugene H. *Working the Angles: A Trigonometry for Pastoral Work*. Grand Rapids, Michigan: Eerdmans, 1987.

Rayburn, Jim III. *Dance, Children, Dance*. Wheaton: Tyndale House, 1984.

PROMOTION

Finley, Tom. *The Youth Worker's Clip Art Book*. Ventura, California: Gospel Light, 1984.

Hunt, Steve, and Dave Adamson, comps. *Youth Ministry Clip Art*. Loveland, Colorado: Group Books, 1987.

Kruback, Rand, illus. *Outrageous Clip Art for Youth Ministry*. Loveland, Colorado: Group Books, 1988.

Rice, Wayne, comp. *Youth Specialties Clip Art Books I and II*. El Cajon, California: Youth Specialties, 1985, 1987.

The Youth Worker's Calendar Kit. El Cajon, California: Youth Specialties, 1985, 1987.

STAFF RELATIONSHIPS

Leadership (Summer 1983 and Spring 1989). (Two issues devoted to staff relationships.)

Mitchell, Kenneth R. *Psychological and Theological Relationships in Multiple Staff Ministries*. Philadelphia: Westminster, 1988.

Schaller, Lyle E. *The Multiple Staff and the Larger Church*. Nashville: Abingdon, 1980.

Youthworker (Fall 1985). (Entire issue is devoted to staff relationships.)

TIME MANAGEMENT

Banks, Robert. *The Tyranny of Time*. Downers Grove, Illinois: InterVarsity Press, 1985.

Christie, Les. *Getting a Grip on Time Management*. Wheaton: SonPower/ Victor, 1984.

WORKING WITH VOLUNTEERS

Christie, Les. *Unsung Heroes: How to Recruit and Train Volunteers*. Grand Rapids, Michigan: Youth Specialties/Zondervan, 1987.

Johnson, Douglas W. *The Care and Feeding of Volunteers*. Nashville: Abingdon, 1978.

McDonough, Reginald M. *Working with Volunteer Leaders in the Church*. Nashville: Broadman, 1976.

Senter, Mark III. *The Art of Recruiting Volunteers*. Wheaton: SonPower/ Victor, 1983.

Stone, J. David, and Rose Mary Miller. *Volunteer Youth Workers: Recruiting and Developing Leaders for Youth Ministry*. Loveland, Colorado: Group Books, 1985.

Wilson, Marlene. *How to Mobilize Church Volunteers*. Minneapolis: Augsburg, 1983.

Youthworker (Winter 1988). (Entire issue is devoted to topic of team ministry.)